A History of the

PIANOFORTE

and

PIANOFORTE PLAYERS

Da Capo Press Music Titles

FREDERICK FREEDMAN, General Editor

University of California at Los Angeles

A History of the
PIANOFORTE
and
PIANOFORTE PLAYERS

Translated and Revised from the German of
OSCAR BIE

By E. E. KELLETT and E. W. NAYLOR

With a Foreword to the Da Capo Edition by
Aube Tzerko
University of California at Los Angeles

Da Capo Press • New York • 1966

A Da Capo Press Reprint Edition

This unabridged republication of the first English edition of 1899 is printed
by special arrangement with the original publishers, J. A. Dent & Sons,
Ltd., London, and E. P. Dutton & Co., Inc., New York

Library of Congress Catalog Card No. 66-28445

© *1966 Da Capo Press*
A Division of Plenum Publishing Corporation
227 West 17 Street, New York, N. Y. 10011

Printed in the United States of America

Foreword

It is remarkable how, in the course of time, a stimulating and significant book can become obscured and neglected. Fortunately, however, man's continuing quest for knowledge often reveals itself in a renewed interest in such works, and this new edition of Oscar Bie's *History of the Pianoforte and Pianoforte Players* represents the culmination of such a process.

Oscar Bie was born in Breslau in 1864. His principal interests were not at first musical. At the University of Leipzig, where he received his doctorate in 1886, he studied the history of art and philology, and in 1890, soon after settling in Berlin, he began to teach art history, finally becoming professor of art history at the Berlin Technical High School in 1901.

Music was never neglected, however. In Berlin, Bie studied musical theory with Philip Scharwenka, and many of his early articles had musical themes. Around 1900, he began to publish books on the subject. These included *Der Tanz* (1906), *Die Moderne Musik und Richard Strauss* (1906), *Die Oper* (1913), *Das Klavier* (1921), *Franz Schubert* (1925), and *Das Deutsche Lied* (1926), and culminated in *Richard Wagner und Bayreuth*, published in 1931. Bie died in Berlin on April 21, 1938.

The History of the Pianoforte and Pianoforte Players was published in Germany in 1898 under the title, *Das Klavier und seine Meister*. It was Bie's first book, but today its validity and force remain clearly evident. For Bie had the capacity for timeless illumination of all aspects of the subject, for clear and eloquent delineation of past and present. Every word breathes his enchantment with the piano, every page reveals the depth of his knowledge. And from the earliest paragraphs, where he speaks of the playing of Queen Elizabeth and Mary Stuart and the music permeating the plays of Shakespeare, there can be no doubt of the presence of an intensely dedicated, mature, and musically sensitive mind.

v

Typical are Bie's perceptive and incisive characterizations of the work of the protean figures who made musical history. Thus, Bach's clavier music is presented in a dual perspective, on the one hand as a complete reflection of the man, on the other as an integral part of a body of work central to the whole history of music:

> Bach's clavier-music is a complete world, a mirror of his music as a whole.... Thus for the first time it came about that the clavier became capable of interpreting the whole nature of a great man. With the early Englishmen it was the embodiment of the whole tone-poet; with Couperin the whole man, indeed, but a man who was nothing but a dancer; with Scarlatti a whole clavier-player; but with Bach the whole nature of a man of whom it is impossible to say whether the musician or the intellect in him was the greater.
>
> A Michel Angelo does not include a Rembrandt, nor a Rembrandt a Monet; but in Bach there is a Beethoven, a Schumann, a Wagner. ... The mysticism of the Middle Ages is there no less than the perspective of the future.... The history of music can be written with almost exclusive reference to Bach.

Of Mozart, Bie's deep musical sensitivity allows him to say that "[n]o music can be less easily described in words than his." But the same sensitivity leads him to emphasize Mozart's "sense for form," his "proportion" and "equilibrium," and "the endless melody and ... free intelligence of his music," and to recognize that Mozart's

> piano concertos ... justly enjoy the reknown of having created an epoch in this class.... The new pianoforte, with its fuller and more subtly expressive tones, is precisely adapted to his aims, and he is the first to launch the pianoforte on its decisive career.

True artists always create an essential language capable of conveying aesthetic experiences rather than merely transmitting indices. In this sense, Oscar Bie is an artist as well as an historian, and the core of his artistry is best revealed in the splendid prose he reserves for Beethoven:

> Music is to him a speech, because it is full of associations of ideas, which bring tones into relation with the outer world, and make them reverberate with a thousand inner meanings.
>
> He cared chiefly for the presentation of the idea, for the inwardness of the piece. Everything that was written down in concrete notes served to him but as a means for that expression, the mastery of which was the mastery of interpretation.

> In this man music spoke in words, not in pictures. He had the un-
> paralleled boldness to tear out his secret feelings, all bleeding as
> they were, and hold them up before his own gaze.
>
> He is ... the first tone-artist who breaks the forms of music to pieces
> on the iron of his emotions.

And how better articulate the classical spirit than to emphasize
that for Beethoven, tricks of technique and virtuosity mattered
little; rather, it was essential that "the *melos,* or latent melodic
air, which lies at the base of the figurations, [be] brought into
prominence, and [that] the rhythmical [and dynamic] presentation of these figurations [be] made as accurate as possible."

Such penetrating insights can be found on almost every
page. In Chopin's *Études,* Bie admires the "mechanical value"
but emphasizes the "poetry" and the ability of the composer to
bring "technique and tune into the friendly relation peculiar
to them." In Liszt, he finds both the synthesis of "[e]verything
that the piano had [previously] experienced" and the creation
of modern piano-playing through ultimate refinement of the
instrument's virtuoso possibilities. And the very vital human
background is never overlooked. Chopin's retiring nature is
brought into vivid focus by noting that he "once said of himself
that he was in this world like the E string of a violin on a contrabass"; and the influence of Paganini on Liszt, inspiring
him with a fanatical zeal to pursue new possibilities, receives
graphic treatment.

Citation of passages could go on and on. The pace is sustained, the excitement and drama continue, revealing a living
world of surprising facts and genial occurrences for the dis-
cerning layman as well as the initiate. And, in the process,
nothing pertaining to the piano is left unexplored. From the
earliest beginnings of the lute to the intricacies of relatively
modern piano manufacture, piano methods, and schools, Bie
takes underlying forces and facts and crystallizes them into
concepts which point to current pianistic developments. And
composers great and near-great, performers from the most
brilliant to the most commonplace, all come under his penetrating light.

Such broad coverage, naturally, must prevent completely definitive treatment in all areas. Thus, Bie's curious evaluations of composers such as Haydn and Mendelssohn appear as flaws in the total picture. And his concept that, for all the vitality of the Lisztian influence, "the piano is no concerto instrument," that in "concertos the delicate ear is outraged," is not a happy one. Even in such areas, however, Bie is never picayune. His judgments are always significant, and while they may not always induce agreement, they do always provoke thought.

As we reach the final pages of the work, it is clear that Bie has made a challenging and truly exhilarating experience from the simple act of reading a book. It is with esteem and gratitude, then, that I pay tribute to Oscar Bie for taking dimly recognizable pianistic concepts and making them clear and trenchant, and to E. E. Kellett and E. W. Naylor for their meritorious comments and their achievement in translating and revising the original so that its richness and power are fully preserved.

Aube Tzerko
University of California
at Los Angeles

A HISTORY OF THE PIANOFORTE AND PIANOFORTE PLAYERS

A

HISTORY OF THE PIANOFORTE

AND

PIANOFORTE PLAYERS

TRANSLATED AND REVISED
FROM THE GERMAN OF
OSCAR BIE

BY

E. E. KELLETT, M.A.

AND

E. W. NAYLOR, M.A., Mus. D.

WITH NUMEROUS PORTRAITS, ILLUSTRATIONS, AND FACSIMILES

LONDON
J. M. DENT & COMPANY
NEW YORK
E. P. DUTTON & COMPANY
MDCCCXCIX

Dedicated

TO

EUGENE D'ALBERT

Editors' Preface

THIS work does not profess to be so much a literal translation as a somewhat free version of Dr Bie's "Das Klavier." The author, writing as he does for a German public, naturally uses a more philosophic style than would be generally intelligible in England. Availing themselves, therefore, of Dr Bie's kind permission, the Editors, with a view to making the book more acceptable to English readers, have allowed themselves considerable liberty both in omission and in addition. For all portions of the text which are enclosed in square brackets they hold themselves responsible. The footnotes, except a few which are specially marked, have been added by Dr Naylor.

E. W. N.

E. E. K.

Contents

Contents

Guido of Arezzo and his protector, Bishop Theodal, playing on a Monochord. Vienna Hofbibliothek.

Old England: a Prelude

[The drift of the remarks immediately following, which the author entitles a "Prelude," is, that Music is at the present time flourishing more at home than in public; that the playing of chamber compositions is more popular than the representation of huge operas; and that therefore it is a suitable time to consider the history and scope of the instrument which, more than all others, has made possible this cultivation of domestic music. He begins then by contrasting the huge performances of Wagnerian drama at Bayreuth with what he calls the "intimate" character of a private pianoforte recital at home.]

THOSE were great days in which the foundation-stone was laid at Bayreuth. Days in which the creative philosopher of the stage threw his sceptre over the Ninth Symphony; days when choice spirits met together, who tremblingly passed through the moment in which they saw something never heard of become reality; days of a joyous intoxication when Liszt and Wagner embraced each other with tears; days that Nietzsche calls the happiest he had ever spent, when something brooded in the air that he could trace nowhere else—something ineffable but full of hope—those days, alas! return no more. In those days music, that music which the million greet with cheers of rapture, stood enthroned on the Stage, which gives to art its public hold upon the world. The living, new-creating music has to-day once more fled to the concert hall, to the haughty and more select rows of aristocratic amateurs who listen to the symphonic poems of Richard Strauss. These are tender and delicate creations beside the dramas of Wagner. They are elves, they elude us, and there are those who see them not. We have been driven to them as the highest musical expressions of our time.

Since the trumpet-notes of Bayreuth died away we have conducted our musical devotions on a smaller, more intimate scale. Already, beyond the concert hall, we see opening the private chamber, holiest of all, and the chamber music, which is to the music of the stage what etching is to painting. It is the old ebb and flow. As we passed from the single instrument to the orchestra, from Beethoven's orchestra with its travail for expression to Wagner's stage with its world-embracing aims, so we are now passing back from the stage to undiluted music first before thousands of listeners, then before hundreds only.

And now, if I had my way, I would bring the pianoforte before a small audience, say of ten persons, not in the concert hall but in the home, where the artist may give his little concerts, in the fitting hour of twilight, playing to a company every one of whom he knows. Under such circumstances, indeed, one can implicitly trust himself to the *intimate* character of the pianoforte. Then stream from it the sweet tones of the harp, then, like strings of pearls, come chains of roses from its notes, or Titanic forces seem to escape from it, and my soul lies wholly in the player's finger-tips. Is it then that the piano is a contemptible instrument compared with the violin or the string-quartet? Do I then remember how it sings so hoarsely, and how its scales are so broken, and how the soul of its melody is so dead without the breath of the rising and falling tone?

Of course, if it expresses itself in the piano-concerto, on the podium of the orchestra, or even if it trusts itself, in trio or quartet, to the company of strings or wind, then it moves my compassion. A foreign atmosphere envelops it even if Beethoven's concerto in E flat major is resounding; and a weakness haunts it, if in chamber music it alternates with the dominating melody of the singing violin. But when once the clang of the violin and of the Cor Anglais[1] has faded from our ears, and all comparison has been laid aside, then, and then only, the soul of the pianoforte rises before us. Every good thing must be considered *per se* apart from all comparison. Is it no good thing to have the whole material of tone before one's ten fingers, to penetrate it, *truly* to penetrate it ; to feel beneath one's nerves all the subtleties of all music—the song, the dance, whispering, shrieking, weeping, laughter?—all, I mean, voiced in the tone of the pianoforte, the epic tone of this modern Cithara, which, in its own kind, embraces the lyrical nature of the violin and the dramatic nature of the orchestra? In such all-embracing power the piano is in the twilight chamber a strange and dear tale-teller, a *Rhapsode* for the *intimate* spirit, which can express itself in it by improvisation, and an archive for the historian to whom it unrolls the whole life of modern music in its universal speech from a point of view which gives us the whole in the average. Then only do I love the piano—then is it faithful, then noble, genuine, unique.

Queen Elizabeth of England is sitting in the afternoon at her spinet. She is thinking of the conversation which she has had this

---

[1] The Cor Anglais is mentioned here as expressing a tone-colour which is entirely foreign to the pianoforte. This instrument is the alto hautboy. Its name is a curious instance of a "ghost" word, viz. : in its original meaning, "Cor anglé," a bent or "angled" tube, German "Krummhorn," it was misunderstood and explained as Cor Angl*ais*, Corno Inglese, English Horn.

forenoon with Sir James Melville—a conversation which the latter has preserved for us in writing. He was in 1564 ambassador from Mary Stuart to Elizabeth. Elizabeth had asked him what was Mary's style of dress, the colour of her hair, her figure, her way of life. "When Mary returns from the hunt," he answered, "she gives herself up to historical reading or to music, for she is at home with lute and virginal." "Does she play well?" asked Elizabeth. "For a queen, very well," was the answer. And so, this afternoon, Elizabeth is sitting at the spinet, and playing Bird's or Dr Bull's Variations on popular airs. She plays from the very (or a similar) copy which to-day is marked in the Fitzwilliam Museum at Cambridge as Queen Elizabeth's Virginal Book. She does not notice that Sir James and Lord Hunsdon are secretly listening. When suddenly she sees them standing behind her she stops playing. "I am not used," she says, "to play before men; but when I am solitary, to shun melancholy."

Fifty years before, Albert Dürer had given an illustration of Melancholy in his famous engraving. Melancholy, as dignified Depression, is sitting in the open air, surrounded by the implements for Manual Labour, Art and Science. It expressed the anticipated pain of the misfortune which lurks in the good fortune of knowledge and intelligence; the pain of the dawning Age of Wisdom, for which Erasmus, in his Praise of Folly, had already shown a just contempt. In his St Jerome, Dürer represents the deliverance from Melancholy. St Jerome, in the contemporary engraving, is sitting quietly and contentedly at home, while the sun shines through the circular panes,[1] the papers, books and cushions being so neatly disposed around, and the lion so wonderfully sleeping beside him. But—in the corner stands his house-organ or spinet!

Something of the spirit of the St Jerome breathes through the Elizabethan music—a tone of the Volkslied, or of that intimate world-sense, alongside of the decaying mediæval counterpoint (decaying as the Gothic architecture was decaying) like scenes

---

[1] Readers who do not know the picture must not be misled by this expression. St Jerome's window-frames are filled with numberless little rounds of bottle-glass.

of popular life or of lyrical beauty, which display themselves chiefly in the drama, in the midst of scenes of historic ceremonial. Everyone has observed what a subtle sense for soft musical tones is revealed throughout Shakespeare's plays. The Duke in Twelfth Night loves the Volkslied, the old song, "old and plain," which "the spinsters and the knitters in the sun, and the free maids that weave their thread with bones, do use to chant: it is silly sooth, and dallies with the innocence of love like the old age." He heard it last night; he will hear it again to-day: "Methought it did relieve my passion much, More than light airs and recollected terms Of these most brisk and giddy-pacèd times." And it is the fool who sings it to him—that typical figure of the love-thoughts and of the love-business of the people: the fool, who in every play has the largest store of old popular songs, and who in this very drama empties a very cornucopia of them. But Shakespeare's holiest encomium on music is sung at night, in that idyllic scene at the close of the Merchant of Venice, between Lorenzo and Jessica. The moonlight sleeps upon the bank; the lovers sit in silence before Portia's house and let the music steal upon their ears. "Soft stillness and the night become the touches of sweet harmony." Lorenzo endeavours to cheer Jessica with the music. We can well believe that his impassioned words express the feelings of the poet himself, who has marked his Shylock, his Cassius, his Othello,[1] his Caliban, with the stain of a heedlessness of music :—

> "The man that hath no music in himself,
> Nor is not moved with concord of sweet sounds,
> Is fit for treasons, stratagems, and spoils."

Portia enters the moonlit garden and hears the gentle tones, not knowing whence they come. She feels keenly the eternal magic of invisible music which lies pillowed in silence and night. The whole scene is a hymn on the infelt soul of musical self-centredness, wherein man finds his best self.

[1] The bagpipers play before Othello's house, and the clown reproves their nasal tone. Othello himself gave them money to go away, which argues rather in his favour. As for Caliban, he was a true musician, except when drunk. Even then he liked howling catches. See especially Tempest, Act iii. 2, 136.

So too, perhaps, stood Shakespeare by the spinet of his beloved, and to his musical sense the tones and the love are blended
together, his loved one becoming transfigured into music :—

> " How oft when thou, my music, music playest,
>   Upon that blessed wood whose motion sounds
> With thy sweet fingers, when thou gently swayest
>   The wiry concord that mine ear confounds,
> Do I envy those jacks [1] that nimble leap
>   To kiss the tender inward of thy hand,
> Whilst my poor lips, that should that harvest reap,
>   At the wood's boldness by thee blushing stand.
> To be so tickled, they would change their state
>   And situation with those dancing chips,
> O'er whom thy fingers walk with gentle gait,
>   Making dead wood more blessed than living lips.
>   Since saucy jacks [1] so happy are in this,
>   Give them thy fingers, me thy lips to kiss."

It is in the Elizabethan age that the clavier begins for the
first time to play a part in the world.   In the English clavier-
music, as in all English music at that time, there is a ravishing
bloom, which vanished just as quickly from the popular concerts,
never to appear again.   Circumstances combined to favour it.
A certain repose, a dependence upon art came upon the London
society of that day, and at such times art penetrates easily into
the privacy of the home.   For centuries had the Low Countries
held the sway of music ; but the art of tone, which had made its
way thither under the stars of Dufay, Okeghem, and Josquin
des Près, remained in the service of the Church.   It represented
the rapid development of contrapuntal vocal harmony, as it had
slowly developed itself into music *per se* from the figurations,
which at the end of the tenth century began to found themselves
on the *canto fermo* of the Gregorian material.   Around the
Gregorian pillars there had arisen a mathematical system of
rules and proportions ; of musical vaultings, symmetries, and

---

[1] This passage is the only one in Shakespeare where the slightest inaccuracy or
looseness in the use of a technical word is to be noticed.   The word "jacks" is here used
carelessly, meaning the " keys," over which of course the fingers walk, and which leap up
to kiss the inward of the hand.   The actual " jacks " are *inside* the instrument.

Orlando Gibbons. After Grignon's engraving in Hawkins.

mouldings, in which the ordering world-spirit seemed to have realised itself. As yet, however, there was no melody whose contour was unifying; no harmony whose development was to be foreseen; no singing voice resting on the support of an accompaniment. The voices ran according to the laws of their *tempi*, all equally important from soprano to bass; and their harmony only aided in reducing them to an average. The *instrument* of this great sacred music was the human voice, at first only the bearer of the tone, but then gradually here and there betraying a greater depth of feeling: and yet this great function of the voice had a value for expression which is not to be underrated. Even in this mathematical tone-system there lay the power of exhibiting nature as she is.

If art was to escape from these rudiments into more intimate circles, the appropriate social surroundings must be provided. *The home* must develop.

The public art of the Middle Ages had divided its favours between church and hall; it was in the church that counterpoint found its development; it was in the hall that the old popular song, without making special advance, maintained itself. The popular song ranged itself over against counterpoint, for it was pure melody, as we understand melody to-day, and it was well arranged as to rhythm in four or eight-bar "strains."[1] In two ways, however, counterpoint and popular song might meet: the first might absorb the second, or *vice versa*. It is well known what took place when counterpoint absorbed the popular song: throughout the later Middle Ages popular songs, even the vulgarest, are taken up in masses or motets as motives for

[1] *Cf.* Shakespeare on "eight-bar strains." See "Shakespeare and Music" (Dent), by E. W. Naylor.

figures; nay, more, when they alternate, while the Gregorian *cantus* holds its own alongside, church hymns are named after popular songs, and we stumble everywhere upon masses named after their underlying melody,[1] " L'homme armé," " Malheur me bat," " O Venus," and the like. But, as might be expected, these are taken up utterly into the framework of the voice-mathematic; their peculiar aroma disappears; they are thrown into contrapuntal form. Far from betraying a worldly element, such as Ambrose conveyed under allegorical paintings of old landscape in religious pictures, they betray on the contrary a total absence of the secular sense. To them the content of the melody is so indifferent that they never once display it.

Secondly, the popular song on its own side stands apart from counterpoint. Since counterpoint is the recognised style of the time, popular song has no choice but to appropriate that means of expression. Hence arises the Madrigal, the most festive form of this appropriation, which sets popular themes to many parts, but with the utmost art. It exhausts all the requirements of better taste in secular music in the sixteenth century. Societies like the Arcadeltian[2] have resulted in an extraordinary growth of published material, and it is no mere accident that this process has continued in England, thanks to the exertions of a Madrigal Society, down to our own time. Yet the popular song was too opposed to the choral setting to feel itself at home in this form long and universally. It tended to unison or to the total absence of words; in the latter case it could still remain contrapuntal and became simply a tone-piece;[3] in the former the counterpoint existed, so to speak,

---

[1] Readers to whom this ancient method of composition is new will find in Mendelssohn's " St Paul," an easily accessible example, viz. : the chorus " But our God abideth in Heaven," where the second trebles sing in long notes the old melody of the Apostles' Creed. No one could recognise it in the midst of the counterpoint of the other vocal parts, and this is the point in question; namely, that the mediæval writers used secular tunes in the same way, and were held blameless.

[2] Named after Jacques Arcadelt, of the early sixteenth century, one of the many natives of Flanders who so distinguished that period of Madrigal composition; a first-rate man.

[3] Doubtless the author refers to the tendency in the sixteenth century for voice parts to be made interchangeable with instrumental parts. Many instances might be given

Young Scholar and his Wife.

Painting by Gonzales Coques (1614-1684), in the Royal Gallery at Cassel.

Lady at the Clavier.

Painting by Dirk Hals (? 1656), in the Rijksmuseum at Amsterdam.

simply at the pleasure of the melody, as it did in hundreds of old melodies throughout the world. These old popular songs, of remarkable origin in their plain melodious orderliness, became finally the precursors of modern music. While they marked the monodic principle, and gave to the expression the full value which it had in all early music, they accustomed the ears to the pleasure of the fully-outlined melody, and compelled the combination with this of an equally well-outlined harmony. Thus the way was prepared for the great discovery of the monodic opera, which arose in Florence about 1600.

But in that wonderful drama, which the emancipation of the secular or popular principle in the music of the sixteenth century presents, the instrument appears as the second agent, with its greater freedom as contrasted with the human voice. Choral counterpoint penetrates into the music of the future in the two ways of the one-part song and of the instrumental polyphony, which form a quite natural whole. In proportion as vocal music became more individual and more full of soul, the absolute instrumental music gained in meaning. But we must mark two impulses which necessarily condition each other. As the one-part song was, so to speak, a victory of the logic of expression over the metaphysic of many-parts, so the latter also was a transference of counterpoint to the instrument.

[In the late sixteenth century, counterpoint can scarcely be said to survive in any popular shape except that of the Catch or (endless) canon, the performance of which, when the complete melody is once learnt, is merely mechanical, and requires no great intelligence or attention from the singer. But to perform continuous contrapuntal music requires very great intelligence, and such concentrated attention as is seldom found in its perfection amongst mere singers. Instrumentalists therefore, as being superior in these indispensable qualities, were naturally called

both in Italy and England, *e.g.* if a tenor voice were absent, the part was played by a tenor instrument, viol, cornetto, trombone, or what not. This was the more easily made habitual since instrumental accompaniment merely consisted in doubling the vocal parts.

upon, first to assist, and then to displace the singers, who had
allowed themselves to rest on their physical gifts rather than on
the accomplishments of the intellect.] [1] Thus it is the instrument
which opens to the popular song and to the dance of the same
kind, within the contrapuntal style, new paths of promise ; and
this principle of popular music, after it had held itself for a
century in the almost neglected plain melody under the wintry
covering of ecclesiastical counterpoint, becomes, in a moment,
conscious of its immeasurable powers.   Still, further, here there
was the ground on which the popular song, so long differenced
from counterpoint, gradually overcame it and was able to develop
its principle freshly and clearly.   In the opera we see it suddenly
break with counterpoint ; but this kind of art suffered by this
suddenness, since it swung uneasily to and fro from the heights of
the stage-reformation to the depths of virtuosity.   Instrumental
music escaped this sudden break, took up into itself counterpoint, transformed it out of itself, and passed on to meet a
development far more regular and advancing with giant strides.
What instrument, then, was best for the reproduction of the
contrapuntal play of the voices ?   Next to choral song stood the
organ, with its power of holding on its tones.   Slowly, therefore,
as we might expect, the organ steps into the contest with the
church-choir.   At first more clumsily, then more gently, its voices
contrast and work into counterpoint.   The organ also offers,
as exchange for the sung chorus, direct transferences from motets
of Josquin and Orlando Lasso.   But so soon as the organ recollects
that it is not vocal but an instrument, it begins—shall we say ?—
to run off into flourishes.   All kinds of adornments and grace-
notes start up, and finally the organist prides himself on departing
utterly from the composer's or author's intention, and embroider-
ing the theme at pleasure.   A Prelude and a Fugue in this style
appeared to the men of that time dreadful enough to linger over ;
as Hermann Finck writes, " they run sometimes by the half-hour,

---

[1] This paragraph replaces some rather obscure sentences in the original, and aims
at conveying their general sense.

up and down over the key-board, trusting thus, with God's help, to attain the highest, never asking where Dan Time, or Dan Accent, or Dan Tone, or Bona Fantasia, are staying in the meanwhile." Further, when the organ had purified itself in the great epoch of German church-music, it had perforce to remain in the service of the Church. It felt the influence of the audience, which was brought into rhythm and harmony by the secular principle of music — that influence which, in the Protestant Choral and in the creations of Bach, made itself felt as a brilliant reaction of the secular musical sense on the church tradition.

Alongside of the organ came the lute, which for so long had been the chief instrument of the home. Yet the lute, with its tones drawn from so few strings, was unable to show itself very productive. It had provided the accompaniment of songs, and music in many parts had very early been arranged for it.[1] At all times, therefore, the lute had imitated the contrapuntal style, though in simple fashion, and occasionally certain passages had been accented with chords thrown in arpeggio-wise. Whether the lute accompanied a voice, or whether it took up the popular melody into itself to produce "absolute" music, it exhibited a style of its own, conditioned by its own limitations, even as, alongside of the organ, it had its own note-script.[2] It was not convenient accurately to retain on the lute every separate voice. An instrumental style was formed; men became accustomed to the sufficiency of this simplicity of tone; dances were written for the lute, as Hans Judenkunig in his lute-book offers a "Court-dance, Panana[3] alla Veneziana, Rossina ein welscher Dantz" and the like. As time went on, all well-known pieces were

[1] An excellent book, which ought to be known widely, containing many examples of early lute music, is W. G. v. Wasielewski's History of sixteenth century instrumental music. Berlin, 1878.

[2] Meaning the "Tablature," a system of writing music for the lute which has nothing in common with our "staff" notation. A set of six horizontal lines (representing six strings), was used, and letters (*a*, *b*, *c*, etc.) on these indicated the semitones, reckoning *a* as the "open string," *b* as the semitone above that, and so on, for each separate string.

[3] Another spelling for Pavana, or Pavan, slow dance in square time.

arranged for the lute, as they are to-day for the piano. Encyclopædias appear—as for example in 1603 the "Thesaurus" in ten volumes of " Besardus nec non praestantissimorum musicorum, qui hoc seculo in diversis orbis partibus excellunt, selectissima omnis generis cantus in testudine (the lute) modulamina continens." Graceful figurations arise, which in France and Italy receive fine names, while the German lute-player sets himself strongly against these complicated "battements," "tremblements," or "flattements," against this or that "passagio largo," "stretto," "raddopiato." But, on the whole, much as the lute achieved, it could not suffice to compel the complete admission of the whole musical material into the home.

The heavy *churchiness* of the organ and the light secularity of the lute were thus constrained to unite themselves in an instrument which was sufficiently flexible to effect the representation of all the voice parts at once yet more easily than in the choir, and which could embrace the whole tonic scale so completely as to expand the limits of the voice both above and below. It must be a light, moveable instrument, a miniature of the organ. The clavier offered itself for this end ; and in it organ and lute met in fruitful wedlock.

Such is the position and the meaning of the clavier in the great struggle for freedom of the secular music-principle which fills the sixteenth century. With this begins the history of the clavier, and simultaneously the history of the orchestra. The orchestra flourishes where the clavier flourishes, and *vice versa*. The combination of single instruments in a body, and that *one* instrument which alone can represent that combination, are manifestations of the same movement, namely, of the transference of the church choral tone-practice into the sphere of the secular, where in place of the counterpoint which ran on by the hour, an interlaced system of harmonies, a strict organisation of melodies, gradually assumed the mastery. The orchestra occupied itself with public representations ; the clavier with the advance of the new music in the home. Already, in Venice, had instruments taken their share with the singers in the church; now chamber-music also began to flourish. Later, in France, the court-orchestra gained a special significance, and very shortly the clavier also made its importance felt. In Naples the orchestra appears simultaneously with the Italian opera, and shortly afterwards arises Scarlatti with his clavier-pieces. In Old England the orchestra was regarded with a special affection; and thus it is that in England the clavier first flourishes.

The early development of instrumental music in Venice cannot have been without its influence upon London, which not only cast an eye on the social and topographical aspect of the city of the lagoons, but also allowed itself to be consciously influenced by Italian culture. So early as 1512 we hear of Italian masques performed in the Palace at Greenwich; and when, in 1561, a tragedy by Lord Buckhurst[1] was performed with introductory pantomimes and orchestral music, we recognise the Venetian touch in the individual character of the instruments. In Act I. the violin, in Act II. horns, in Act III. flutes, in Act IV. oboes, in Act V. drums and pipes are set down.[2] The orchestra of Queen Elizabeth exhibits strong features of the mediæval physiognomy: there are sixteen trumpets (about equal to the number of the singers in the associated chorus) and three kettle-drums stand in close relation to them. It is the old official festival music once more. Eight violins, one lute, one harp, one bagpipe, two flutes, and three virginals are the relatively weaker supplanters of the more intimate orchestral type. The respective costliness appears from the account: the lute, £60; the violin, £20; the bagpipes, £12. The Italian operatic orchestra started on the opposite path, gradually getting rid of the stringed instruments and adopting wind. It was, however, very thin, and even in France the orchestra of the sixteenth century appears hardly

---

[1] The play was *Gorboduc*, otherwise *Ferrex and Porrex*. The author is better known as Thomas Sackville.

[2] See "Shakespeare and Music," pp. 169-171, for other English examples.

more elaborate than a Papal orchestra of the fifteenth. It is the English orchestra that at this time stands at the head, not even the thirty instrumentalists of Munich being equal to it. Above all there seems to be growing a division of labour between orchestra and chamber-music, so much so that Prätorius, when in his great musical work (1618), he mentions such combinations of lute-choirs, calls this style of chamber-music especially English. "Die Engelländer nennens gar apposite à consortio ein consort,[1] wenn etliche Personen mit allerley Instrumenten, als Klavicymbel und Gross-spinett, grosse Lyra, Doppelharff, Lauten, Theorben, Bandorn, Penorcon, Zittern, Viol de Gamba, einer kleinen Diskant-Geig, einer Quer-Flöt oder Bock-Flöt, bisweilen auch einer stillen Posaun oder Racket zusammen in einer Compagny und Gesellschaft gar still, sanfft und lieblich accordiren, und in anmuthiger Symphonia mit einander zusammen stimmen." Hence it appears that the orchestra and the chamber-music of old England were the chief things. In the former the wind prevailed, in the latter the strings; but the clavier had its place in both kinds. For the clavier, during many years, even when it had made good its position as a solo instrument, still took its part in orchestral combinations. Even in Hasse's time the *Kapellmeister* at Dresden sat at the clavier.

Under such circumstances it is no wonder that the old English clavier should have flourished, or that it was in England that it first recognised its mission. The influence of this was great enough to bring about a speedy development on the continent. The cultivation of music was not only wide-spread, but also very ancient; so much so that the old musical writer Tinctor (1434-1520) expressly ascribes the origin of all contrapuntal music to England. The compositions of the thirteenth century were, in grace of melody, simplicity of rhythm, and modernity of harmony, far in advance of their age. (Compare the canon in six

---

[1] "The English call it quite appositely by the name 'Consort' (from Latin consortium) when several persons with various instruments, such as . . . etc. . . . play together in sweet concord with one another."

parts,[1] "Sumer is icumen in" of the Monk of Reading, before 1226.) It is noteworthy that the English possessed of old a popular, simple, melodious tendency in music which reminds us of Mendelssohn. This has made English music great and also small. Great, for at a time when the whole musical world struggled with the contrapuntal want of system in harmony and melody, the English were capable of preparing the way, in systematic, plastic form, for the new conquering secular principle. Small, because so soon as this principle became universally recognised, they laid themselves to sleep in the luxurious enjoyment of their tradition, and set up foreign ideals, such as Mendelssohn and Handel,[2] who were endowed with the like gifts.

Madrigals of Elizabeth's time are so familiar to us that Dr Ambros, of Prague, could produce them in Prague with great success, drawing from J. J. Maier's German collection. That free geniality of the English in its ancient dress, which conceals all triviality, overcomes us even to-day. With the clavier-pieces it is the same. We are charmed with the extreme simplicity of their musical form, and we love them because they come before us in an archaic dress. They exhale an aroma whose popular sweetness mingles beautifully with the slight harshness of their naïve style. Allowing ourselves a touch of triviality, we find ourselves wondering that these works seem to be quite outside their own time, and in the modernness of their spirit surpass even the renowned contemporary performances of Gabrieli and the other Venetians.

In this London, the imitator and rival of Venice, we fall upon the first clavier-books that, as such, were ever collected in the world. Strictly speaking, they are not the absolute first. We read on the title-page of a collection of Chansons, Madrigals and Dances, issued at Lyons in 1560 by S. Gorlier: " Premier Livre de tablature d'Espinette." We learn from Prätorius that the inscrip-

---

[1] It is misleading to say "in six parts." There are six voices, but the canon proper only takes four. The other two sing, independently of the canon, a "bussing bass," founded alternately on Do and Re.

[2] In the early seventeenth century it was matter of complaint in England that " French songs " and instrumental music " in the Italian manner " were more popular than necessary.

tion, " For an Instrument," which appears so often on old works, is not to be understood universally, but to be confined to the clavier. Nevertheless, it is in England that we first find in any numbers collections of expressly-marked clavier-pieces, springing from a special impulse of musical enthusiasm. First in interest stands the so-called Queen Elizabeth's Virginal Book, one of the chief treasures of the Fitzwilliam Museum, lately transcribed into our own script for Breitkopf and Härtel. Granting that it may have been written after the time of Elizabeth, it yet, with its three hundred pieces, goes back to the earliest names of this school— Tallis, Bird, Farnaby, Bull. Next, in the library of the late Rimbault, an important English historian of music, we find, in manuscript, a Virginal Book of the Earl of Leicester, and another of Lady Nevill. Doubtless great lords and ladies had many manuscript collections of this kind, including copies of the favourite pieces of the day. But soon manuscript gave way to print. In 1611 appeared the first copper-engraved set of pieces ever seen in England. This was " Parthenia, or the Maydenhead of the first Musicke that ever was printed for the Virginalls. Composed by three famous masters : William Byrd, Dr John Bull, and Orl. Gibbons, Gentilmen of His Majestie's most illustrious Chappell." A modern edition of this collection was issued in 1847 by the indefatigable London Musical Antiquarian Society. From the materials collected by this Society Ernst Pauer, whose contributions to the history of the clavier have achieved a great repute, formed his collected edition of Old English Composers, which presents, in modernised form, special pieces by Bird, Bull, Gibbons, Blow, Purcell, and even Arne, who, though later, is not uninteresting.

The pieces in these collections are of three kinds. First, free fantasias,[1] such as were also composed for organ and lute under the name of prelude, preamble, or even toccata (here denoting simply piece). In their essence fugal they are broken and inter-sected by florid passages. In the second class, a canto fermo was

[1] These were also called by the plain English name "fancies."

PARTHENIA

or

THE MAYDENHEAD

of the first musicke that

euer was printed for the VIRGINALLS

COMPOSED

By thee famous Masters William Byrd. Dr: John Bull & Orlando Gibbons.
Gentilmen of his Ma:ties most Illustrious Chappell

Ingrauen
by William Hole.

Lond: print: for M. Dor: Euans. (Cum priuilegio.) Are to be sould by G.
Lowe printe in Loathberry

Title-page of the first English engraved Clavier Music, 1611.

taken from a church melody, and developed after the approved
fashion in fugal or figured style.   Or, finally—and this is the most
usual case, and the style most appropriate to the clavier—a number
of variations, or even groups of variations, if the theme has several
sections, are formed into a series.   The theme itself is a popular
song or dance.   Popular songs, as they swept uncounted through
England and Scotland, are inexhaustible.   Even to-day they retain
their freshness.   To the whole piece they impart their tense and
melodious rhythm.   The dances—in common time called Pavans,
in triple, Galliards—are frequently named after noblemen,[1] and are
in their variations adorned with the same encomiastic flourishes as
the songs.

The clavier, for which these English musicians wrote their
pieces, was of the kind called a virginal.   The virginal was a
peculiarly handy kind of spinet.   It is not to be assumed that,
after the quibbling and flattering fashion of the time, it was so
called in compliment to the Maiden Queen.   The name is older.
Possibly it is due to the fact that the small size of the instrument
made it specially suitable for young girls.   We find scarcely any
pictures of *men* sitting at the clavier.   In Italy the same name
was in vogue ; but we are not here concerned with the whole
history of the nomenclature of old keyed instruments.   We are
only so far interested in the history of the instrument as it forms
the basis for the rise of the *literature,* i.e. *style of composition,*
which concerns us in its human aspect.   The histories of the
clavier, those of Rimbault, Oskar Paul, and others, place the
history of the instrument in the foreground.   Even Weitzmann
has appended to the last edition of his " History of Clavier-Playing
and Clavier-Literature," a comprehensive chapter on this subject.
But the history of the clavier is a very complicated matter if we
are tedious on it, and a very simple matter if, without becoming
inexact, we are brief upon it.

---

[1] When Sir Toby says to the caper-cutting Sir Andrew : " I did think, by the
excellent constitution of thy leg, it was formed *under the star* of a galliard," may he not
refer to one of these dedications of dances to noblemen ?

It is a union of the harp with the mechanism of key-action. Harps, in which the strings are plucked with the plectrum, are in some form or other as old as music itself, and appear in the most various shapes in the first dawn of civilisation. The mechanism of the keyboard, which by means of an easy leverage adapted to the human fingers, gives the player control over the sounds of pipes or strings, is not quite so ancient, since it presumes a certain inventive capacity; but it is old enough to be equally beyond our chronological powers. In Europe we find keyed organs as early as the first centuries after Christ. The application of this action to stringed instruments was completed in the monochord. The monochord, an instrument well-known to the earliest theoretical musicians, was a board with a string stretched across it on which the intervals could be clearly marked and sounded by mathematical division : the half marking the octave above the pitch of the whole length of the string; the third part of it giving a fifth above that octave; the quarter part giving a fourth above that fifth, namely a note two octaves above the pitch of the whole string; the fifth part sounding a major third above the last named note, viz., a seventeenth above the pitch of the whole length; and so on.

The simple monochord developed itself after the tenth century in two directions, the musical and the technical. Its development was musical, inasmuch as three or four strings took the place of the *one* in order to produce a chord instead of a simple arpeggio; an aim which the church music attained by the multiplication of instruments sounding only one note each at a time. It was technical, inasmuch as, in place of the constant alteration of the "bridge" which divided the string, *keys* were introduced, which not only divided the string at the desired spot, by a flat metal pin (called "tangent" from its action in simply "touching" against the wire), but also caused it to sound. With twenty keys and only a few strings, of course it was necessary for several keys to divide the same string, and to sound it at different points in its length; whereby the simultaneous

From the Weimar " Wunderbuch," a Clavichord of about 1440.   One of the oldest
representations.

sounding of several notes was brought into the proper limits.
Though thus really many - stringed, the instrument still retained
its name of *mono*chord.   Gradually the number of keys increased,
and in increasing proportion the number of strings, which still
remained of equal length.   About the year 1450, probably, the
clavier attained this, its earliest form of the monochord.   It
served an educational purpose.   Virdung, Abbot of Amberg,
who in 1511 published his German " Music with Illustrations,"
is our authority for the development of the monochord up
to the first true clavier-form—that of the *clavichord*—which is
nothing more nor less than the many-stringed many-keyed
" monochord " which we have just described.   The self-contra-
dictory " mono " was rejected, and ' *clavi* ' substituted (Lat.
clavis, a key).   The *clavis* is the key which in the organ
admits the wind to the pipes, in the clavier sets the strings
in motion.

The clavichord introduced a new means of " expression," viz.,
the " Bebung " (trembling, shivering), which could be applied to

any of the notes by a gentle after-pressure of the key, a mournful, soul-moving *vibrato*, which was only possible with the peculiar mechanism of the clavichord, where a "tangent" both divided the string and at the same moment instantaneously created the sound. A slight relaxation of this pressure on the key caused a slight lowering of pitch; a slight renewal of pressure a corresponding heightening. The German players of the eighteenth century could scarcely find it in their hearts to resign this delicate effect, even for the advantages of the modern pianoforte. Here for the first time the keyboard mechanism had succeeded in producing a modification of the tones by "touch" alone, and the keyed instrument had gained its soul. How confined were the old eight keys of the Hurdygurdy,[1] the favourite instrument till the rise of the lute, where the strings were strained against a rosined wheel turned by a crank (a sort of everlasting fiddle-bow), while the keys divided

---

[1] *Drehleier.* The instrument referred to is of the ninth century.

From the Weimar "Wunderbuch," Primitive Spinet, of about 1440.
One of the oldest representations.

the strings into notes—an antiquated compromise between clavier and violin ! How clumsy was the treatment of the organ-keys so late as the fourteenth century, in which, according to Prätorius, the keys were struck with the fist ! But from this time the art of mechanics develops quickly, and the rapid increase of the number of keys in the clavichord shows us how speedily its supremacy was attained. The fall of the key was shallow, the quick-sounding tone encouraged ornamental flourishes, which were more easily played on the clavichord than on our heavy-touched pianoforte. Yet it was long before the number of strings became equal to that of the keys. Not till the eighteenth century (about 1725) do we find clavichords with a string to every key. (These are called *free* instruments, in contra-distinction to the old *tied*.)[1] It is obvious that the " tied " clavichords did not admit of *all* chords ; but those which were impossible were discords, avoided on other grounds by the older music. To sound C and D flat together was impossible ; but no one complained, for no one, for reasons of style, wished to try it. But, on very old clavichords, C and E are also incapable of being simultaneously sounded—a fact which gives us many a hint for the criticism of the oldest pieces.

In the form of a simple case, fit to be laid on the table, and later when fitted with its own stand, frequently painted on top and sides, or with its keys set in ivory and metal, the clavichord continues to the beginning of the nineteenth century. Although the strings were then duplicated, although it was possible to attain in the touch stronger or weaker, louder or softer, expression, yet it could not, with its far too great simplicity of tone, hold its place in the rapidly hurrying development of music. It had taken one thousand years to improve the monochord, five hundred more to produce a clavichord, two hundred and fifty more were required to bring the clavicymbal[2] form to its perfection ; and yet a hundred and fifty for the clavicymbal to emerge into a Steinway or a Bechstein.

---

[1] *Bundfrei* and *gebunden*, the former only was capable of striking any combination of notes at once—*e.g.*, four or five adjacent semitones.

[2] One of the many names of what we know best as " harpsichord."

The Clavicymbal 23

The *clavicymbal* represents a second form of the clavier, which begins its career about 1400. Its invention is directly due to the influence of the organ. When the clavier began to replace the organ in the home, a desire was felt for the stronger notes of the great wind-instrument. The clavichord was unequal to the task. A new technique was required. The strings, instead of being touched and divided, were plucked with quills, which stood out at the side from the jacks, at the end of the key-lever. For this purpose it was necessary of course that the strings should be tuned each to its proper note, and therefore have each its due length. The mechanism of plucking, and the measurement of the strings, give to the clavicymbal its character as distinct from the clavichord. The tone becomes rippling, metallically glittering, firm and yet rattling; nay, it might be called romantic, if it could sustain its poetical air, which it gains for us in the first instance by its strange character. But it was a defect that the tone was unsuitable for *nuances;* for, unlike the clavichord, it was unable to produce *forte, piano,* or the "Bebung." Here a hint was taken from the organ. Stops, as with the organ, were added; these, as they were drawn out or pushed in, made it possible to use either one, two, or three strings on any single key, thus offering three gradations from piano to forte. Or, by the same means of a stop, a damper of leather or cloth was put on the strings, and thus an imitation of the lute was effected. Or, thirdly, both these appliances were united by providing two keyboards placed one over the other, on which at will the player could play loud or soft. Hence arose dozens of combinations. Strings were coupled in unison or octave, registers were made either for hand or foot, keyboards were made to shift, the shapes of the cases were either rectangular or in the "flügel" form (like our grand pianos) to accommodate the gradual shortening of the strings as they reached the higher octaves, the cases were either small, or larger, and furnished with magnificent stands, such as were brought out by the first famous clavier-manufactory, that of the Ruckers at Antwerp, who flourished at the end of the sixteenth century; there were almost as many names as shapes. Those with smaller cases were called Virginals, those in the shape of a swine's head were called Spinets ("Spinet" referring to the plectrum of quill); while the larger instruments were "Clavi-cymbals" (cembalo, a "dulcimer"; though the clavicymbal was a *harp-with-keys*, not by any means a dulcimer, which is the progenitor of the pianoforte, a very different matter), or in Italy "Gravicymbels," in England "Harpsichords," in France "Clavecins." The keyboard, at first incomplete in the lower "short" octave,[1] gradually spread itself over three or even five octaves. The fulness of tone was greater, but the touch necessarily heavier than of old. The new instrument was unsuited for the quick development of a natural system of "fingering."

The technique of clavier-playing advanced but slowly from the mere tapping of the finger-ends to the dexterity of to-day, which lays under contribution the whole arm as far as the elbow. In the first clavier and organ "school," which was published by Girolamo Diruta in Venice about 1600, and which bears the title, "Il Transilvano, sopra il vero modo di sonare organi e stromenti di Penna," are already to be found rules for the use of the fingers, for the holding of the hands, and as to the differences of organ and clavier-playing; but fifty years later, according to Weitzmann, Lorenzo Penna,[2] in his "Albori musicali," knows no other rules than that the hand should be raised high, and that, as the right

---

[1] What were known as "short octaves" were to be seen almost in our own time in certain old organs. For three centuries the following or a similar arrangement was practised. Supposing the lowest notes of the keyboard ran thus: E, F, F sharp, G, G sharp, the first E being that under the bass staff. But when the E key was put down, the note *sounded* was the C a third below ; when the F sharp key was played, the resulting note was the D below ; the G sharp key produced the low E, which should have had its own key to itself. Thus the keyboard, which apparently stopped at E under the bass staff, really had D and C below, arranged to sound on two other keys. So to produce a diatonic scale beginning from the low C of the violoncello, the keys actually played had to be : E, F sharp, G sharp, F, G, etc., which would produce C, D, E, F, G, etc.

[2] Penna's name should not be connected with the word "Penna" in the title of Diruta's book, where it merely means "quill," and "stromenti di Penna"= "harpsichords."

5- Iucundo tristes oblecto carmine mentes,
Depelloꝗ graves curas, relevoꝗ labores.

A Concerted Performance.   Engraved by H. Goltzius (1558-1617).

ascends the scale and the left descends, the third and fourth
fingers should be alternately used, and *vice versa* with the third
and second. Old pictures confirm this statement. In England
we meet notable examples of the influence of this Italian fingering.
The thumb, as the finger that passes under the others, is still for
a long time an *enfant terrible*. The technique is still that of the
zither, simply transferred to keys. It is not till the time of Bach
that the special technique of percussion springs into existence.

It is astonishing to see what feats were attempted by the old
English masters of the virginal in spite of their scanty means.
We feel how they love this instrument, which, in spite of itself,
pointed out to them the way to the Promised Land of music,
namely, to the stiff rhythm and arrangement of the secular music.
For example, we actually find in the virginal books pieces by
the famous Amsterdam organist, Sweelinck, and arrangements of
compositions by Orlando Lasso, as well as all kinds of transcriptions of Italian works ; but the gems are the variations on popular
songs and the dances. In the contemporary virginal music of
Venice this relation is reversed. There the Ricercari (pieces for
lute, organ, or harpsichord, displaying the tricks of counterpoint),
the Toccatas, the Preambles, are overlaid by the heavy, clumsy
harmonies of the Middle Ages ; they stagger about in uncertain
syncopations, dabbling with $\frac{5}{4}$ time, and confused with the most
intricate figurations. It is only towards the end [1] that they yield
a clear formal idea. Not until the younger Gabrieli do we see
rhythm more clearly defined.

In England, however, the fruitful songs and dances admit
none of these flabby harmonies ; all the ornamentation of the
variations is accommodated to the simple fabric of the piece ;
the clear melody is allied with an equally clear harmony ; and
they are woven, by the quick and light tone of the virginal,
into a musical movement which, in order to live, must include
a thousand delicately elaborated *nuances* of thought.

---

[1] This is also the case with the English variations. The last one is commonly the
most valuable and convincing.

Compared with the lute dances, which necessarily retained the stiffness of their fabric, there is here a blossoming field, a veritable new world. The organ gives the voice parts their character, the lute supplies their tone-colour, but the child of these two parents has its own standing and its own future.

About 1500 we meet with the first Old English clavier-pieces, as well as Aston's Hornpipe, a variation on a popular song. A manuscript collection in the British Museum, known as the "Mulliner Book" (Mulliner was a master in St Paul's School), offers us the earliest specimens of clavier-works of this kind, by various masters, from the middle of the sixteenth century. Many of the pieces by Thomas Tallis, the old master of this school, are exceedingly rhythmical. He was organist under four reigns—those of Henry VIII., Edward VI., Mary and Elizabeth. There is a canon in two parts, in lines which can be grasped at a glance, and which makes full use of sequential repetitions—a sure sign, from the early times of church music, of the advancing rhythmical consciousness. Gradually there is added to the canon a running bass, which at first sounds twice, and finally rolls forth quite unhindered, rendering the whole picture easily grasped by the eye. The unaided eye indeed, in these old pieces, is a good judge. Without being preoccupied by the archaism, which perhaps wearies the ear, it detects the intellectual art of the composer, as it were, at a certain distance. It observes the great and small curves of the voice-contours, sees the succession of the canonic themes, notices the parentheses in which long passages are confined, and the delight of the composer in the clearness of the pattern. It is indeed as a finely-sewn, carefully-fashioned pattern that we see an exercise of this kind, simply worked out, but richly adorned with broken chords—such, for example, as the figuration of the "Felix namque" which Tallis has as the third piece in the Fitzwilliam Virginal-Book. The *nuances* of the accompaniment rejoice in their ornamental existence.

William Bird, the pupil of Tallis, whose life reaches from 1538 or 1546 to 1623, would be reckoned as the father of modern piano-music, if only this English school had exerted some influence on art, and did not stand so isolated in musical history. We shall call him the first of the clavier-masters. Both organist and singer in the Royal Chapel, where both services were alternately demanded from all the adult musicians, he had a considerable interest in the monopoly of music printing and of the music paper duty which was granted by Elizabeth first to Tallis and then to him. A happy man he was not ; he appears to have suffered more than most in the religious persecutions of the time. We have hardly a word in the authorities as to the hours of work of these old musicians ; but indirectly we learn from the Act against Rogues and Vagabonds that private instruction was a not unusual *parergon* of the musicians.

Prosniz, the collector of all clavier-literature, in his " Handbuch der Klavierlitteratur "—a work not to be implicitly relied on—calls Bird's music coarse and tasteless. Weitzmann agrees, saying that it is composed with intelligence and art, but heavy and without soul. But this is the fate of all transition styles. If we observe, from the standpoint of modern music, the traces of the old style, as for instance the change of time and the " flabbiness " of the harmony in the Fantasia, which comes eighth in the Virginal Book, or the cross-passages in the interesting Piece 60, they are indeed coarse and tasteless. But we must endeavour in such things to put aside the modern point of view. Mediæval music is not a preliminary step to the modern, but something quite different. It is pictorial, as the other is plastic. If we would hear their " molluscous " harmonies, and their indistinctness of rhythmical arrangement, we must lay aside the rhythmical canons of modern music ; we must accept the molluscous nature and want of distinctness as something purposed, and we must follow without preoccupation this web of voices, enjoying it note by note. The piece is so delicate, so quite in colour, that the last note is a shock to us. In fact, the conclusion of these pieces, with its formal clash, under which the harmonies and voices assemble themselves in a stiff group, is a contradiction to their inmost being, a desertion of

Page from " Parthenia," the first English engraved Clavier Music, 1611.

the pictorial principle and—in a word—the germ of the coming style. In a greater degree than we can bring ourselves to believe, the ultra-modern expression-music is allied to this conception of the art of tone.

It is true that we justly judge Bird chiefly from the modern point of view, since we are investigating the progress of history, and therefore work for the new, the developing, rather than for the old. But it is precisely from this point of view that he presents such surprises that we are not at first able to form a decisive opinion about him. I find a quiet pleasure in observing his harmonies, which are felt rather than calculated, as, for example, the sudden D major chord in the famous song, "John, come kiss me now" (Virginal Book, No. 10), and in studying the delicate parallel legato passages, the gradual change of melody, the growing complexity, the unusual variations, the alternation of hands, the rhythmical developments. In the ninth variation there run together plain quavers, dotted quavers, and the melody above all.

New suggestions, aroused by the clavier, are constantly being introduced. Prelude xxiv. has a stiff structure. The Passamezzo-Pavan and Galliard (Nos. 56 and 57) present broken chords as a genuine clavier-motif, and the most delicate canonic repetitions by means of a thematic modulation from the key of F to that of G. Very neat is the descending D C A in the seventh galliard-variation alternating with E D B. Bird is particularly fond of writing a passage based on a chord of F, and immediately followed by another based on G. This is akin to the practice of the drone in bagpipes, and has analogy with the ancient " Pes," or " pedal " two-part vocal accompaniment in " Sumer is icumen in." The similarity to the bagpipe drone is rather striking in " The woods so wild " (Fitzwilliam Virginal Book, No. 67) or in " The Bells," where the lower bell voices repeat themselves in a way that reminds us of the pedal bass of Chopin's Berceuse.

The rich technique of " Fortune " (No. 65), the wealth of figures in " O Mistress Mine " (No. 66), the harmonies of the Passamezzo dances (Nos. 56 and 57), cling to the memory.

But chief are his two most modern clavier-pieces—the variations
on "The Carman's Whistle" (No. 58) and "Sellinger's Round"
(No. 64, where the piece is complete, not abridged as in Pauer's
edition). These have often been issued in popular form, and
in Pauer's collection are provided with modern execution marks.

"The Carman's Whistle" is a perfected popular melody, one
of those tunes which will linger for days in our ears. At the
beginning of the third and fourth bars Bird sets the first and
second bars in canon, in the simplest and most straightforward
style. Next come harmonies worthy of a Rameau, with the
most delicate passing notes. In the variations certain figures
are inserted which are easily worked into the canonic form, now
legato with the charm of the introduction of related notes, now
diatonic scales most gracefully introduced, now staccato passages
which draw the melody along with them like the singing of a
bird. Finally fuller chords appear, gently changing the direction
of the theme. From first to last there is not a turn foreign to
the modern ear.

The "Sellinger's Round" is more stirring. Its theme is in
a swinging $\frac{6}{8}$ rhythm, running easily through the harmonies
of the tonic, the super-dominant and the sub-dominant. It
strikes one like an old legend, as in the first part of Chopin's
Ballade in F major, of which this piece is a prototype. The first
variation retains the rhythm and only breaks the harmonies. Its
gentle fugalisation is more distinctly marked in the third variation, which at the conclusion adopts running semiquavers, after
Bird's favourite manner, anticipating at the conclusion of the one
variation the motive of the next. The semiquavers go up and
down in thirds, or are interwoven by both hands, while melody
and accompaniment continue their dotted $\frac{6}{8}$, in a fashion reminding us of Schumann. In the later variations the quaver
movement is again taken up, but more florid and more varied
with runs which pursue each other in canon. This piece, perhaps
the first perfect clavier-piece on record, which had left its time
far behind, was written in 1580.

Alongside of William Bird stands Dr John Bull (1563-1628). These two represent the two types which run through the whole history of the clavier.   Bird, the more intimate, delicate, spiritual intellect; Bull, the untamed genius, the flashing executant, the restless madcap, the rougher artist.   It is noticeable how these two types stand thus together on the very threshold of the clavier-art.

John Bull, at nineteen, became organist of Hereford Cathedral, and at twenty-two a member of the Royal Chapel.   In the following year he becomes Bachelor of Music of Oxford, three years later Doctor of Music of both Oxford and Cambridge.   When, in 1596, Sir Thomas Gresham founded his College in London, he was made Professor in Music, and that without (as the statute demanded) lecturing in Latin.   But he held this post no more than five years.   We find him, "on grounds of health," travelling in foreign countries.   His playing created the greatest enthusiasm. The French, the Spanish, and the Austrian courts were in a furore. Like all later executants, he is the subject of myths.   There is an anecdote that a kapellmeister of St Omer showed him, as an extraordinary curiosity, a piece in forty parts.[1]   Bull, nothing daunted, added another forty parts to it.   The kapellmeister stares, and takes him for the devil himself.   After an absence of six years he returned to England, where, like his satanic prototype, he resists all authority.   He resigned all academic positions, threw up his post in the Royal Chapel, and in 1613 again set out, without permission, for the Continent.   Four years later he emerges as organist of Notre Dame in Antwerp, where he died in 1628.

From these few biographical notices we figure him as a restless ambitious spirit.   As the peaceful life of a mediæval painter is to the splendid existence of the seventeenth century artists, so is the relation of Bird to Bull.   And Bull's works

---

[1] It is right to mention here that Thomas Tallis actually did write a motet in forty parts, "Spem in alium non habui," which, thanks to the enthusiasm of Dr Mann of Cambridge, has been published (1888), and performed in public on more than one occasion during the last few years.

John Bull, at the age of 26, after Caldwall's engraving in Hawkins.

exhibit many of the lineaments of an elegant *faiseur*.[1] He is not so fond as Bird of the primeval freshness of the popular songs and dances, nor does he work out his pieces with Bird's virgin purity. The side-issue is often with him the main object; the figuration is often licentious, and both hands vie in the performance of the closest and most difficult passages. Often, indeed, his pieces assume a grotesque appearance, hard and antiquated harmonies, in which the leading note is conspicuous by its absence, being crossed with runs in semiquavers, dotted rhythms, rapidly intruded chords, four-fold imitations, syncopated grace-notes, mingled two and three-time passages in wild and bewildering confusion. The eye looks as it were on a specimen of Indian ornamentation, in which, among the confused lines, a pure human feature is almost indistinguishable. From the first piece of the Fitzwilliam Virginal Book, Bull's thirty "Walsingham" Variations, which later Bird treats so much more simply, the executant shines out in his whole personality. There

[1] Meaning a "manufacturer" of show pieces.

are thirty studies on figure motives which in Bird are reduced to a dozen. The semiquavers run like will of the wisps in their most unsubstantial courses, resembling endless chains, which are here and there interrupted with leaps of a sixth or seventh, to knit them together in the self-same run higher up or lower down. The ornamentation is richer than with Bird, melting in its *sfumato*[1] the lines of the voice almost after the manner of Couperin. The clavier, even more than the organ, lent itself, with its isolated tones, to such trills, slurs, and mordents,[2] which give to the sound an apparently longer existence. It is these that, down to the time of the German classical music, give the stamp to the special physiognomy of the clavier-piece. I called them just now *sfumato*. As in painting the sharp outline of the body gradually gives way to greater truth to nature, and in Lionardo is replaced by the specifically pictorial obliteration of the *sfumato*, by which, so to speak, we see round the corners ; so the ornamentation in these pieces, in which the clavier is seeking its own means of expression, assumes the habit of obliterating its thin outlines until finally the figures thus obtained regulate the lines of the melody as a fixed motif, or even become an end in themselves. It takes an inner effort before we can transplant ourselves into this old world of ornamentation. We must learn to feel it as it would be played by the old masters : we must, if possible, play it ourselves on old and lightly-responding spinets. Our heavy and serious pianos are unsuitable to them ; they sound too forcibly and harshly. The average pianist cannot play them ; and hence, in his new edition, Pauer has for the most part cut them out.

Doctor Bull's flying fingers, utterly altering as they did many a church-tune and many a dance, were constantly making discoveries among the clavier-figures, just as the worst of executants has since done. Thus, in Bull's somewhat bewildering forest, we find many a germ of future wealth : broken triads,

---

[1] *Sfumato* means " smoky," and refers, in painting, to the blurring of the outlines.

[2] The mordent is a grace where the main note is alternated rapidly with the note below.

which even in the contrary motion of both hands delight us in the midst of all kinds of consecutive fifths; broken octaves, of which Beethoven was so fond, a greater frequency of the crossing of the hands, by which the voice-part gained a wider field, and finally endless repetitions of the same note, either singly or in the middle of a passage,—this last a genuine clavier-device, for which later the new repeating mechanism was invented. Also, in harmonic relation, Bull seeks out many novelties, boldly bending the voice-part to his will; as he does in the truly stupendous Prelude No. 43, in the Virginal Book, or in the bold enharmonic modulation in Piece 51, an exercise in DO, RE, MI, FA, SOL, LA, a theme which appears a tone higher at each repetition, starting from G, in the midst of close figuration, until the C sharp simply changes to D flat.

There is a Lute Book of Bull's in Vienna which gives us pieces like the following: "Miserere Mei," "Galliard," "La chasse du Roy," "Salve Regina," "Canon perpetuus, carens scriptura, notulis in systemati positis scriptus," and so on. Let us not think too badly of them. The Virginal Book also has a variegated collection. In the time of variations, "variatio delectat," there are collections for household use, which are not necessarily an indication of a want, on the part of the originator, of the sense of the characteristic in an instrument. At this epoch the instrument delivers men from the mediæval love of grouping instruments. And I even find that Bull in certain pieces has shown a note-worthy sense for characteristic. He has once a simple bag-pipe melody e f e d e f d c, called "Les Buffons," with a series of variations in humorous style. There are at first chords with simple broken accompaniment, then hopping semiquaver figures, then a popular canon, then slurred sixths, and similarly right on to the conclusion, which is as usual fully harmonised, in the turns of which, of course, his want of plasticity, as contrasted with Bird, is clearly shown. More striking still is the working out of his best-known piece, the variations on the fresh delightful song, the "King's Hunt," giving us a romantic reminiscence of horns and

Henry Purcell, 1658-1695.

trumpets. Something of this romance runs through his figures. He uses the horn-motive of the second part specially for a longer variation, which is simple and full of character. The flourish of runs in quavers, which he also uses in Galliard No. 17 of the Virginal Book, and the systematic answering of right-hand chords by the left hand, which appears also in Galliard 11, are here specially characteristic. We seem to see tramping horses and waving flags delineated in ancient technique. He was specially good in such hunting pieces. On the musical side, as his somewhat awkward variations on the fine " Jewel," though among his best pieces, clearly show, he cannot be compared to the magical Bird ; but his sense for characteristic and for technique has aided the advance of the clavier. Both of these superiorities are parts of his nature, which expressed itself most completely in this style. The clavier needed both types.

The most characteristic and notable piece of this school is the third in the Virginal Book, a Fantasia by John Munday, which represents no less a phenomenon than the changes of the weather. Over its sections, which have no thematic connection, but have various distinctions of rhythm—*e.g.*, quietly moving semibreves and minims ; jerky dotted quavers interspersed with semiquaver rests ; extensive runs in semiquavers, etc.—he writes in this succession four times each, " Fine Weather," " Lightning," and " Thunder." Instead of "fine" appears once "warm" weather ; and a slow passage, marked "a clear day," forms the conclusion. The characterisation is of course extremely superficial, and the last time the lightning rolls just like the thunder. But this novelty, as a symptom, ought not to be overlooked. It reveals to us the consciousness of characteristic, and the increasingly intimate character of the clavier. Technically, Bull inaugurated a school. Of the various authors of the Virginal Book, Ferdinand Richardson (who exhibits pure part-writing), Giles Farnaby, Orlando Gibbons, Peter Philips, to a large extent follow his footsteps. Farnaby thus early writes pieces for two virginals; he darts, in the midst of his technique, through a graceful " Spagnioletta," and often lights on interesting modern passing chords, as, for example, running upwards, b, f sharp, d, a, where a follows b and c d. In the use of chords Peter Philips (who arranges many pieces of Orlando Lassus in the Virginal Book) stands in the first rank. In the Pavan (No. 76), which is dated 1592, he has in the conclusion [1] unheard-of simple alternating triads ; in the Galliard he deals with the most beautiful suspended chords ; and in the " Galiarda Dolorosa " (No. 81) he introduces chromatic colouring.[2] We can perceive how much he must have learnt on his Italian and Dutch travels from the flourishing art of the Continent. The spirit of Bird does not exert so powerful or so enduring an influence as that of Bull. The anonymous Piece 14 of the Virginal Book is a famous Alman (German dance), which in the severity of its subject reminds us of Bird, and its working-out is done by means of single-note passages of melodious motive.

In their clearness of arrangement and harmonious development, so far as they do not deal with dance or song, the majority of the pieces of the Virginal Book are marked by the spirit of the Toccata of the great Dutchman Sweelinck, which appears as Piece 96. Here the spirit of Bach is seen before its time. Gradually the distinctive edges of individuality fade away. A piece by Thomas Morley on the theme, " Goe from my window," whose

---

[1] This is a really fine passage, and (by the way) bears every mark of the madrigal for double chorus.

[2] The passage has four times over a chromatic scale of six notes, *every note* properly harmonised. Neither Purcell (a century later) nor Bach (later still) could have done it better.

melody he himself partially employs again in his "Nancie," appears again almost unaltered in the same Virginal Book, and is then ascribed to John Munday. With John Blow, Henry Purcell, Thomas Augustine Arne, in the following generations,[1]

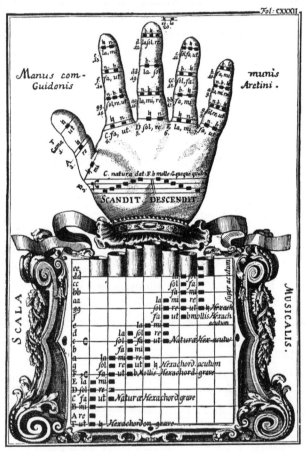

The so-called "Hand" of Guido of Arezzo, with an early and extensively used diagram of the scale-notation.

[1] The author here makes a startling leap of a century or so in his chronicle of English composers. From Munday, who was a grown man in 1586, he suddenly goes to Blow and Purcell, who flourished in 1690, and even mentions Arne in the same breath, who died in 1778.

The "isolation" of the early English clavier school is fairly explained by the

English clavier music blends with the general Continental stream, till it is absorbed and must seek its nourishment from without.

immense amount of attention that was now given, from 1600-1695, in England, to the development of the dramatic scena or cantata, for one or two voices, to the song, and to the cultivation of concerted music for strings and keyed instruments. It is only to prevent any one from supposing that there was *no* "secular" music in England between the days of Elizabeth and the coming of Purcell that I give a few names, all of which have a real claim to remembrance. Songs—Campion (flourished 1600), Johnson (1600), Cæsar (early 17th cent.), Couper (1612), Laneare (1620), H. Lawes (1630), Wilson (1640). Cantatas or "Scenas"—H. Lawes (1630), C. Colman (1640). Instrumental music—Gregorie (mid. 17th cent.), Jenkins (1630), W. Lawes (1630), Lock (1650), Sympson (1660)

D'Anglebert, Chamber Musician to Louis XIV., after Mignard.

Old French Dance-Pieces

THE independent musical fame of England—omitting Purcell, the evening star—rests solely on this early period. Hence we have been led to trace the musical history of England further back than that of countries where the stream spread over a wider area. Old English music, indeed, had no influence worthy of the name. It stands, like a half-mediæval prelude, before the actual history of the piano. It is true that it shows the forces which are to work in the future; but they are not yet brought into the line which they are constantly and exclusively to follow. This process begins rather in France; it unites itself later with a second movement which comes from Italy, and follows a broader and more lively path through Germany until it reaches our own times.

Oskar Fleischer, the founder of the splendid Berlin collection of old musical instruments, has endeavoured, in his book on Gaultier, the great French lute-player, to describe English and French relations in the seventeenth century. But the hints which, in his view, the elder Gaultier[1] gained in England, are only matters of execution. Flourishes which in England were marked, without precise discrimination, with / or //, found a more exact representation among French lutenists. I do not mean that every performer did not put his own interpretation upon them. Every lutenist or clavier-player issues a new code of these *agréments;* but the basis remains essentially the same, and it is possible that the flourishes were adopted, by an impulse derived from England, into lute-music and thence into clavier-music. Thence they soon spread themselves over the whole musical field. But it is a mistake to imagine that these *agréments*, which infest old French compositions like locusts, were a peculiarity of the country, the "style galant" of France. The peculiarity lies elsewhere, in the form, in the dance.

English clavier-music had attached itself to the song. From the song it derived its stiffness of form and the grace of its melodic outline—two important aids in the advance of music. But its treatment of these pieces was conducted in a manner which reminds us of the middle ages of music. The form, a continuous succession of variations, sprang from the idea of figuration, which constituted the essence of mediæval music; and the voice parts were worked out in general on the fugal principle or in canonic imitation, both factors of the mediæval music. The early ripening of English music, and its close connection with the old Dutch vocal or organ composition, brought it about that the *form* rested still partly on tradition, while the *content* already pointed towards the future. Even dances were worked out in this manner, which belonged especially to the time. In France the system was the

[1] Gaultier "the Elder" was a French lute-player, who also published (in collaboration with his cousin Pierre Gaultier) a collection of pieces for lute, with instructions for playing. He flourished *temp.* Charles I. References to him may be found *inter alia*, in Herrick, who calls him Gotiere or Gotire.

exact opposite. There, the form of the variation, and the absolutely fugal clavier-exercise, are as seldom found as the simply-harmonised song.

The emancipation in France was due to the attainment of a point of departure which was as distant as possible from anything vocal. The dance—although of course there were some sung dances—had early allied itself with the purely instrumental exercise. It has never been treated so entirely "à plaisir des gorges,"[1] as Gargantua expresses it. It had a stiff arrangement in common with a stiff harmony. It never showed much affinity with the contrapuntal twists and turns of the voice, to which song associates itself so easily from its close connection with choral music. If we compare the earliest instrumental dances of the sixteenth century with the dances, in several parts, of the old song-books—the "Rat's-Tail," the "Crane-Bill," "Fox-Tail," "Cat's-Paw," "Peacock's-Tail," and the like, we see how rapidly the influence of the instrument over a clear and light vocal current was increased in France. Here especially does the dance, from the very earliest times, enjoy great popularity. It is very early set to the lute or the clavier, other instruments being but rarely employed. Men grew accustomed to pieces in a condensed musical style, harmonised simply and melodiously, contracted in form. These were regarded on their own merits, and not as subjects for variations and figurations. It was for this reason that the French clavier-piece was more fruitful, more musical, and more capable of development than the English.

The dance then is the darling conception of French music ; and French dances are the nucleus of all instrumental music. So early as 1530—for we can go back a great distance—the Paris printer, Attaignant, the oldest of French note-engravers, published all kinds of musical volumes "reduict de musique en la tablature du jeu d'Orgues, Espinettes, Manicordions,"[2] etc.

---

[1] *Anglicé*, "for the sheer fun of howling."

[2] Manicordion = Monocordion = a clavichord in which *one* string had still to provide several notes. See full explanation elsewhere in this book.

We wonder to-day how M. Attaignant could transcribe his pieces "out of music" into the script of organs, spinets and monochords. But by "music" he meant nothing more nor less than song, and song, down to his day, was nothing more nor less than music. A few years after the German music-publisher Agricola[1] wrote:—

> "Drumb lern singen du kneblein klein
> Itzund inn den jungen jarn dein,
> Recht nach musicalischer art
> Las aber keinen vleis gespart."

> "Thou little boy, come learn to sing,
> Now, ere thy youth has taken wing.
> Let all be done with art refined,
> And give thereto thy heart and mind."
> [E. E. K.]

For music, he had once before said, is the foundation on which all instruments rest. Attaignant was one of the first to make transcripts of this "music" for keyed instruments. Nay, more; as far as our knowledge goes, he was the first who in general printed for such instruments. On his title-pages stand for the first time the words spinet and clavichord, although the claims of the organ are allowed. And it is noteworthy that the dances play the principal part in his books. Here the Frenchman already peeps out. Galliards, Basse-dances,[2] Branles, Pavans, are brought into a clear and relatively good harmonic form, without much complication of the instrumental parts. They are often, as for example in a charming Galliard in F major, of entrancing *naïveté*. Not too many runs in the treble, not too much harmony in the bass, and all exquisitely adapted for the instrument.[3]

A hundred years after, the dance still rules French music, and not merely French music, but French life. The forms of social intercourse, as they were fashioned for the universal use of Europe at the court of the Parisian princes, were modelled on the broad

[1] Agricola. Pupil of J. S. Bach.

[2] Galliard, in triple time, with a "leap" in every other bar (second beat); Basse-dance also in triple time, but "sans sauter," all solemn sliding.

[3] For examples of these pieces, Wasielewski's book on sixteenth century instrumental music is invaluable. Also see Arbeau's "Orchésographie," and my "Shakespeare and Music."

rhythms of the dance. Going and coming, bowing and sitting, complimenting and smiling—all the pleasure in the formal beauty of hollow conventionalities, all this is nothing but the light and yet regulated step, the theatrical and yet sympathetic essence of the dance. The French people, having resolved to live their life, determined to do it prettily; and therefore to put even their ordinary motions and common gestures under the mild rule of the dancing master. Even in rough and ready England, traces of this are extant; witness the would-be grace of the formula of "introduction."

In lute-music the dance takes the form of ceaseless corantos and sarabands; on the stage it supplies the framework for the love-representations of the time. In 1671 appeared *Pomona*, Perrin and Cambert's first French public opera. In it, cattle drivers and agricultural labourers ply their dances. The great Lully, most fertile composer of the nobly tedious French national operas, is inconceivable apart from the school of the dance. His tunes, at every possible opportunity, run off into the beloved dances of three or four strains, now inserted in airs and prologues, now as episodic dances. By this means the flexibility of the voice parts increases year by year; and since Lully is a composer for the clavier, many of his dances easily adapt themselves to clavier-arrangements, to which indeed they are very early subjected. Lully is the most vigorous teacher in the rehearsal of opera-dances. The style and the school of dances reach such a height in Paris, that they give the law to the whole world just as their social etiquette does. "France," writes Mattheson, "is and remains the true school of dancing."

After the time of Lully, who had done so much for the development of the characteristic dance, the art advances with rapid strides. The Pantomime was invented by the Duchess of Maine: it was in 1708, at her famous festivals, "les Nuits de Sceaux," that the last scene of the fourth act of Corneille's "Horace," was pantomimically represented with musical accompaniment.

Of old the parts of women in the dance had been taken by

Le Maître de Musique.

Painting by Jan Steen (1626-1679), in the National Gallery, London.

Concert.

Painting by Gerard Terborch (1617-1681), in the Royal Museum at Berlin.

men. Lully ventured to introduce female dancers. Here begins
the epoch of famous " danseuses" who, in accordance with a natural
law, become the centre of public interest. We owe to Castil Blaze
a list of those *grandes dames* who took up the profession. Henceforward the art of song and that of dancing divided equally the
popular affection, for the two were not always separate callings.
La Prévost was the first to essay a solo dance, which she set
to a violin solo of Rebel. La Pélissier inaugurated costume-
dances. She had purchased the whole wardrobe of Adrienne
Lecouvreur, lately deceased, and was thus able to appear in the
ballet " Le Carneval et la Folie," in the characters of Jocasta,
Mariamne, Zenobia, Chimène, Roxana, Paulina, Célimène, Agatha,
and Elvira. Next we see rising the star of La Camargo, who
from her début in the ballet "Caractères de la Danse," was the
amazement of the world, the discoverer of operatic airs set to the
dance, the glass of fashion, the arbitress of mode, against whose
decisions there was no appeal. But, as Castil Blaze tells us in
his history of the French theatre, all were surpassed by La Sallé,
with her noble figure, her lovely form, her perfect grace, her dancing so full of expression and voluptuous languor. Not only does
she dance ; she writes dances. She invents a Pygmalion, in which
the divine statue assumes life, and engages in a long pantomime
with the sculptor, who teaches her to assume her humanity by
means of the measured motions of the dance. La Sallé brought
this ballet on the stage in London first and then in Paris ; and the
London correspondent of the *Mercure de France* writes to his paper
of the extraordinary furore created by the new art. For Sallé had
at last rejected the lingering relics of the old ballet—the anachron-
isms of costume—in order to be able to give full expression to the
spirit of the dance. "She ventured," says the correspondent, "to
appear without skirt or bodice, with loose hair, and absolutely unadorned. Over corset and undergarments she had only a simple
muslin dress, and seemed the very image of a Greek statue."
Sallé appears to have practised her dances without virtuosity,
as a mere artistic representation. She essayed no acrobatic

leaps, no *entrechats*, no pirouettes.   Contrasting her with Camargo, Voltaire exclaimed :—

> " Ah, Camargo, que vous êtes brillante !
> Mais que Sallé, grands dieux, est ravissante !
> Que vos pas sont légers, et que les siens sont doux !
> Elle est inimitable, et vous êtes nouvelle :
> Les Nymphes sautent comme vous,
> Et les Graces dansent comme elle."

The victories of the dance were universal.   Even public ceremonies were taken up in its advance.   The " Messe des Révérences " was altered into the " Ballet des Écrevisses."   In their first delight of dominion, love and the pleasure of life revel in the light and magical rhythms of the dance.   The great and flourishing masked balls of the opera, acquiring a new rapture, lead on to new dances—the Calotins, the Farandoule, the Rats, Jeanne qui saute, Liron Lirette, le Poivre, la Fürstemberg, le Cotillon qui va toujours, la Monaco—old songs of universal popular origin ; or, like wines and laws, named after towns and races, and now, as dances, naturalised on the parquet.   How ancient is this connection between song and dance, in which the name of the song remains attached to the dance !   This is a process which is of daily occurrence in our music-halls.

Famous *danseuses* received characteristic nicknames.   The elder Duval du Tillet was called " La Constitution," because her father was an eminent clerical constitutionalist ; the younger was affectionately dubbed " Church Calendar."   La Mariette was called " the Princess," on more private grounds.   It was the same with their male companions.   The three brothers Malter were called " the Bird," " the Devil," and " Knickerbockers."   I stay to refer to this as this French nickname-mania explains the bizarre inscriptions of so many clavier-pieces.   An amusing story is told of a certain Cléron, who, in the demi-mondaine circles from which her beauty and seductive arts had brought her to the opera, was known as " Frisky " (Frétillon).   In the opera she greeted her new friends very affectionately, but added, " I shall do my best to be agreeable to you ; but if any one calls me Frisky, let him know I

will give him the best box on the ear he ever had in his life."
Mademoiselle Cléron was no boaster, adds the narrator, and was
pretty likely to keep her word.

The due understanding of old French clavier-music then,
must start from the knowledge of the dance. Almost all its
pieces are dances, whether they declare themselves as such or
not. They take up the numerous existing dance-forms and
develop them in the ways already described. But in addition
to this formal principle we must notice a second, the symbolic.
The pieces *mean* something, and mean more and more the
further the century advances. As if to console themselves for
the want of content which belongs to the dance in itself, composers are fond of indicating in their titles and dedications all
kinds of relations which give to their pieces a more marked
physiognomy or a more comprehensible expressiveness. For
this purpose they had not only at their disposal the old song-
names which clung to the dances, but a hundred other associations.
They loved the dance, but they loved associations also. Nicknames and allusions flew from the smiling lips, and men had
the fairest inducements to take the abstract in a concrete sense.
The chief inducement was the stage with its representative music,
the stage, so passionately loved by the French in the middle
ages that even from the thirteenth century we have dramatic
lyrical plays with the most delicate songs by the trouvère Adam
de la Hale. These stand like flowers in the midst of their
time, and penetrated so deeply into the life of the people that
the little song of Marion " Robin m'aime " is still, they say, sung
in the Hennegau. The fairies, which had already played their
part in the works of this mediæval opera-composer and writer,
had in the later French opera their rich harvest of beings of
symbolic meaning. In Lully's works there is quite a swarm of
abstract figures, gods, demi-gods, personifications, which in small
scenes or great airs bring out this characterising function of music
to the utmost degree possible. But what such things as the
good and bad Dreams, or the nymphs and Corybantes in the

"Atys," entering as chorus, performed in characteristic music was as nothing to what was done by the great ballets which drew heaven and hell into the circle of their representations. "Le Triomphe des Sens," "Les Voyages d'Amour," "Les Génies," "Le Triomphe de l'Harmonie," "L'Ecole des Amants"—all these are titles of operas and ballets of those times which had as their aim to represent musical things as symbols of sensuous incidents. From the lists of ballets and operas performed from Lully's time right into the eighteenth century the application of fêtes, rococo-amusements, love-pictures by Watteau, or idyllic porcelain-orna-mentation, to stage purposes, speaks with no uncertain sound. In such an environment, recollecting the renowned fantastic art of the contemporary Callot, we are led to understand the unusual preference for the direct association of clavier-pieces with particular persons or things.

But here we must speak specially of programme-music.

A Pavan called "La Bataille," full of vigorous trumpet-signals and horn-echoes, was inserted by Tielman Sufato in his collection of 1551. Shortly before that date a Zürich lute book included dance-songs, "mitsampt dem Vogelgesang und einer Feldschlacht." The song of birds, the imitation of animals, and all kinds of con-fused shrieking—a comic counterpoint—offers rich material to the programme-music of the sixteenth century. Even before an Italian had written the famous fugal chorus, in which the scholars, with a comical employment of the dismembered canonic voice-exercise, declined *qui, quæ, quod*, in the ears of the raging schoolmaster—even before this, contrapuntal janglings were well known. Jannequin, the Frenchman, depicted in *chansons* with many parts the battle of Marignano, the capture of Boulogne, war, jealousy, women's gossip, the hare and hounds ; or, on the other hand, the song of birds, the lark or the nightingale. We hear in the music of this time the thirds of the cuckoo, the clucking dactyls of the hen, the chromatic mewings of the cat, the trills of song-birds. The boldest of these pieces—an earlier Howleglass—was perhaps Eckard's representation of the turmoil in St Mark's

Place at Venice (1589), in which noblemen, beggars, hawkers, soldiers, appear with all the artistic counterpoint appropriate to their respective classes. Thus programme-music, in the sixteenth century, enjoyed an international repute. It must not, however, be regarded as an achievement of modern music, but rather as something as old as music itself. The tempest which the Greek Timotheus represented on the kithara, and the fight of Apollo with the Python, which Timosthenes depicted on the flute and kithara, in all its stages—the challenge, the struggle, the hissing, the victory—had a renown in very ancient times. Programme-music belongs to all ages of musical development, and appears always as a natural phenomenon, never as a revolutionary movement. It marks the *ne plus ultra* of the need of musical expression, which cannot find satisfaction in pure musical forms, and seeks to justify itself by extra-musical titles. Thus on the extreme limit of ancient hymn-music stood a Timosthenes, on that of mediæval choral-music a Jannequin, on that of modern instrumental music a Berlioz.

We can trace the psychology of this programme-music with great ease in the French instrumental art of the seventeenth and eighteenth centuries. From the first definite orchestral programme-piece—the storm in Marais' opera Alcyone—to the volume of François Dandrieu, "contenant plusieurs Divertissements dont les principaux sont les caractères de la guerre, ceux de la chasse, et la fête de Village"; from the lute-dances of Gaultier to the clavier-pieces of Rameau, we see nothing but an endeavour of the developed dance-form to enter into relations with actual life—an endeavour which leads to the manifold names of the pieces. Formerly the dances had taken their names from the songs. Now, as definite pieces, they are so full of special significance, so rich in all kinds of characteristic figures and harmonies, that the composer feels his mind insensibly drawn to incidents of life, of persons, of characters, humours, landscapes, and calls upon all his fertility in association to fashion decorative titles out of them. Music, which has arrived at the limits of the traditional dance-forms, passes over from the formal to the characteristic. As

Berlioz' Queen Mab is nothing but a further development of Beethoven's Scherzos, and not a heaven-descended music, discovered
in Shakespeare, so the pieces of the great clavierist Couperin,
whether they have descriptions of humours or personal names for
titles, are merely the developments of dances, which, so fertile were
they, reminded the composer of life itself. Couperin himself
declares that he gives in his pieces portraits, which appear to give
to others also, before whom they are performed, the actual features
of the models.   But it is obvious that he could hold himself as
a portrait-painter, only so far as his music was rich enough, by its
definite relations to actual life, to give clearer definition and a distinct picture to its stream as it flowed in a thousand forms.   Like
all programme-musicians, he is such, not from poverty in musical
invention, but from wealth.   The French are a people that revel
in the fulness of forms, and find their very life in the special magic
of the formal presentation of all things, whether social or artistic.
Thus in their hands all musical forms, melodious, harmonic,
rhythmic, grew so luxuriantly, that at all times, from Jannequin
to St Saens, in order to live they have necessarily turned to
programme-music.

   Yet the titles of the clavier-pieces are not fully explained by
this reference to the value of programme-music for the French
mind.   We must take into consideration also an old decorative
tradition.   Let us open the magnificent volume of lute-pieces
by the famous Denis Gaultier,[1] which came into the Berlin
Museum of Engravings along with the Hamilton collection.   It
is fantastically called "La Rhetorique des Dieux," because only
gods could speak so movingly by music, and equally fantastically
he introduces all kinds of titles for the pieces, such as " Phaethon
struck by lightning," "le Panégyrique," Minerva, Ulysses, Andro-
meda, Diana, "la Coquette virtuosa," and the like, besides several
"Tombeaux," by which term dedications to deceased persons were
generally indicated.[2]   If we compared these sixteenth century

---

[1] This is yet a *third* musician of the name, according to Hawkins.
[2] Called a ''knell'' in England.   See Shakespeare, Henry viii., iv. ii. 77.

pieces with their names, a certain nimble fancy is required to find actual programme-music in them. Of a genuine representation of the content there is no pretence. Minerva, Echo, and the Coquette would seem to have more in common than they ever suspected. The titles are nothing but decorative stamps, resembling those medallions of Aphrodite which are so often engraved over a love-poem. The interpretation is always in the widest spirit possible. It is amusing to see how the editor of the collection labours to explain the names while confining himself exclusively to the vaguest generalities. On "l'Homicide," or The Fair Murderess, as it is also named, he writes : "This fair creature deals death to every one who sees and hears her; but this death is so unlike the usual death that it is the beginning of a life, not its end." It could not easily be more plainly indicated that there is no clear representation of anything to be seen in the piece, and that the title is a piece of self-flattery in the dress of the fantastic. Already had the elder Gaultier, the founder of this lute - school, recognised, or perhaps even invented, these decorative titles, such as "le canon," "la conquérante," "les larmes du Boset," or "la volte," "l'immortelle," "le loup." This last, it is certain, is no ordinary wolf, but howls so musically that it is really a man.

The custom of adding decorative titles was made universal by the lute-players, but the tone-painting must always have been of the slightest. Otherwise the old historian of the lute, Baron, could not have been so irritated at them as to write, some decades later, "Gallot has given such strange names to his pieces that we have need of close study to see their relation with the subject. For example, when he wishes to express thunder and lightning on the lute, it is a pity he has never added a note to tell us *when* it lightens and *when* it thunders." (We are reminded of the old English clavier-piece on the same theme.) "We shall seldom," he adds, "light on a French piece but the name of some noble dame is attached to it, after whom, if she so pleases, the piece is named."

The clavier-players adopted this custom all the more willingly as their instrument, so full of resource and so capable of expressing shades of meaning, allowed them to raise these titles from their decorative and shadowy existence into genuine programme-inscriptions. We see this remarkable process clearly exhibited in Chambonnières, a clavier-player who towers in solitary grandeur, and marks an epoch by his introduction of the clavier *suite*, by the clear adaptation of his dances to the clavier, by the first realistic use of these titles, and by the establishment of a precise character in the clavier-piece, which holds its ground even to-day. He is not, like William Bird, the original of modern clavier-music, but its actual father, from whom a straight unbroken line stretches down to the present day.

Jacques Champion de Chambonnières sprang from an old family of organists, and was born at the beginning of the seventeenth century. The year of his death seems to be fixed as 1670. Titon des Tilliers, who in 1732 wrote his "Parnasse Français," a work of great antiquarian research, says of Chambonnières that he played the organ very well, but the clavier with special genius, and that his pieces as well as his execution gained a considerable renown. His fame increased until Louis XIV. appointed him his chief clavier-master; and his compositions appeared in two volumes. In Titon's times these pieces were still admired. Copies of these works are very rarely to be found to-day; but the great French historian, Farrenc, had the good luck to get possession of one of them, and he has freshly edited it in his famous collection of old clavier-music, "Le Trésor des Pianistes." While Attaignant still bound his dances together according to their classes, there are here mixed sets of dance-pieces after the example of the lutenists, in simple setting, but with the adornments of the time. The succession is not yet so elaborate as in later *suites*, and *courantes* stand often one on top of another. The construction of the melodies has still a certain gentle, unforced charm, which gains our attention though its influence is scarcely irresistible. The canonic element appears strongly only in the Gigues, three-time dances with a lively movement. Every piece has its dance-inscription, and some have in addition their special titles, as La Dunkerque, La Verdinguette, la Toute Belle, Iris ; or more distinct indications as the Slider, the Barricades, the Young Zephyrs, the Peasant Girl. A Pavan with slow conclusion in three sections is called " The Conversation of the Gods." Here the sliding, the zephyr, and the peasant, are easily to be recognised in the music. Nevertheless, complete liberation from the merely decorative framework of the fantastic title was not yet attained.

The man to accomplish the great work was François Couperin, called by his time " the Great." The piano-player of to-day hardly knows his name ; and yet it is only two hundred years since men spoke of him in the same breath with Molière and Watteau. A genial, smiling, clean-shaven man—so the somewhat unsatisfactory portraits depict him — with half-length peruke, polite and yet slightly subtle, with a certain priestly sobriety of demeanour, his light fingers run over the hundred adornments of his spinet-pieces. He seems half astonished at his fame, and wholly ignorant that a whole art is one day to rear itself on his shoulders. It was only with difficulty that the pressure of his friends induced him to print his dances, which he wrote for himself in memory of his experiences, or the preludes which he wrote as exercises for his numerous pupils, or the concertos which he composed for Louis XIV.'s Sunday musical evenings. He watched with painful anxiety the tedious process of engraving. As we to-day inspect these prints, we are struck by the joyous *naïveté* of the art, by the graphic awkwardness with which the notes overflow the five-lined limits of the clef, and by the soul which breathes from the delicately-engraved prefaces. He thinks that his portraits are accurate pictures, and thankfully acknowledges his indebtedness to the intimate character of his instrument. His notes as to execution, his " gaiement," " tendrement," and " sans lenteur " (he is always warning the performer against slowness) and all the other guides to interpretation which he inserts, he excuses

François Couperin, " Le Grand."

by saying that the pieces seemed to express something which could not be embraced in accurate language. In spite of all this pedantry of teaching he appeals to the sensitive musical appreciation which will find the right way of interpretation ; and in spite of all this reference to the spiritual momentum of music he is a stern disciplinarian in form and technique. In the midst of the utmost freedom of movement we discern a strong feeling for style, just as in the contemporary architecture the most playful license of the rococo is strangely mingled with the most sober attention to classical rules.

The Couperins, like the Chambonnières, were a widely spread musical family. It was old Chambonnières who, in a noteworthy fashion, had discovered Louis Couperin, the uncle of François. One morning the father of François and his two brothers who lived in the neighbourhood of the old master, brought a serenade for his inspection. Chambonnières was struck with it, asked after the composer, brought him to Paris, and thus laid the foundation of the fame of the family from which the great perfecter of his work was to spring. François was born in 1668. He lost his father when he was ten years old, but in Tomelin, the organist of St Jacques-la-Boucherie, he found a teacher and a second father. His life, as its details have come down to us, was simple and uneventful. He became organist of St Gervais and chamber-clavierist to the king, and died in 1733. But the dedications of his works enable us to conceive him more definitely. He appears in them as the professional artist and man of the world, pampered by noble ladies, and kissing their hands with graceful flatteries.

We see him as he moves in the salons of Paris, which were then beginning to realise their mission. He is the admired artist of the court which he charms with his chamber-music; the intimate of the Duke of Burgundy and of the Dauphin, of Anne and Louis of Bourbon, giving his lessons and receiving pensions of a thousand francs. A true lady's man, he thinks the hands of women better adapted to the clavier than those of men. He is the first to sanction ladies in his own family as clavier-players. His daughter Marguerite Antoinette, and his cousin Louise, played at court. Marguerite even became the teacher of the Princesses, and was official royal clavier-player — in France certainly, and probably in the world, the first woman to hold such a post.

The music of Couperin has something of this feminine quality. It is more truly "virginal" music than that which Queen Elizabeth once played in her quiet chamber. But its grace is not hidden; it is coquettish and conscious of itself. It is the high style of grace which belongs to the French culture of the eighteenth century. A spinet stands on a smooth parquet, and the ladies sit around with their roguish eyes and tip-tilted noses, smiling at all the well-recognised allusions, as the then flourishing pastel-art has fixed them for us in light colours. It is light, entertaining music, in which the thoughts of their own accord run on bright and re-splendent paths. Short pieces; *courantes* with their lively, scarcely broken triple-rhythms; *allemandes* in their decorous and inter-woven quadruple time; *minuets* with their pretty, melodious triple rhythm; *chaconnes* and *passacaglie* rearing their piquant erections on slow-moving basses; *sarabands* in their triple movements and interesting national colouring; *gavottes* with their graceful move-ment in soft two-time, the hurrying fugal *gigues*, and all the many other unnamed dances—all these give the ear, without exertion, a subtle delight. The rondo-form takes a supreme rank; it is con-stantly growing from a simple round-dance with refrain into a genuine clavier-composition, seeming to forebode the sonata which still remains unborn within it. Its theme, like a Ritornel, recurs among the "couplets" or episodical passages; but it is only seldom that the couplets set themselves in conscious opposition to the theme. Usually they adopt its rhythm or the character of its melody, and play with it until, neatly and gracefully, they glide back into the theme itself. There is no iron rigidity of thematic handling. A delicate colour - sense holds the parts together. Couperin does not regulate his pieces according to any definite scheme of dance-successions; he binds the dance and the non-dance, the piece in one or more sections, together into one bouquet which he offers to his lady-friends, often with a polite dedication appended, under the general title of " Ordre." Twenty-seven such " Ordres," in four volumes, were published by him between 1713 and 1730.

The music of Couperin is as simple as possible. But we must not judge its sound by the somewhat heavy pianofortes of our time, which, even in the playfulness of a rapid passage, seem conscious of an *arrière pensée*. No ; the spinet, which, even at its saddest, had a joyous exhilaration—this was the instrument of this playful music. The passages glide on, usually in two voices, of which the one is played by the right hand, the other by the left ; and whether these voices are tied in chords or chord passages, or whether—as occurs more rarely—full chords, usually arpeggio, stand between, in either case there is a delicacy which recalls to us the origin of French clavier-music in the sweet-toned lute. But Couperin advanced yet further. In his last " Ordres " his compositions increase in depth ; the more luxuriant conceptions and deeper feelings of a lesser Beethoven show themselves ; the playful and ornamental element recedes into the background, and the compositions become those of a master who has summed up whole centuries of music in himself. From the insipid melodies of Lully's time Couperin has fashioned more graceful and charming turns of expression ; not only roguishly dancing-melodies, in which the vigorous popular songs seem to live again, but also melodies of the intellect, in which the soul of Mozart might seem to dwell. He prefers to advance in the diatonic scale ; and the sense for the general outline of

the composition, which is so often wanting in the older generation, is in him so unerring that he permits, with inimitable skill,
the semiquavers of his "papillons" to sway up and down through
entire bars. Yet occasionally his melodies seem ashamed of
their nakedness, and, as in the "Sailor's Song," draw the flowery
robe of adornments so closely round them that we can scarcely
trace their limbs. There are the well-known short and long
grace-notes, upper or lower, the *pincés, ports de voix, tremblements,*
and the whole apparatus of ornamentation, which was then larger
than it is now, and which, in spite of the stern admonitions of the
composer's marks, was frequently at the mercy of the performer.
Like almost all composers of that day, Couperin gives in his first
volume the table of his ornamentations, but he insists strongly on
their exact carrying out. To players of to-day his *agréments* are
anything but pleasant. They seem to destroy our sense for the
pure run of the voices, and are painful in their superabundance.
But we must play them with *historical* fingers, and seek to understand the psychology of their expression. They give to the quick
clavier-tone a significance of its own ; they are, so to speak, running drills, cutting the tones deeper into the relief of the piece,
some more, some less, until they bring out the light and shade
which serve to aid expression in the material of the clavier. Could
we hear Couperin play, we should certainly hear the pure voice
more distinctly than we imagine, enfolded as it would be here and
there by deeper or brighter shadows of the ornamentations which
bring out its form in plastic manner. His was a technique which
was lost to us with the thorough comprehension of this music.
Couperin took pains to bring it to the highest perfection. At
times he introduced a slight tempo rubato; he took from the note
at the conclusion something of its length, and gave to another at
the beginning a short pause for breath, inventing for the former
the mark of aspiration, for the latter that of suspension. Here the
endeavour was the same as with Prall-triller[1] and grace-notes.

---

[1] *Prall* means rebounding quickly, or springing back. The Prall-triller consists of
the main note, the note *above*, and the main note again, and should be executed *fast*.

Instead of the ornamentation, the short pause, like the white mounting of a picture, raises the important note, giving to it its meaning and with the meaning the due expression. But later, in the last "Ordres," Couperin must have felt the inadequacy of these marks. The aspirations and suspensions retreat into the background, while the sign) becomes more prominent. This sign simply marks off an independent musical phrase in order to resign its due interpretation to the sympathetic feeling of the player. Such is the trouble he takes with the traditional style of ornamentation and its spiritual expression.

But the remaining musical peculiarities of his composition follow the simplest lines of development. Freedom of motive increases. Tremolo accompaniments, interesting sequences, a playful counterpoint—this latter especially in the pieces for two claviers, or in the "Pièces croisées" for clavier with two manuals— in fact an inexhaustible array of new forms arises. Thus the harmonisation simplifies itself along with the advance of the entire musical development. Couperin modulates, into the dominant or sub-dominant, by means of their related notes, in major and minor keys. By his turn for repetitions of short figures on changing basses—a truly modern motive—or by bold passages of passing notes—for instance, in the saraband "La Majestueuse," we find once e flat, d, f sharp, g, a, one over another—he gives us interesting harmonies, which appear, especially in the *allemandes*, as full, heavy chords, already anticipating Bach.

The theatre of Couperin is rich and varied. The representations which we see in this theatre under the innumerable titles of the pieces, range over the whole world. Some of the characters are also not strange to us ; others we soon learn to know ; a few remain unintelligible to us since the relations they betoken are too subjective. But all lend to the pieces a personal value and an intimate charm, as Goya's editions present them to us ; and it is from them that the clavier derives its great significance as interpreter of this intimate personal art.

"Nanette" greets us with her pleasant quavering melody ;

" Fleurie " is more subtle, and sways delightfully in richly-adorned $\frac{6}{8}$ time; the " Florentine " blooms in graceful, gentle play of quick triolet-figures; but the "Garnier" has the dress of the confined fantastic time, having not yet cast off her heavy folds. " Babet " is " nonchalamment " contented; " Mimi " has a temperament which the many slurs and points of the ornamentation can scarcely fully exhibit. " Conti " (or " les Graces incomparables ") works lullingly out her counterpoint; " Forqueray " (or la Superbe) has a physiognomy of almost academic severity. Many ladies pass by us in these pastel-portraits. We are amused with the divine Babiche (Les amours badins) and the beautiful Javotte (or the " Infanta "); but the most beautiful in melody is Sœur Monique, an intellectually delicate creation, and the most beautiful in construction is " La Couperin " (perhaps the musician's cousin Louise) who poses before us in a masterly, stately, and slightly fugal movement.

Then follow the troops of nameless ones. First the nuns— the blondes in the minor and the brunettes in the major section. Then the charming and melodious representatives of landscapes : Ausonian, Bourbon, Charlerois, Basque. Then the " Enchantress," who of course in process of time suffered much from her magic. Then the " Working Woman," who finishes her course, but is surpassed in it nevertheless by the " Diligent One." The " Flatterer " and the " Voluptuous Woman " are a relatively quiet pair. The " Gloomy One " is sharply defined, with her dismal, jerky passages, and the heavy full chords. The " Sad One " exhibits the light sentimentality of all archaic melodies. The " Spectre " sweeps past in slurred thirds. Close behind come the " Gray Women " with their ponderous sad march. The " Fox-Tail " has tripping broken chords ; the " Lonely One " shows her caprices in the rapid successions of grave and gay. Then follow, in endless succession, the " Princesse d'Esprit," " l'Insinuante," " l'Intime," " la Galante," " la Douce et Piquante," faithful ones, *risqué* ones, bold, visionary, mysterious ones, with their chromatic descents. " Le Turbulent " is one of the few men in the list.

His more general portraits are the most satisfying. They depict emotions, characters, animals, plants, landscapes, occupations, bits from all kinds of life, which are often inscribed with the favourite antique titles. Thus "Diana" with her broken chords leads us into the forest, and shortly after in the second part we hear her horns sounding; while in the "Hunt" a more romantic note is struck. In a broad violoncello-like "Romance" the wood gods are singing and the satyrs dance a very melodious and attractive Bourrée. The Amazon rushes on in thirds, which bear a striking likeness to the *leit-motif* of Die Walküren; and Atalanta runs past in rapid figures. Hymen and Amor sing a marriage-song, the former in the first part more firmly, the latter in the second more delicately and tenderly. The Bells of Cythera sound to us from the holy island, rising and falling alternately, enlivened by glissando-passages. This motive Couperin adopted a second time in "Les Timbres."

The Bees hum and revolve round one point; the Butterflies flutter past in ravishing triplets; the Fly buzzes and dances round her own melody; the retiring Linnet hurries through restless triplets; the complaining Grasshopper chirps in endless imitative short grace-notes; the Eel twists itself now tightly, now loosely; the Amphibian creeps along in legato notes, winding itself through bar-sections of Schubertian length; the Nightingale in Love sings her piercing plaintive accents in quick and ever quicker trills, or as Victor chants more joyfully and triumphantly. Or, again, blooming lilies rise before us in delicate self-enfolding figures with petal-like ornamentations; the sedge rustles eternally to its melody; the poppy spreads abroad a wonderful secret mysterious tune, with many slow arpeggio thirds; and garlands twine themselves in festal guise on a canonic trelliswork.

Life unfolds itself in its entire wealth. Here we have the rolling play of the waves, there the purling and rippling of the brooks, and the twittering of the birds—a foretaste of the slow movement of the Pastoral Symphony. Then again, under the name of "Bontemps ou l'étincelante," an appeal is made to the emotions of springtide or fair weather; we live as it were in a small forest of enchantment. In the second part—Les Grâces Naturelles—one of Couperin's most intellectual melodies breaks forth, showing all the chaste delicacy of Mozart. There rises the blooming landscape of St Germain en Laye; farther off we catch a sight of teeming orchards from which the music of bagpipes sounds forth. The reapers draw nigh with cheerful song; the buffoons—males in minor and female in major—stir their happy limbs; the jugglers appear and ply their tricks;—we can hardly distinguish the trick and its solution, or the rapid intermingling of left and right hand—the knitters lace their rolling semiquavers together right to the "falling meshes" at the end; the click-clack of the lace-makers—tic, toc, choc, tic, toc, choc—beats joyfully hither and thither in the broken chords of a *pièce croisée*. Even the milk-maids of Bagnolet have their appropriate pieces. There the gossipping wife—a reminiscence of Jannequin—beats her rapid bubbling motive; there the short rolling courses of the famous little windmills play their humorous part; here hobbles a cheery lame man along; there staggers a *bizarre*, syncopated, now swift, now slow Chinese. "The Man with the queer Body" makes his springs, in scattered notes, and close by stands the idyll of "Dodo," or "Love in the Cradle," the bass of which rocks itself to and fro in a *pièce croisée*. "Wavering shadows" glide ghost-like in sadly-sounding movements throughout this play of life.

The "Sentiments," full of feeling, with their beautiful "anticipation" notes, the long legato-movement of the "Idées Heureuses," the "Regrets" and "Amusements" musically darting to and fro, the syncopated tender "L'Ame en Peine," the wonderful "Langueurs Tendres," the somewhat lengthy "Charmes," the "Agréments" with *their* agréments, the free diatonic of the various morning melodies,[1] the gentle toying of the "Bagatelles," of the "Petit Rien," of the "Brimborions," the rapture-like "Saillie"— these are inward reflexes which have not quite the clear sensuousness and realism of the outer experiences. The following are

[1] *Aubade*, English "morning music" or "hunts-up."

the most elaborately worked out, and are presented in "cycle" form.

The " Earlier Ages " appear in four figures—the first exercise gives the syncopated " Muse naissante," the second the rocking " Enfantine," the third the rioting " Adolescente," the fourth the " Délices " in violoncello style, which is Couperin's favourite for the attainment of the most delightful effects.

Or the great " Shepherds' Feast " with the twanging musettes of Taverni or Choisy, and the lightly rocking rhythms.

Or the five-act Ballet of the " Pomp of the great and ancient Menestrandise." [1]   Act I., the pompous entry of the Notables and sworn probationers.   Act II., a bag-pipe song of the hurdy-gurdy-men and beggars.   Act III., a joyous dance of the jugglers, clog-dancers, and Merry-Andrews with bears and monkeys.   Act IV., a duet of the crazy and the lame.   Act V., breaking up of the whole troop by the animals—furious étude in semiquavers.

Next, the cycle of the old and young men ; the former sober, the latter happy.

But, before all, that original of Schumann's Carnival, " Les Folies françaises ou les Dominos."   Maidenhood in invisible colours, Shame in rose, Impetuosity in red, Hope in green, Faith-fulness in blue, Perseverance in gray, Longing in violet, Coquetry

[1] The " Pomp " is the " Masque," as it would be called in England.   The " great and ancient Menestrandise " is the old association or guild of Minstrels.   The Charter of the King of the Minstrels, granted by John of Gaunt, King of Castile and Leon, and Duke of Lancaster, dated 1381, may be seen in Hawkins's History of Music.   An old verse in " Robin Hood's Garland " alludes to the festive sports of the Minstrels in these words, which almost reproduce the above description of Couperin's piece :—

" This battle was fought near Tutbury town
When the bag-pipers baited the bull,
I am king of the fiddlers, and swear 'tis a truth,
And call him that doubts it a gull ;
For I saw them fighting, and fiddled the while,
And Clorinda sung Hey derry down :
The bumpkins are beaten, put up thy sword, Bob,
And now let's dance into the town.
Before we came to it we heard a great shouting,
And all that were in it look'd madly ;
For some were a' bull-back, some dancing a morrice,
And some singing Arthur a Bradley."

J. PH. RAMEAU

Né à Dijon le 26 septembre 1683.
Mort le 12 Septembre 1764

J.J. Cassieri S.D.R. del.   J.G. Sturm sculps. Nürn.

A Clavier Lesson.

Painting by an unknown Dutch Master, 17th century, in the Royal Gallery at Dresden.

in a domino of many colours, the old gallants in purple and gold, the cuckolds in brown, silent Jealousy in dark gray, Rage and Desperation in black. Externally the form is that of a great ballet of the time; internally it is the variation of collected pieces on a single harmonic succession, its contents are the allusions easily comprehended at the time; the characterisation is carried through with great skill; but its musical setting is even shorter than is usually the case with Couperin's clavier-pieces.

The Preludes, which Couperin appended to his "Art de Toucher le clavecin," he named, in accordance with their *ad libitum* performance, the Prose of clavier-literature. These dances and pictures were to him the poetry, rhymed and rhythmical. And it was precisely their formal completion which was of importance for the future of clavier-literature. We see the forms developing. In his best pieces the Sonata is already fore-shadowed. The fulness of motives, as they occur to him in his two best compositions, the splendid "Favorite" and the stupendous "Passacaille," is elsewhere thematically limited. In the recapitulation of the main theme at the beginning of the second part of the pieces, in the rhythmic similarity between the rondo-motive and its "couplets," in many a thematic working-out, shown for example in "La Trophée" with its wonderfully modern sonata-style, lies the promise of thematically-developed music of succeeding generations. To the same purpose is his increasing sense for the association of several pieces. The many slow second pieces, or the popular dances such as the Polonaise, the Sezile, the Musette, which form the concluding parts of a group, the repetition of the first part after the second, the divisions into slow movement, slower, and lighter, which are specially visible in "La Triomphante," and "Les Bacchanales"—all these are as much the germ of the future sonata arrangement, as the severer thematic was the germ of sonata-playing. The charm for us lies in observing, in the springtime of art, the natural uprising of these forms which appear to us almost laws of nature.

His "Art de toucher le clavecin," the first school-book

specially devoted to the clavier, was published in 1717 and dedicated to the king. This was a noteworthy advance. There was to be no longer a teaching of mere notation, but a teaching of technique and execution. "The method which I here propose," says Couperin, "is unique, and has nothing to do with the tablature, which is only a counting of numbers. I deal here chiefly with all that belongs to good playing. I believe that my observations are clear enough to please connoisseurs and to help those who are willing to be helped. As there is a great difference between grammatical and rhetorical rules, so there is an infinite distance between tablature and the art of good playing." Such a general musical "fabrication" and grammar, in spite of many advanced ideas, had been the work of St Lambert, which appeared from 1702 to 1707, and which in its first part (called " Principes du Clavecin ") devotes only a few lines to actual clavecin playing, and extends the second part (called " De l'accompagnement ") also to the organ, and other instruments. It is painful to him that his experience is treated lightly and turned into a " school." The parents of the pupils, he says later, ought to place the most implicit reliance on the teacher, and yield him the completest powers. The teacher even takes the key of the instrument with him, and no playing should be attempted without his supervision. The scholar sits with his fore-arm horizontal before the clavier, elbows, hand and fingers in a line—the fingers thus lying quite flat on the keys. He has his body turned very slightly to the right, and the right foot a little stretched out. In order to prevent grimacing while playing, he often places a mirror in front in which he can watch his motions. A bar over the hands occasionally regulates the equality of their height; for the holding of the hands high makes the tone necessarily hard. Looking about of any kind is forbidden, and above all, coquetting with the public as if the playing were no trouble at all. And although, finally, everything in the performance depends on experience, taste, and feeling, yet rules are given for performance to which the player must conform. Couperin frequently disregards the fingering of his predecessors, and to the examples which he gives of his new art he adds confidently in a side-note that he is convinced that few persons in Paris have the old rules in their heads —Paris being the centre of all good. Step by step we have harder and harder studies developed from a single figure, and directions for finger exercises fill the rest of the volume. The change of fingers on one note, the avoidance of the same finger twice in scale passages, the first application of the thumb in passing under are his characteristic points. These are all symptoms of the endeavour to form a legato style suitable to the clavier; they are the external indications of the suppression of the lute. Couperin's abhorrence of a vacuum runs through his whole teaching of the clavier. The adornments, the avoidance of too long note-values, the legato finger-exercise—all are the systematic development of the powers which arise from the necessity of *short* tones in the clavier. He once introduces a charming short fugal *allemande*, in which both voice-parts work in contrary motion in most flowing style in order to show what "sounds well" on the clavier, and opposes to it the one-sided broken chords of the Italian sonatas of whose light style he has on other grounds the highest opinion. "The clavier has its peculiarities as the violin has *its*. If its note cannot swell, if the repetitions of one tone by striking do not suit it, it has advantages on the other side, precision, neatness, brilliancy, and width of compass." Perhaps Couperin was the first who had an absolutely good ear for the clavier.

In comparison with him his elder and younger contemporaries must give place. Dumont, le Begue, D'Anglebert, Loeilly, Marchand, Dandrieu, and even the brilliant Rameau, composer of operas and founder of modern musical theory, are his inferiors. It is now demonstrated that Rameau published his first clavier-compositions in 1706, seven years before those of Couperin. But these pieces had just as little meaning and result as those of Marchand which appeared the year previously. They must have differed little from the style of the old school of Chambonnières.

LOUIS MARCHAND
Organiste du Roy.
Né à Lion, Mort à Paris le 17 Février
1732. Agé de 61 ans

Rameau in later years is much freer and more developed, like Couperin, whose work he continued with the happiest results. He is no pioneer, but an improver of the ways. How powerful are his *allemandes*, how dainty his *gigues*, how brilliant the conduct of the thematic in his Cyclopes and his Trois Mains! What a depth of invention appears in his variations on Gavottes, in his Gigues, and in his splendid Niais de Sologne! How wonderfully melodious is his "L'Enharmonique," what a realism is there in his "Hen" and in the "Call of the Birds"! How clear, how penetrating, how rich in promise is his technique! In him there are musical conceptions of extreme penetration and melodious harmonic turns which live for ever in the ear. From the "twenties" to the "sixties" all kinds of new editions of his works were produced, so popular were they, as they would still be, if the public knew these enchanting little works.

Thus the fame of the clavier is fixed in the Paris of the beginning of the eighteenth century, and its future assured. It is a kind of symbol of history that from the guild of violinists, founded by a king of violin-players, which reigned throughout the seventeenth century, should have proceeded, first the dance-masters, for reasons of independence, and then the organists and clavierists, who actually maintained that a musician was he only who played an instrument with full harmony. The orchestra went its own way, the "grande bande des violons" and the "petits violons" of Lully's time having laid the foundation. The clavier was again the opponent of the orchestra, and concentrated the whole body of tone in its keys. An intimate, personal interpreter of musical emotions, it chooses to perform its functions in itself. Its consciousness of its own importance grows to a height. No longer will a clavecin-player when accompanist be the Cinderella among a company of proud sisters. "The clavierist," cried Couperin indignantly, "is the last to be praised for his share in a concerto. What injustice! His accompaniment is the foundation of a building which supports the whole, and of which no one ever speaks!"

Rameau, out walking. Old engraving from the
Nicolas-Manskopf collection, Frankfort.

Old engraving after Wagniger's design. The true musician is climbing up the Ladder of Contrapuntal Art ever higher and higher (see in the engraving the words *plus ultra*) to the Concert ot Angels (legitime certantibus). From the "Basis and Fundamental Tone" the musical notes are being carried to the Gold-furnace (various flames in which are labelled, *e.g.* motet, canzonet, canon, etc.). The enemies are seen up above breaking the tritone, the false fifth, and the ninth; arrows are being shot at the Artist on the left as he writes (volenti nil difficile, "nothing is difficult to the willing mind"), but they are shattered on the Shield of Minerva, on which is represented the Austrian Eagle.

Scarlatti

DOMENICO SCARLATTI, perhaps the greatest clavier-player that Italy ever had, prefaces a collection of thirty sonatas, which appeared at Amsterdam,[1] with the following words: "Amateur or professor, whoever thou art, seek not in these compositions for any deep feeling. They are only a frolic of art, intended to increase thy confidence on the clavier. I had no ambition to make a sensation; I was simply requested to publish the pieces. Should they be not utterly unpleasing to thee, I shall all the more willingly undertake other commissions, in order to rejoice thee in a lighter and more varied style. Take then these pieces rather as man than as critic; so only shalt thou

[1] Before 1746. Burney says they were printed in Venice.

68

increase thine own content. To speak of the use of the two hands—D denotes *dritta*, the right, and M *manca*, the left. Farewell!" It is noticeable how here in a few words the whole essence of Italian clavier-music is summed up—the fresh, cheerful disposition of the artist ; the respect for the amateur ; the pleasure in mere sound and in musical construction ; the thorough working-out of intellectual motives (in the manner of the Étude) ; and the stress laid upon the equal participation of both hands as essential factors in the "concert," [using this word in its older sense as expressing the association of two or more vocal or instrumental "parts"]. The word "concert" was well understood in these early days to mean the combination of two viols ; and music of such a kind was, in form and in content, the true precursor of clavier-music, in which the right and left hand "parts" are strictly on an equality both in difficulty and importance.

These are the distinguishing marks of Italian clavier-art, and within these limits it works.

But Scarlatti is especially remarkable to us in the present day, in that he occupies the position of an early writer whose pieces still play a part, though a small one, in modern public concerts. Liszt, for example, was partial to him, and arranged his "Cat's Fugue" ; while Bülow edited a representative selection from his pieces. Czerny published (through Haslinger) two hundred of his so-called Sonatas—though, by the way, the last of these pieces belongs really to the father, Alessandro Scarlatti. Before that time the remains of the master had formed no inconsiderable part of private manuscript collections, such as those of the Abbé Santini in Rome, and others.[1]

Domenico Scarlatti, the famous son of the not less famous

---

[1] The engraving and printing of music was rare, even in the case of popular masters, till late in the eighteenth century. In most cases short and simple clavier pieces were copied privately. This method of spreading works about in our own time when printing has made everything democratic is not lost, but made aristocratic. When Wagner copies the Ninth Symphony, or when a scholar copies an old, unpublished work, we have an instance of the personal love of manual labour in a dilettante or scholar—the work of the hand in an age of machinery.—[Author's Note.]

Alessandro, who was a composer of operas and chief of the Neapolitan School, exhibits in old portraits a serious, severe, even pedagogic countenance. There is also much of the pedagogue in his pieces; yet I think him fresher, gayer, more happy in life and mind than this face would lead one to suppose. His "Exercises" move with vigorous strides, and are far too full of esprit to be pedantic. His life was that of an artist universally honoured, and rejoicing in his fame, a type of which his contemporary Handel is the model; and his biography reveals no less activity than his works. A pupil of his renowned father, in the midst of the volatile, melody-loving, easily-stirred Neapolitan world, he set out early for Rome, in order to become the scholar of the great theorist Gasparini and of the organist and clavier-player Pasquini. In 1709, at the age of twenty-six, he made the acquaintance of Handel at Venice, and in sheer admiration, followed him to Rome. There he remained ten years, and became kapellmeister of St Peter's, gaining a reputation by the works of his genius. In 1720 we suddenly find him in London as clavicymbalist of the Italian opera. Here his "Narcissus" was performed. A year later again he was in Lisbon, where the King of Portugal made efforts to detain him, and where for a time he gave lessons to the Princess. At this time the fame of his playing and of his compositions reached the farthest bounds of Europe, and he ranked thenceforward as the first executant of the age. He returned again to Italy, and from Italy to Spain. He remained in Madrid from 1729 to his death in 1757. Here all kinds of honours were showered upon him; he was Knight of St James, and chamber-player to the Queen, who still retained a grateful memory of the lessons he had given her at Lisbon when she was Princess of Asturias. To her he dedicated his first-published pieces, prefixing to them the lively preface above quoted.

Italian music has to French the relation which Bull has to Bird, or the virtuoso to the poet. In Scarlatti we seek in vain for any inner motive, nor do we feel any need of an emotional rendering on the part of the performer; his short pieces aim only at *sound* effects, and are written merely from the love of brilliant clavier-passages, or to embody delicate technical devices. They are not denizens of Paradise, who wander, unconscious of their naked beauty, under over-arching bowers; they are athletes, simply rejoicing in their physical strength, and raising gymnastic to a high, self-sufficient art. We admire them, as we admire an acrobatic troupe of strong and stout character; we admire them—not too much, yet with a certain eager anticipation of the next interesting and unusual feat of skill. We wonder at their mastery of technique, and the systematic development of their characteristic methods; we rejoice that they never, in their desire to please, abandon the standpoint of the sober artists; but our heart remains cold. There is an icy, virgin purity in this first off-shoot[1] of absolute virtuosity, which kindles our sense for the art of beautiful mechanism, for the art of technique *per se* —an art which, after all, the historian of the clavier must not depreciate by comparing it with that of the *inner* music.

The Scarlatti style is a genuine product of the Italian musical emotion. The Italian is not born for heavy, contrapuntal, "vain ticklings of the ears"; nor, on the other hand, for too intimate effusions or symbolic mysteries. He is sensuous through and through; delight in playing and in sound is the very life of his music, as delight in outline and in colour is the very life of his painting. The intoxication of absolute tone runs through the masses of his churches, the operas of his theatre, the chamber-music of his salons. Delight in sound gave the impulse to every Italian musician in his bid for fame. It created virtuosity, which loves playing for its own sake; it created the dramatic choruses, with which the Venetian school began its career; it created the melody predominating over the harmony, with the discovery of which in the Florentine opera the greatest blow was struck for the new principles of "secular" musicianship. From love of sound

[1] A far earlier exponent of pure virtuosity is found in England in Dr John Bull, whose pieces, written a century and a half before Dom. Scarlatti's, bear every mark of devotion to "pianistic," as Bülow would call it. The author seems to recognise this a few lines back.

the Venetians cast the instruments free from their old corporate unity, and gave them an individual meaning and value. From love of sound Frescobaldi led the organ, Corelli the violin, Scarlatti the clavier, to undreamt-of technical creations. And the *bel canto* of the human voice almost attained the capacity of an instrument; so small was the influence of the mere words. They were en-

Adrian Willaert, of Venice, after the engraving
published in 1559 by Antonio Gardano, Venice.

amoured of melody, which, unlike the ecclesiastical counterpoint, sought its new objective not in the manifold transformation, but in the natural development of a motive: they were captivated with the "da capo" repetition of concerted pieces or arias, a habit grounded on the psychological law of the higher effectiveness of all repeated passages. They rioted in the multitude of forms, in which they found a place for every kind of music, for every "tempo," every rhythm, and for all kinds of expression. Through-out all this was to be perceived the sensuous Italian love for

music, which expressed in this manifoldness its freedom of artistic activity,
and in that freedom the unity of thematic construction and consequently
the unity of formal repetition.
Technical ability was appreciated
in Venice earlier than elsewhere. The
registers of organists at St Mark's go
back to 1318. In Venice not the
office only, but the art, was honoured.
The musician was not, as he was much
later at Florence, interrupted by the
ringing of a bell, if he continued his

Frescobaldi.

performance too long. The emancipation of artists, which in
our own century we have seen carried out in the person of the
orchestral conductor, was in Venice effected by the instrumental
musician ; and as to-day the orchestra has grown in repute
by the agency of the conductor, so in those days the prestige
of instrumental music advanced alongside that of the performer. At the beginning of the seventeenth century a
Frescobaldi could already gain so important a position as player
of the organ and clavier, that it was said that no clavier-
player was respected who did not play after his new fashion.
When he gave his first recital in St Peter's, thirty thousand persons were there to hear him. What Frescobaldi was in the first
half of the seventeenth century, that was Pasquini in the second
half. In Italy, Austria, and France he was treated like a prince ;
and his tombstone bears the proud inscription, " Organist of the
Senate and People of Rome." With Scarlatti the art of clavier-
playing reaches its height, and begins to decline. It is not
clavierists but violinists, the wordless rivals of the singers, who
have carried the type of Italian virtuosity into our own times—
Corelli, Vivaldi, Locatelli, Tartini, Paganini.

This sensuous devotion to music apart from inner meaning,
this passion for poetic beauty, the Italians have not yet, even under

Wagnerian influences, wholly forgotten. The victorious rule of absolute tone, while it constituted their greatness, carried with it the germ of their decay. Virtuosity is the mark of their art and of their life. We must take them as they are, in the whole light-hearted temperament of their existence. This Bohemian type of the Italian musician of the time may profitably be compared with the similar French type. What a seductive brilliancy there is in the adventurous career of a Bononcini! His operas are received at Vienna with unparalleled enthusiasm. Queen Sophia Charlotte is the clavier-player at the production of his "Polifemo" in Berlin. In London he enters upon a contest with Handel, in which social intrigues are involved with high political aims. Next, he appears in a lawsuit, and is unmasked as a common plagiary[1] of a madrigal of Lotti's; shortly after he is away to Paris with an alchemist, who swindles him of all his property, and leaves him to make his living by the sweat of his brow to his ninetieth year. Stradella's fate is well known— how he ran away with the mistress of a Venetian before the first performance of his own opera;[2] was more than once attacked with a dagger, and finally actually murdered.[3] What, compared with this, is the story of Rameau's youthful love and its punishment, and of his tardy attainment of the haven of fortune, or what the anecdotes of Marchand, with his love affairs, his expulsion from Paris, and his smiling return? The dangerous glitter of this Italian Bohemianism is the fitting framework of that sensuous, lively, irresponsible music.

It was inevitable that the Italians should invent the opera —the opera, in which every thing tends rapidly to the spectacular; singers, scene painters, musicians, and the public. Apart from its relation to opera all Italian music is unintelligible, and it is

---

[1] Plagiarism of the most thorough-going character was common in the eighteenth century, and can hardly have been accounted disgraceful, considering how frequently Handel himself practised it, appropriating subjects of fugues, long passages, and whole movements, from Stradella, Kerl, Urio, Steffani, and others.

[2] A "spiritual" opera, or oratorio.

[3] A doubtful story. S. died *circa* 1681, probably in his bed.

no accident that for centuries the Italians stood in the forefront of opera. Those lucky misunderstandings are well-known, which led, about the year 1600, to the rise of this form of art. A circle of Platonic dreamers (led by Giovanni Bardi, Count of Vernio) in Florence, anxious to revive the ancient tragedy, engaged certain musicians to compose monodic songs with accompaniment. They merely meant by this to be antique; but as a matter of fact they were unconsciously acting along the line of the most modern of needs, which had long tended towards isolated melody. The dainty and delicate songs, which took their origin in this, the Venetians, and afterwards the Neapolitans, accepted eagerly as a material on which to construct forms of ravishing virtuosity, until a Jomelli, with his dashing bravura passages on the most solemn words, finally arrives at that very " laceramento della poesia "[1] which the Florentine reformer Caccini had once fanatically combated as a madness of the ancient song in several parts. In a very short time the opera runs through the whole gamut of the joys and sorrows of virtuosity. The sweet charm of sound, exhibited by a voice which bears the melody, so suited to the narrow outlines of poetry, is found in the old vestal airs of Caccini and Peri. The delight in a multitude of forms, in an alternation of different rhythms in short portions of the aria, lived in the songs of the Venetian Cavalli, in which we are reminded of the alternating tempi of the old instrumental pieces[2] —the toccatas, fantasias, and canzoni. Yet empty vanity shows itself all too soon. The original simplicity was overlaid by various corrupt accretions, first by songs, introduced in loose dependence on the action, then by complete concerted pieces, which are indicated in the libretto—together with directions to tailors, architects, and decorators, and alongside of the titles and orders of the performers. In Naples, worse still, the music gradually declines into a stiff and wearisome form and sweet playful nothingness.

[1] " Tearing the passion to tatters."

[2] For instance, in the numerous seventeenth century English "cantatas" for solo voice, and the contemporary instrumental fantasias, where it is common to find short sections in triple time breaking the continuity of the more ordinary quadruple time.

The well-defined outline of the aria appears, now regularly written "da capo"; it alternates to a tiresome degree with the accompanied recitative; the chorus recedes into the background before the soloists. It is the old typical form, skilfully adapted to virtuosity, precisely as a sonata of Scarlatti is differentiated from a toccata of Frescobaldi or Pasquini. Originality is vanquished; elegance has created a set of formalities in which technique can freely exercise itself. The substantive style, so to speak, has given way to the adjective, and matter is conquered by form. This Neapolitan class of opera, which thus exalts the virtuoso, begins with Alessandro Scarlatti. He is the father of that species of art which is afterwards included in the name of Italian opera, in which we see a contempt for the words, a love of vocal bravura, the supremacy of the aria, and a delight in the human voice as an instrument. In the forms of his ornamentations we discover again in antitype the passages of Domenico; in his love of the *da capo* and instrumental repetitions of vocal phrases we see once more in antitype Domenico's repetitions of shorter or longer groups of bars. In the "Alessandro nelle Indie" of the Neapolitan Leonardo Vinci the hero sings arias full of slurred "divisions," syncopations, unprepared sevenths, which to a man acquainted with Scarlatti's sonatas appear to bear a strong family resemblance to Scarlatti. Old rubbish bears germs of new creations; released from the heavy burden of the words, the light play of the voices in the clavier-pieces introduces a fresh, youthful life that is full of promise for the future.

The isolation of the voice and of the instrument, the sensuous delight in sound, demands a chamber-music and a chamber-style. Chamber-music demands the Maecenas of the great house, and the wealthy amateur, who is so powerful a factor in every advance of art. Roman musical life, for instance, draws its strength from the practical encouragement of the Pope's, or from the concerts and operas performed in aristocratic houses. A Venetian nobleman, Benedetto Marcello, became a distinguished and favourite composer, a poet and a satirist. A Roman nobleman, Emilio dei

Cavalieri, became the founder of the modern oratorio, an opera-composer of the advanced school, perhaps even the very earliest composer of vocal monody. Vincenzo Galilei, the father of the astronomer, became known by his monodies in that circle of Florentine Platonists, to whose worthy amateurism is due the origin of the opera ; and he wrote a work on the technique and fingering of all instruments.

Music in the home is in Italy not too intimate, but proud, splendid, mere pastime. Like the opera of the virtuosos, like the secularised church-music, it tends to rely upon effect, and lives on applause. It depends chiefly on the performer, and knows little of the mutual intelligence of souls. A subtle aristocratic love of music runs through the Italy of the Middle Ages. Many are the names of high-born men and women who had mastered the art of the lute by ear—for a notation was as yet unknown.[1] In the Decameron (1350), alongside of the novel-telling, it is song, lute-playing, viol-playing, dance and choral refrain, with which that pleasant company loves most to kill the time.

The music of dances, songs, and instrumental pieces, which was soon to find its proper home in the clavier, is a child of the world, and, in the view of a serious theoretician like Pietro Bembo, it is exposed to all the dangers of emptiness and vanity. In 1529 he writes to his daughter Helena, who like many of the women in her position, intended to receive instruction on the clavier in her convent : " As to your request to be allowed to learn the monochord,[2] I answer that you cannot yet, on ac-count of your youth, understand that playing is only suited for idle and volatile ladies ; whereas I desired you to be the most pure and loveable maiden in the world. Also, it would bring you but little pleasure or renown if you should play badly ; while to play well you would have to devote ten or twelve

---

[1] A notation for the lute was published as early as 1512.

[2] " Monochord " is synonymous with " Clavichord " here. The word was often used for the keyed instrument, probably because the " German " clavichord had tangents at the ends of the levers, which cut off the right length of the string, just as the moveable " bridge " of the acoustician's monochord of one single string does.

years to practice, without being able to think of anything else. Consider a moment whether *this* would become you. And if your friends wish you to learn to play in order to give them pleasure, reply that you do not wish to make yourself ridiculous in their eyes; and content yourself with the sciences and domestic occupations."

A hundred years later chamber-music is at its zenith. The great Carissimi (d. 1674) put the flourishing chamber cantata [1] —that half-dramatic, half-lyric song of the seventeenth century —by the side of the monodic church-songs of Viadana; and Steffani added his renowned chamber-duets. The case was precisely similar with instrumental music; by the side of the "sonata da chiesa," with its free and independent style, came the "sonata da camera," as a suite of favourite dance forms; [2] and the "concerti," with their several instruments playing to a small accompanying orchestra. Above all, the possibility is now realised of suitably accompanying monodies and concerted works on the clavier, from the figured bass; and this in its turn contributes not a little to the victorious advance of the melodic song. But as a solo-instrument, the clavier suns itself in the light of the chamber-style, in which brilliancy, dexterity of hand, and elasticity of form are not less admired than the many small and spirited caprices, which in the "grand" style of music have perhaps not yet been attempted.

Among all the instruments of tone which achieve an independent existence in Italy, the clavier naturally takes its stand last. From its first movement towards this independence, in Venice in the sixteenth century, to the full liberty of a Scarlatti, stretches an interval of a hundred and fifty years. It was in fact partly too much occupied in the orchestra, and partly too dependent on the technique of the organ. We find it already

---

[1] Our modern notion of a "cantata" includes the free use of a chorus; whereas the seventeenth century "cantata" was for a solo voice with accompaniment of a single instrument, harpsichord, lute, or viol da gamba.

[2] For instance, Corelli's trios, two books (out of four) of which are "suonate da camera," chamber music, the rest being "da chiesa," for church.

in the orchestra in the first operas of Peri; under Monteverde, the first of all great orchestral geniuses, there were two claviers, on the right and left of the stage. They serve to accompany solo singing, or, along with small organs, to fill up the harmony of the orchestral body. As a rule the operatic composer writes only the figured bass, but occasionally adds some of the melodic voice-parts; the conductor completes the score, leaving to the several players, however, a certain freedom of improvisation in colouring, a freedom which a well-trained musician would not abuse to the detriment of the *tout ensemble*.

But clavier-pieces pure and simple had a characteristically *dependent* existence. Even in that Venetian circle where Willaert (1490-1563) Gabrieli,[1] and Merulo moved, in which instruments were first emancipated, in which they were boldly introduced into church-music, and solo-pieces were written for orchestral or for keyed instruments, even here the soul of the clavier lay still fettered. It is the organ that indicates colour and takes the lead. In the pieces of the two Gabrielis, or of Merulo, the old contrapuntal, pictorial fashion lives still almost untouched by external disturbances; and the picture seldom allows us to anticipate that stiff adherence to the theme, and that well-wrought harmony which, in the England of the same age, we found so full of promise. Down to the time of Frescobaldi, organist at St Peter's in 1615, who stands as a landmark in this development, the Italian sense for absolute music is far too strong for an "applied" music to be able, as it did in France and England, to *modernise* the instrumental pieces by their necessary dependence on song and dance. Canzoni[2] are treated in a light fugal style; the so-called Ricercari[3] represent another and freer fugal form; the toccatas, capriccios and fantasias are variegated attempts to

---

[1] Two Gabrielis, uncle and nephew; the former, Andrea, dating 1510-1586, the latter, Giovanni, 1557-1612. Andrea was a pupil of Willaert and he succeeded Merulo as "second" organist of St Mark's, Venice, in 1566.

[2] "Canzone," a sixteenth and seventeenth century term for a sort of vocal madrigal.

[3] "Ricercari" (compare French "recherché"), the name of a class of pieces for organ or cembalo in which the object was to include as many ingenuities of counterpoint as possible.

unite all tempi and all kinds of playing in one piece. The composers are aiming at typical forms, and only attain an unrestrained formlessness which all these pieces with their trifling differences alike exhibit. The juxtaposition of chords, successions of canonic imitations, free alternations of tempo, piquant applications of the newly-discovered chromatic possibilities—all these interest these writers much more than character or expression. All these ricercari, canzoni, fantasias, toccatas, are alike " sonatas " —pieces which exist for the sake of their *tones* and technique, and, as Couperin says, not in the least for the sake of their soul or content. Dance-suites and variations on songs, which as time went on gained in popularity, sharpened, here as elsewhere, the sense for form ; but these never became the predominant class. The free form of the fantasia always ranked as the principal species of the higher clavier-pieces. In Frescobaldi we already see the process of crystallisation. His canzoni and fugues not only exhibit for the first time the good fugal style familiar to us, but also betray the modern sense for arrangement and method in their frequent division[1] into three movements, and in their progressive quickening of tempo. He it is also who reduces under a distinct law of arrangement the various movements of the whole instrumental fantasia.

With Pasquini in the second half of the seventeenth century, we meet the visible line of demarcation between organ and clavier. Hitherto the organ had been in everything the predominant partner. The whole aspect of the clavier-pieces was that of the organ. The old Venetians had frequently written for it in three or four parts and brought the instrument into popularity. But even Frescobaldi had written no piece for clavier alone. Diruta, organist at Chioggia, the pupil of Merulo, wrote a dialogue between 1597 and 1609 on the best method of playing organ and clavier, and had of course drawn attention to the characteristic features of clavier-playing ; but all his observations on hold-

---

[1] Compare Byrd's Cantiones Sacræ, 1575, where the pieces are divided in this way, *e.g.*, Pars Prima, Pars Secunda.

ing the hands horizontal,[1] on the good and bad fingers (the second and fourth are the "good," and fall on the strong accents of the bar), or on the ornamentations and their execution, are

in the first instance written with reference to the organ. Indeed, he actually begins his book with a panegyric on that instrument. As a matter of fact the true emancipator of the Italian clavier was Pasquini. He wrote for the clavicymbal alone; in

Virginal in shape of a work-box.

The same opened, showing the instrument within, which can be taken out.

his figures and thus early showed the clavier; he practice of setting runs in close juxta-borated out of the clavier style; he connection with a and slower parts of set them clearly other; and he at- style of play he a genuine sense for abandoned the chord passages and position, but ela-two the proper brought into strong theme the quicker his sonatas, and over against each tempts, as in his

Capriccio on the motive of the cuckoo's song, to draw from the clavier all kinds of characteristic effects, still wild and confused, but full of the freshness of spring.

So far is the early Italian clavier (when the violin begins its victorious career) from assuming a leading position, that the cembalo can do nothing better than make use of the experiences of the violin. For we must give up the legend of the genius of Michel Angelo Rossi. This story is one of the most

The instrument taken out. Constructed in 1631 by Valerius Perius Romanus. De Wit collection, Leipsic.

[1] Meaning that the fingers were held straight out, and consequently only the first, second, and third (in so-called "German" notation, 2, 3 and 4) would be in common use, the ends being nearly of a length.

amusing freaks of musical history. We find in many popular collections of old music an andante and allegro in G major by this man, who is tolerably well known as an operatic composer and violinist. He was a pupil of Frescobaldi and died in 1660. This piece is so captivating in its melody, so decided in its form, so restrained in its arrangement, that it would have done honour to Mozart. Had these pieces truly sprung from the *intavolatura* of Michel Angelo Rossi, the modernity of their form and melody would give such a shock to musical history that it would be shivered into fragments. Yet a man like Pauer, who published them, could actually believe that this music was possible before 1660.[1] A later historian, Rolland, in his "Histoire de l'Opéra avant Lully et Scarlatti," led astray by the same mistake, fancies he detects in the choruses of Rossi's opera of Hermione anticipations of the Zauberflöte.[2] Parry alone, the author of the brilliant article on the sonata in Grove's Dictionary of Music, has boggled at this pseudo Rossi. Heaven knows to whom the pretty little pieces really belong. It is not unlikely that Scarlatti wrote them in his old age.

The thematically precise sonatas and concertos of Corelli, the old violin master; the pieces of Vivaldi, so wonderfully rich in melody; the intellectual suites of Locatelli; it is in these violin works that the form of the Italian instrumental piece first appears, deriving itself from the joint experiences of the free toccata and of the fettered dance. Corelli, who died so early as 1713, was one of those strange phenomena in the history of art, which reach the utmost heights of an epoch, without freezing into an icy classicism. His pieces are even to-day of a ravishing sensuousness, and must be produced in the flowery dress of

---

[1] It is difficult to set the limits of what is possible in such matters ; *e.g.*—John Jenkins wrote a "Fancy" for three viols, before 1667, which modulates from F major through the whole set of flat keys, up to G flat, whence he coolly turns a rather sharp corner home to F. No one would have dared to suppose this possible.

[2] This might well be. Compare the first phrase of the Recitative, which precedes Dido's dying song in Purcell's "Dido and Æneas," with the first phrase of Wolfram's recitative before the "Star" song in "Tannhäuser."

an improvised *coloratura*.[1] They mark the highest point in the monodic style of the virginal Italian music. From the point of view of melody they are the freshest dances and arias written about 1700, full of unparalleled invention and of a rhythmical freedom which anticipates the scherzi of Beethoven. They are indeed the works of a genius in form. But they never stiffen into one shape, like the operatic overtures.[2] In Corelli the sonata still stands in the full bloom of its manifold forms. Among his numer-

Italian cembalo, from a monastery, of the 18th century. Made of cypress wood. The pictures on the lid represent a concert of monks and a landscape. On the sides of the case are Cupids and garlands. De Wit collection, Leipsic.

ous pieces there are not many which exhibit precisely the same arrangement of the movements and of their tempi, or of the various dances. Even the number of these movements varies, so that one can lay down no precise rule. Slow movements begin, or stand

[1] This *coloratura* means the elaborate ornamentation with which Corelli used to overlay the plain written violin part. Joachim's edition gives Corelli's own version of the sonatas as he himself used to play them.

[2] These in France were usually arranged adagio, allegro, adagio ; in Italy, allegro, adagio, allegro, but in both countries they had found very early a stereotyped form for the succession of their movements. —[Author's Note.]

in the middle, or come at the end ; or even, with a modernised reminiscence of old times, introduce themselves for a few bars[1] between the allegros and the vivaces. This is, from the point of view of form, the same rhythmic freedom which Beethoven, on deeper material grounds, reintroduced in his latest sonatas and quartets. All is held together by an ornamental, delicate, and thematic filigree-work. More rarely, as in the fourth Sonata da chiesa and in the fifth Sonata da camera, a certain thematic relation between the several movements is to be detected ; but within the movement the thematic conception is so worked out that it is treated with natural modulations and appropriate intermediate passages. The movement falls into two parts which are repeated as a matter of course ; the second part begins with the modulated main motive of the first. Occasionally, as in the allemande of the tenth concerto and in the allegro of the twelfth, we find an exact return to the first theme. This combination of the da capo system with the modulation of the theme ; and in the midst of this the miniature da capo system of the concerted violins imitating each other ; and especially the favourite concluding repetitions of bars, alternating from forte to piano,—all these became the groundwork of the Scarlattian style.

The da capo is in fact the scaffolding of this formal music. To our modern minds it appears pointless ; but in those days it was natural enough. Some day the history of musical repetition ought to be written ; it would be indeed the history of quite half of music. Even in Greek writings we meet melodic repetitions ; it is on the principle of imitation that the contrapuntal style of the Middle Ages[2] is built ; from the repetition of parts, or the rearrangement of the themes, musical sentences become capable of new effects ; and further, there was the germ of progress in the thematic conception of whole bars, whole groups of bars and whole

---

[1] Such things are found as late as Mozart ; cf. overture to Zauberflöte.
[2] The true origin of imitative counterpoint is almost certainly the *Rota*, what is nowadays called a Round. This sort of infinite canon was already perfect in the thirteenth century in England. No doubt the *Rota* itself was invented by an accident.

De ces grands Maitres d'Italie
Le Concert seroit fort joli,
Si le Chat que l'on voit icy
N'y vouloit Chanter sa partie.

CONCERT
ITALIEN.
6 Le Chat de Cafarelli, chantant
une Parodie Italienne.

De deux cœurs que ta chaine lie
C'est ainsy, petit Dieu d'Amour,
Que quelque Animal chaque jour
Vient troubler la douce harmonie.

1. Scarlatti.
2. Tartini.
3. Martini.
4. Locatelli.
5. Lanzetti.

Old engraving representing Scarlatti playing a Harpsichord with two rows of keys; and certain well-known contemporaries of his. A satire on the unheard-of successes of the famous Italian Soprano, Cafarelli. From the Nicolas-Manskopf collection, Frankfort-on-Main. Cafarelli's cat is sitting in the foreground singing an Italian parody. The persons represented are named on the right. The two verses are as follows: "The concert of these great Italian masters would be beautiful, if the cat did not join in. Just in the same way, the sweet harmony of two souls joined by the god of Love is constantly being interrupted by some animal or other."

movements, which finally, whether arias or sonatas, were taken da capo. This is the last step of thematic music which has shaken off the contrapuntal forms. To-day we are in a period of repetition which, for want of a better word, we may call "Thematic." In dependence on the old beginnings of programme-music, which were greatly developed by Beethoven, the new *subjective* repetition takes the place of the older. This new form works chiefly in the *idée fixe*, in the Leit-motiv, which is subtly treated and varied according to the situations represented. Founded deep in the essence of music, the principle of repetition has at all times been an ever-changing, ever re-incarnating characteristic of the condition of the tonic art.

It gave to the Italian sonata of its time the same character of unity which the rhythm of the dance gave to the French clavier-piece. But, before the separate movements could reach their full formal development, the emancipation of the thematic subjects from counterpoint, and their absolute self-dependence, must be completed. The Italian ear, from its mere pleasure in motive and its development, released the subject from obligatory contrapuntal treatment. From the old thin forms of toccata and capriccio sprang fugal exercises with poor and limited themes, to which, so early as 1611, the old Francesco Turini gives the sounding title of sonatas. They are full of the passages associated with solo-instruments; they sound with flexible melodies; they run off in the measured steps of the dance, and circle round with repetitions of motives, groups, and movements. The point which a Rameau, in his "Cyclopes," attains by an extension of the rondo-form—perhaps under the gentle influence of the sonata—is reached by the Italian by formalising the free fantasia, under the influence of the dance. It is *form* at which everything on all sides aims.

In Scarlatti's sonatas we have very rarely more than one movement; the two-movement groups of the sonatas, numbered by Czerny 122 and 123, are exceptions. The pieces might be combined into sonatas on the Corellian model but for the lack of slow movements, which Scarlatti did not willingly write for the brilliant and spirited clavier. The structure of the movements displays that perfect freedom which still reigned in that springtime of the age of musical form. If we are so inclined, we may often detect, as in the prototype, a[1] first and a second theme; but the signs of this later form of the typical sonata are still so hidden that in many pieces we might, with equal justification, detect five or six themes in the more melodious or decorative passages. All is in transition, but the thematic conception is never

---

[1] The "first" and "second" subjects are often very clearly distinct in the binary form of Scarlatti. The "second subject" is not a mere continuation of the "first" in the subordinate key, as more generally it is in J. S. Bach, but it is another melody altogether.

LES CLAVECINISTES

DOMENICO SCARLATTI

Né à Naples en 1683. — Mort à Madrid en 1757.

J. S. Bach.

Bust by Carl Seffner.   Modelled on the actual skull.   After His, J. S. Bach (Vogel, Leipsic).

left utterly in the background. The motives come out in apparently reckless profusion, but scarcely one remains without its adequate treatment. We observe all possible arrangements. Sonata 110 has a perfectly incongruous middle movement; in Sonata 111 a moderato alternates with a presto, and both are repeated in fuller elaboration. On the other hand some sonatas preserve throughout the same rhythmical movement. As a rule the second part of a movement concludes like the first, but in a different key, just as it began like the first, but again in a different key; or sometimes Part II. begins with some different motive from that of Part I., or even with one absolutely new. Usually the beginnings of both parts are somewhat stiff in their thematic, while their later course is usually more free. The development of a main motive—which in later times begins the second division of a movement in sonata form—is as yet confined to no definite part. Not rarely it is despatched in the first part, as in Sonata 169, where the dactylic-trochaic motive is so taken up, more or less decidedly, in the first part, that only the very briefest reminiscence is left for the second. The general construction is well illustrated in the eighth sonata— runs of five semiquavers (*sic*) in A minor[1]—a fugal movement proceeding in crotchets, diatonically rising and chromatically descending—groups of diminished sevenths descending to C— conclusion, the semiquaver motive again. Part II.: the latter motive modulating from C, through G minor to D minor, with an insertion of the former figure in crotchets, developed as in the conclusion of Part I., and returning from D minor to A minor.

Formal structure is the be-all and end-all of the Italian sonata. Technique is its very life. An inexhaustible brilliancy and exclusive adaptation to the clavier is the characteristic of Scarlatti. He has in his eye the thousand possibilities of

---

[1] The movement here described is apparently the "Presto" on page 25 of the first volume of Mr Thomas Roseingrave's edition of Scarlatti. The groups, so-called, of "five semiquavers," are of four descending semiquavers, followed by a crotchet, making five notes altogether.

clavier-technique, and throughout his pieces there breathes a glow of enthusiasm which draws us easily from beginning to end with the sweet grace of an irresistible rhythm. The successive retardations, as in the arias of his father Alessandro's Rosaura, the changes of hands, the rivalry of concerted violins, the delight in passages of quavers with thirds and sixths as their harmonic accompaniment, such as is seen in the pieces of Corelli, long-sustained notes with sudden leaps which seem to be derived from the violin—all this is yet treated from the point of view of the clavier, and, so to speak, new-born from it. There is little song in Scarlatti, and a singing phrase is preferably repeated with brilliant decorations; for the *leggiero* is much better adapted to the spinet than the *arioso.* As a rule, both hands roll on in a two-voiced exercise in pure and simple move-ment without any additional encumbrance of heavy harmonies. It is a spectacle of fireworks. Deep bass-tones are suddenly introduced; high thirds fly off; thirds and sixths are darted in; close arpeggios swell into monstrous bundles as they are filled in with all possible passing-notes; octaves are vigorously intro-duced; the hands steer in contrary motion, to one another, away from one another; they are tied into chains of chords; they release themselves alternately from the same chords, the same groups, the same tones; unison passages in the meanwhile run up and down; chromatic tone-ladders dart through, then slowly moving phrases or still-standing isolated treble notes are seen confusedly dotted over the changing bass as it runs up and down, in a kind of upper pedal point; harsh sevenths one after another; repeated notes, syncopated effects, parallel runs of semiquavers with leaping side-notes, such as we know so well in Bach; sudden interchanges from major to minor, a device of which the Neapolitan operas are so fond; bold char-acterisation by means of sudden pauses; startling modulations by means of chromatic passages; embellishments rarely introduced; a delicate arrangement of tones from the severest fugues to the most unrestrained bourrées, pastorales, or fanfares—such is the world of Scarlatti's clavier-music. The "plucked" clavier (clavichord)[1] as yet does not admit of the delicacies of touch[2] which delight us in the pianoforte; and its technique, too, will have to consider the three main problems—how to arrange the musical conception in the light and lively style suitable to the clavier, how effectively to combine the two hands, and how to use the opportunities which spring from the divided movements of the single hand. These three problems—what the fingers can do, what the hands can do, and what the clavier can do—are solved by Scarlatti with all the readiness of his Italian temperament. His style luxuriates in the liveliest crossings of the hands—a practice he is said to have diminished as years increased his bodily dimensions; and his ideas blossom out into a captivating, often eccentric freshness, as, for example, in his fugal theme G, B♭, E flat, F sharp, B♭, C sharp [D] (ascending), which he has taken as the foundation of his best known and perhaps most splendid composition, the Cat's Fugue. Legend indeed asserts that these boldly combined tones were suggested to him by a cat gliding along the keyboard.

The most distinguished names of those who have laboured with success at the Italian clavier are those of Alberti,[3] whose preference for the skilfully broken chord-accompaniment has given rise to the title "Alberti Bass"; Durante, who was dry, calculating, and destitute of emotion; Galuppi, the graceful and courtly; the somewhat superficial Porpora; the subtle Paradies; and Turini, who is by far the most brilliant of all the Italian inheritors of the mantle of Scarlatti. They take two or three movements for

---

[1] The action of all these keyed instruments, whether called virginal, spinet, clavecin, clavichord, harpsichord, cembalo, is the same, namely, a "plucking" of the string by a projection of quill or leather. The exception is the *German* clavichord, which was not a keyed harp, but a keyed "monochord," with key levers in connection with "tangents" of metal, which sounded the string and cut off the right length of it at the same time.

[2] The *German* clavichord referred to in the note was able to produce a most delicate effect of tremolo or repetition, called *Bebung*. This was possible simply on account of the "tangential" action of the German instrument.

[3] Alberti rather deserves the title of an early "decadent." His broken-chord formula is mainly a way of avoiding trouble in writing real passages.

Scarlatti

a work; they combine dance-pieces and sonata-pieces; they pursue new melodic and rhythmic graces; but they all group themselves around or after their hero, Domenico Scarlatti, who, as first and greatest, has ushered in the pure Italian delight in sound as voiced by the clavier.[1]

[1] Pieces by Durante, Galuppi, Porpora, Paradies, and Ferdinando Turini (1749-1812), also the disputed movements mentioned on p. 82, which bear Rossi's name, may be found in Litolff's publication "Les Maîtres du Clavecin."

An Octave Spinet (tuned an octave higher than usual).
18th century.   De Wit collection.

German Clavichord, 17th century, "gebunden" (explained on page 22). De Wit collection.

Bach

IN 1717, when Scarlatti as yet dreamed not of his Spanish renown, and shortly after Couperin's first little pieces had appeared, the Parisian clavecinist Marchand made a journey to Germany. At the Polish court of Dresden he created a furore by his playing, and a famous contest was the result, got up, as it appears, by intrigue, between Marchand and an organist of Weimar, Johann Sebastian Bach. The King was present in person. Marchand began by improvising variations on a French song, and was loudly applauded. Bach then took the same theme, but varied it twelve times over so marvellously that without further contest he carried off the palm from his famous adversary, who, when Bach proposed a competition on the organ, incontinently fled from Dresden.

Who was this Bach, and what was this sudden development of German music? Hitherto not much had been heard of it in foreign countries, and on looking at the German tablatures [1] of the older

---

[1] The word "Intavolata" was used about 1600 to describe the "arrangement" of a many-voiced madrigal for the keyed instrument. Hence "intavolatura" comes to mean a "copy" presenting all the parts at one view, and such "arrangements" for clavier were common and popular.

time one could only recognise an honourable but somewhat clumsy struggle. In the sixteenth century, perhaps when, in wider circles, some mention was made of the great vocal compositions of Isaac and Senfl, a certain Nürnberger, Hasler by name, proposed himself to Gabrieli in Venice as a pupil, and later his renown was heard at the courts of Vienna and Dresden. In the next century another German, Johann Jakob Froberger, was associated with Frescobaldi in Rome, and his fame also was afterwards heard at the Viennese court. He cannot have been unpopular, for a number of anecdotes clustered round his name. Froberger, and with him Pachelbel of Nürnberg, began the emancipation of the clavier in Germany. In the Hanse Towns of the north were good organists, such as Buxtehude in Lübeck and Reincke in Hamburg; but no one in Italy or France troubled himself with them.

The fame of Italian sonatas and French suites was such a matter of course, that the Leipzig organist, Kuhnau, when he in 1700 published his collections of genuinely German clavier-pieces, plumed himself mightily, in his chatty prefaces, on the fact that now at last, even in Germany, good music was to be had, which could take its place by the side of the foreign. " Even in Germany," he exclaimed, " oranges and citrons at last bloom ! " The excellent Kuhnau ventured to give the title of sonata to a piece on the model of the Italian sonata da camera, although it was written not for violin but for clavier. Hence it is often said that he was the creator of the clavier-sonata. But this piece has nothing in common with the later popular composition of that name ; it was a cento of several movements in various tempi, as the suite was a cento of several dances. Nay, the Cyclopes of Rameau stands nearer to the later type than this. The suites and sonatas of Kuhnau are pure clavier-pieces, somewhat marred by the usual failings of youth, and running every theme to death, but clear, vigorous, and adapted to the fingers, smooth in feeling and modern in technique. But the most curious work of Kuhnau is his " Biblical Histories." Here he illustrates on the clavier all kinds of Scriptural stories, like the death of Goliath, the cure of Saul, the marriage of Jacob, Hezekiah's recovery, the life of Gideon, and Jacob's death, in sonata-form, on the model of the programme-music [1] of the time, and with the assistance of verbal elucidations. Yet Kuhnau is as little as Froberger or anyone else a forerunner of Bach, who so overshadows the work of his predecessors that one may almost say he is independent of them.

It is indeed hard to compare Bach even with the other wonders of the history of art. For there is scarcely one who is so identical with his art as is Bach with music. A Michel Angelo does not include a Rembrandt, nor a Rembrandt a Monet; but in Bach there is a Beethoven, a Schumann, a Wagner. I believe that if the Almighty had wished to offer to men in sensible form what at that time was called music, he would then have given them the work of Bach. In it there are the deepest secrets of musical poly-phony, as well as the most intense degrees of decadent expression; the mysticism of the Middle Ages is there no less than the per-spective of the future. But content and form are not dissociated as they are in history; they are identical, they are one and the same, as they are in the philosophic concept of music. Once, and perhaps once only, in this world has the "Thing in Itself" been realised, and the difference between concept and actuality been reduced to nothing. The history of music can be written with almost exclusive reference to Bach. We might show how it has converged towards him and again diverged from him in search of its special partialities. We might point out how it revolves round him, comes to him, and goes from him in the course of the centuries, just as in the case of the imitative arts we show that they come from Nature and go to her.

Bach's life was the most uneventful conceivable. He made no journeys to Rome and Paris; he learned musical literature by studying and copying. A true "Old Master," he sits with his serious, almost severe countenance, in the midst of his large

---

[1] More than a century before Kuhnau, an English clavier composer, John Munday, composed a piece of "programme-music," with the various sections labelled, *e.g.*—Faire Wether, Lightening, Thunder, Calme Wether, A Cleare Day. It is the third piece in the Fitzwilliam Virginal Book.

family of twenty children, all musical, and composes for instruction or for his own pleasure, without seeing many of his compositions printed. His renown had no wide extent;[1] his bold extravagances aroused only that hostility which does not bring honour, and in his successive posts at Arnstadt, Weimar, Köthen, and Leipzig, he had little opportunity for sunning himself in the rays of princely favour. A single moment of his life perhaps stands out prominently, when Frederick the Great at one of his concerts received the list of strangers in Potsdam, and interrupted the playing to say to his officers, "Gentlemen, old Bach has arrived." He was instantly summoned, and, in his travelling dress as he was, improvised on a theme of the King's, which, when completed and published, he dedicated to the King as " Musikalisches Opfer." When two great men meet, the whole world feels the electric shock.

With the appearance of Bach the whole history of music turns to Germany. And clavier-music, so far as it has a particular meaning, is henceforth German. England, France, and Italy, sink either gradually or suddenly into the background.

Bach's clavier-music is a complete world, a mirror of his music as a whole. As Nature is her whole self in every leaf, so in every piece or group of pieces Bach is the whole Bach. Thus for the first time it came about that the clavier became capable of interpreting the whole nature of a great man. With the early Englishmen it was the embodiment of the whole tone-poet; with Couperin the whole man, indeed, but a man who was nothing but a dancer; with Scarlatti a whole clavier-player; but with Bach the whole nature of a man of whom it is impossible to say whether the musician or the intellect in him was the greater. This was the first outstanding peak attained by the clavier.

The natural creative principle from which Bach works, that which gives unity to his being, is the conception of counterpoint.

---

[1] Bach died in 1750. Hawkins published his great History of Music in 1776, and in spite of the fact that he had his information direct from Bach's son, John Christian Bach, then living in London, he appears quite ignorant of any of his works but the Clavierübung (1731-42), from which he prints three short harpsichord pieces.

Music can be written in which every
single voice is treated as an independent line, and in which the art of
combining these lines reaches the
highest possible development, as in
a picture of Holbein—and this is
counterpoint. Or music could be
written, in which an upper melody,
clearly illuminated, runs on an advancing basis of accompanying harmony
without much attention to purity of
voice, as in a work of Ribera—and
this is the style resting on "accompaniment." Bach's essence lies in
the contrapuntal method. He con-

Konrad Pau(l)mann, the first German
writer for keyed instruments, blind.
Died 1473. After a modern drawing
by Wintter.

ceives the voices *over against* one another; and at the very
moment in which he interjects a motive, there is a second or
third motive introduced, embracing the other in contrapuntal wise.

Yet he has taken the accompaniment-style also into himself.
Just as little as he can ever be censured for defect in melody, so
little has he ever neglected the newer "secular" harmony—rather,
he has carried on his counterpoint in accordance with its laws.
He has of course as little respect as any other first class musician
for the common Italian accompaniment with its singing melody
alone. If he adopts it, it is in very discreet fashion; the richly
decorated arioso soaring above the vigorously moving *basso continuo* in such delicate arrangement that we think rather of an
ornamented contrapuntal passage than of a light singing voice
accompanied by the cembalo with *figured* bass.

In this secularisation of counterpoint by means of the contrasting features of an arioso, the foundation of a bass, and the
modern system of a network of harmony, he exhibits the characters
of both musical styles in one, and gives us the unification of two
epochs, which necessarily opened a boundless prospect into the
future.

Two or more voices running alongside are treated in their relation to one another. Here the simple contrapuntal exercise, which sets them neatly together, and enfolds their rhythms into each other, will soon cease to satisfy. The best-sounding contrapuntal relations are those in which the voices show some slight traces of imitation. From the lighter imitations rises the stricter canon,[1] and at last the exact and regular succession of canonic repetitions is reached. The ideal is then an exercise in which every note of every voice has its imitative relations, and in which the whole is so interconnected that not a stone can be removed without bringing about the fall of the whole structure.

We see Bach himself at this work. He works more lightly and elegantly, or more heavily and massively, not by arbitrary choice, but according to his subject. He begins with a Prelude, in which a gentle interlacing of voices answers to his mood ; imitations, arising as if of their own accord, are inserted here and there. Then there is the final gigue of a suite, in which a rapid $\frac{6}{8}$ theme has to be treated, in spite of its rapidity, with a certain canonic severity, which gives solidity to the conclusion of the whole suite. Then again we have a slow movement of intertwining voices, such as is found after the first preluding bars of the F sharp minor and C minor Toccatas ; the voices alternately take up the mournful themes, with no strict regularity of exact succession, wonderfully floating, according to a fixed purpose, and gently swimming in their harmonies, with no recognisable support, almost a fairy-like echo of mediæval counterpoint. Or, finally, there is a regular fugue, which stands there like a monument, with hardly a superfluous note ; in regular succession the voices present the theme in single or double counterpoint, always alternately imitating at the fourth or fifth, with a never-failing reference to the tonic key ; and near the close, where still greater closeness of imitation is demanded, proudly and stiffly vaulted over with diminutions or augmentations of the theme.

[1] This is certainly not so, historically speaking. The strict canon is far older than what we understand by "imitation."

Bach has left us clavier-works in which we see perfected the simplest form which the contrapuntal conception could assume in his hands. These are the fifteen "Inventions" and the fifteen "Symphonies," which in the manuscript appear with the inscription, "Straightforward directions, by which the amateur of the clavier, but especially the one anxious to learn, is shown a plain method, not only of playing properly in two parts, but also, on further progress, to undertake three obligato parts; at the same time also not only gaining good inventions, but also personally performing them, and, above all, attaining a cantabile style in playing, as well as a good foretaste of composition." This curious preface ends, "Verfertiget von Joh. Seb. Bach, hochf. Anhalt-Cöthenischen Capell-meister, Anno Christi 1723."

The simple homeliness of the time speaks in this title-page; and it is well to appropriate to-day as much of this as possible, in order to lose nothing in the enjoyment of these fifteen two-voiced Inventions and these fifteen three-voiced Symphonies. Even to-day Bach demands the desire of learning in amateurs, who should feed their pleasure with diligence, and enter into the feelings of the composer. One who sits at the clavier with a zeal worthy of Bach's compositions, will find in these thirty simple contrapuntal pieces a small storehouse of treasures. He will be captivated by the elegance of this canonic music as soon as his fingers are able to play in parts; but he will never be released from the influence of the many-coloured glittering character of these compositions. They are the drawings of a master, which in a few strokes depict great objects; sketches of a great artist, so full of scholarship that they cover the whole of life. The solemn Invention in F minor, the eccentric one in B flat major, the Symphony which sounds so mournfully in E flat major, or the chromatically gloomy F minor, the sprightly staccato G minor, the graceful A major whose traces are to be found in so many works of a later time, and the rhythmical, freely-singing B minor, with its harp-like strokes, in which Beethoven and Chopin, yet unborn, seem to meet—these pieces were then unique in literature, and still remain so.

In these fantasy-pieces the fugal conception is dealt with on a small scale; in the Toccatas on a large scale. The clavier-toccatas of Bach are free pieces of that wonderful many-sidedness of construction which a music might still possess that had not yet stiffened into conventionalism. When we sit down to play the Inventions and Symphonies, we point our fingers as if for miniature work. But when we sit down to the Toccatas, we dispose our arms and hands, as would have been said in Bach's

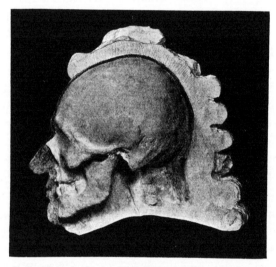

Skull of Sebastian Bach, with Seffner's modelling of his features.

time, " in einer gewissenen grossartigen Freyheit," with a certain large freedom. These Toccatas will be eternal favourites, because of their air of improvisation which develops the fughetta out of the preludic movement, and scatters the playful, pleasant technique in the midst of the severities of imitation. Inexhaustible in the apparent formlessness of their form, they stand on the threshold of modern literature as the great models of that true clavier-style which will always have a touch of the extempore as one of its characteristic features.

In the Toccatas it can be seen how Bach permits his fugal

conceptions organically to grow. It is in them that we see the psychology of the fugue more purely than in the strictest formal fugal movements. Take, for example, the F sharp minor Toccata. Here the fingers preludise over the keyboard, gradually growing slower, the passages differentiate themselves into motives, which gently imitate each other, until at length they come to rest on a solid bass. This is the moment of lyric inspiration; and the soul sighs itself out in a slow movement, which weaves itself in fugal style, speedily sweeping forth in its own free, harmonious woven-work. A staccato-motive breaks in; rolling semiquavers soon crystallise around it; it grows and swells in a three-voiced fugue; loosens itself, becomes lighter, and passes off into an operatic joyousness, circling round in repetitions, which to us seem almost too wide for the narrow significance of this motive. A pause, and in the new-won freshness emerges the first chromatic adagio-motive as a lively floating fugue, soon breaking forth into four voices, and ending in a stirring finale.

Take the D major Toccata. Here there is a joyous prelude of ascending scales, running off in chords and tremoli. An insertion of a fresh capriccioso motive follows, which pursues its course mingled with playful figures. A pause in adagio; mournfully moving melodies, freely accompanied by tremoli; softly passing over into a quiet three-voice fugue, which again leads to preluding passages, speaking recitatives, broken chords, till the great wild hunt of triplets surges in its fugal power. This D major piece is in content and technique Schumann all over.

Similarly, one easily recognises the development of soul in the solemn C minor Toccata, which is dominated almost throughout by a charmingly-constructed fugue; or in the D minor Toccata, with its stirring and beautiful adagio-movement; the G minor with its bacchanalian finale; the rapid G major; and the never-to-be-forgotten E minor with its clearness and restraint. They are all built up on an inner meaning, and show a grandeur in their intimate nature such as only Beethoven has dared to express on the clavier, and a soulfulness never surpassed by a programme-

musician in our century in his own style. But the fugue has in
them become the indwelling soul, and the whole speech of music
has absolutely ascended into their form. We see it come, grow,
and depart.

One who has investigated the psychology of Bach's fugue in
the Toccatas, will no longer fail to recognise it in his pure and
absolute fugues. A fugue of Bach—this sounds to the *lay* musical
ear as the very sum of all that is academic. But in reality never
were fugues written which were developed less academically, or
which flow so entirely from the soul. Only take the fugal form not
as the end in itself, and not as a mere example of musical architecture—only take pains to discover the spirit of its unfolding—and
we shall be astounded at the endless variety of the inward musical
life which is profusely showered into this form. The essence of
a fugue of Bach is just this freedom from all architecture, this
suppression of all calculation in favour of the spiritual development. The fugal form, that well-known series of enlargements
and arrangements of the pure canon, is to him a prime *datum*,
from which, nevertheless, he has formed no unbending principle.
But he works with this material in such a way that he keeps the
development of a piece always subordinate to the character which
the fugal theme imposes on him. The theme is the title, the piece
the contents.

His genius reveals itself in perception of the thousand possibilities of unfolding which lie in his themes—some advancing
diatonically, some studded over with pauses, some with sudden
stops on sevenths, some marching on in massive choral style,
some humorously staccato, especially those with startling false
accents, others drawn in large outlines which excite curiosity and
scarcely stand forth in their clear rhythm till the ninth or tenth
bar, and which he was so fond of because they gave the strongest
stimulus to the coming development.

Let the "layman" accustom himself not to be frightened
by fugues. The fugue in the grand style of Bach, constructed
with that unparalleled art which the first C major fugue in the

"Wohltemperiertes Klavier" displays, or which is shown in the C sharp minor fugue, with its three themes gradually stratified one above the other, or rolling themselves off with that extraordinary ease which we daily admire in the famous A minor—this kind of fugue is a necessary speech of music : it is melody, it is a natural language which can never disappear. To grasp it, to assimilate it, until the many voices or even many themes of its development stand clearly before our eyes in their full characteristic value, is a feast for the musical epicure to which hardly anything else can be compared. Bach's fugues are *playable*. They are not too easy ; but they are so in the spirit of the clavier that the fingers soon lose their timidity, and the work is as a mirror in which they speedily recognise the necessary nature of their motion. And there is an eternally fresh animation in this activity, in which no deception, no dilettantism, no superfluity can exist for a moment.

The great artist, to whom the " Fantasy " is a presupposition, does not work on it, however much it may seem to the crowd a chief aim ; he works on the form which requires this kind of work. We see Bach, through his whole life, labouring at the fugue ; and the encyclopædic work, in the midst of which he died, " The Art of Fugue," shows us heights of power in this form which make us dizzy. Besides certain scattered fugues, he has made a collection of different periods in the two volumes of the " Wohltemperiertes Klavier." Here every major and minor mode of every semitone is doubly treated, with a prelude and fugue—a comprehensiveness of arrangement which was partly due to the taste of the time,[1] and

---

[1] Long before Bach was born, we find an English composer anticipating this comprehensive treatment of the scales. Before 1667, John Jenkins wrote a series of " Fancies " on each degree of the alphabetical scale, three movements to the set. The keys actually used are C, D, E, F, G, A, B flat, all minor except F and B flat. But, as is mentioned in a previous note, in one of the three movements in F, Jenkins modulates nearly through all the flat keys, at any rate as far as D flat, thus showing that already in the middle of the seventeenth century an Englishman contemplated Bach's accomplished work of using the scale on every semitone. And this by no means fixes the ultimate limit. Bull's fantasia on Ut, Re, Mi, Fa, Sol, La—piece number 51 in the Fitzwilliam book—modulates into all the twelve keys. Though this does not *prove* that instruments were as yet tuned with an equal temperament, it does prove that Bach was

partly can be referred to the secondary aim of the work, which was the introduction of a system of clavier-tuning which should be sufficient for practical purposes, in which no acoustic solecisms should be committed to suit convenience, and in which all the keys should be used indifferently and in their completeness by pupils. It is not hard to detect that the unity of these two volumes is not very complete. Even Spitta, a meritorious but somewhat tasteless biographer, who seeks to find the "higher" unity in all Bach's works, is compelled to grant that there are varieties of style and intrusions of alien matter in the "Wohltemperiertes Klavier." But that is no loss. The brilliant many-sidedness of its contents can support even this discontinuity of style (which, by the way, is but a slight discontinuity) and this artistic fusion of certain preludes and fugues, which originally were not composed with a view to each other. No one will fail to perceive how wonderfully the preludes combine with each other and with many of the fugues. The whole, perhaps, gains something of the character of the old composite epics, such as Homer or the Bible. Bach's autograph of the first part bears the date 1722; there is no complete autograph of the second part, and this Bible of clavier-playing was first printed in 1800, two or three generations after its production.[1]

If we look at the original editions of the six works which were printed in Bach's time, they speak in no uncertain tone of the taste of the age. From 1726 to 1730 appeared the "Klavierübung"— the first part, with the suites which are known as "Partiten." In 1735 we have the second part of the Klavierübung, containing the Italian Concerto and the "Ouverture nach französischer Art" (also a suite). In 1739 appeared the third part, in which are found organ chorales along with four duets for two claviers. In these the distinction between organ and clavier is as feebly marked as it always was before the invention of the pianoforte.

in no sense the originator of the idea, and the probability is very great that the system was in practical use in England in Elizabethan times. Bull was flourishing in 1590.

[1] The date of the first edition of the "Forty-eight" is uncertain, namely, 1799 or 1800, London. (Author's note.)

The fourth part, which appeared in 1742, contains the great Variations for clavicymbal with two keyboards. Besides these, in 1747 appeared the "Musikalisches Opfer," in which the theme of Frederick the Great is elaborated; and, in 1752, two years after Bach's death, was published the "Kunst der Fuge." He could only venture on the printing of the "Kunst" in his later years, when the Bach fugue had made some way in the world. The "Musikalisches Opfer" came ·out under the protection of the King; all the other clavier-pieces which seemed to him likely to pay for the printing are of a lighter kind—suites and concertos "for the delight of amateurs," as it stands on the title-page. The three types of the great Bach counterpoint— the miniature Invention, the free Toccata, and the absolute Fugue—then, as now, appealed to too select a circle to attain the popularity of dances and concertos.

If Bach's greatness is in the former works stupendous, in the latter it is loveable. Here we learn to know his other side. It is his "other manner." Here, instead of the severe canonic development of a theme, attention is paid to the voices as parts of a harmonious whole; he steps down from the cothurnus, and moves familiarly in pleasant comedy. Still, the contrapuntal conception is the basis of the structure; but simply harmonised floriations of melody are interwoven, so that the clavier almost rivals the arioso of a violin. Between the extremes of the first movement of the "Chromatic Fantasia," with its free rhythms, arpeggios, recitatives, and song-passages, and of the second movement, the regular fugue—extremes which mark the two limits of Bach's style—there is an endless abundance of methods of treatment, in which now the contrapuntal element and now the arioso takes the lead. We see Bach in this second group of his clavier-works, the suites and concertos, pass over into the enchanting fields of Italian sensuous music. But it is remarkable how he never loses for a single moment his unique depth and his insatiable delight in form. There is a very abyss between a suite of Bach, founded on the Eternities, and one of Handel's, owing its popularity to the transitory charms of dexterous trivialities.

There are three great groups of Bach's clavier-suites : the so-called Partiten, which appeared in print in his own life-time, the "English Suites," and the "French Suites." The Partiten, which were first published separately, must, as the earliest work of this author known to the public, have struck the whole world with bewilderment. It was the first bound of a unique genius, the elevation of a traditional form of art into quite unparalleled shapes, a storm of intellectual lightning in a region long regarded as exclusively owned by Frenchmen and Italians. Even to-day the Partiten belong to the most select class of clavier-literature ; and I cannot for a moment conceive how they are not to be regarded as superior by many degrees to the English and French suites. In no book is the future of music more clearly foretold. To see in the B flat major corrente, Chopin; in the B flat major gigue, Schumann ; in the C minor sinfonia, Beethoven ; in the C minor Rondo and Capriccioso, Mendelssohn ; in the A minor Scherzo, Mozart, is no mere enthusiastic fancy.

The Partiten outgrew the ordinary scheme of the suites (allemande, corrente, saraband, gigue) as Beethoven's sonatas outgrew the old scheme of sonatas. They have given a new life and a new spirit to a traditional form. The suite, which at the end of the seventeenth century has become merely conventional, is so elevated by the spirit of Bach that it thenceforward stands in the world of actuality. Even Schumann selects a similar form for the expression of modern emotions. The suite having been thus despatched, the sonata is in similar fashion put into precise and regular form, to be transfigured later by Beethoven with the same modern spirit. Bach had the fortune and the genius to relegate the traditional suite into the past, and to see the conventional sonata dawning in the future. Thus with him the dance-piece and the free piece remained fresh and lively. Suite and sonata were only different external ways for reducing several pieces to unity. There, men took their stand on the old

The Fifteenth Sinfonia of John Sebastian Bach, from the Royal Musikbibliothek, Berlin.

familiar series of dance-tunes, without ever thinking of the dances themselves ; here, they found for the first movement a practical form, and, in the event, ranged the adagio, scherzo, and rondo together, just as their predecessors had used the saraband, minuet, and gigue. On this tendency to unity on the part of the clavier-pieces, from the first English variations, through Couperin's Ordres, to Bach's suites, Italian sonatas and German sonatas, Chopin's Albums, Schumann's Scenes, Liszt's Epics, too much stress need not be laid. Even more than the orchestra, the clavier leans to short pieces, but the intellect demands some excuse for binding them together.

If we take a striking liveliness as the characteristic of the Partiten, we indeed find a feature in which they are distinguished from the French Suites, but which is far from exhausting their qualities. Solid melodies, humorous capriccios, enchanting dances, tuneful airs, everything is included in these works. In their pages we realise how the spirit of Bach strives to utter the very utmost of which it feels itself capable. And in these introductory preludes, toccatas, or symphonies, in these flowing allemandes, gliding correntes, heavy sarabands, filigree-worked gigues, in those numerous intermezzo movements, such as burlesques, rondos, airs, minuets, and passepieds, there are turns of genius, the form of which is impressed for ever on the mind. I think of the sweet running movements of the astonishing B flat major Gigue ; of the brilliant structure of the C minor Capriccio, which concludes the Partita in place of a Gigue ; of the D major aria, in which breathes the whole grace of the eighteenth century ; of the bold and rhapsodical Saraband in D major; of the rich colouring of the introductory E minor Toccata ; the rocking melody of the allemande, the sombre glow of the saraband, the wayward syncopations of the gigue.

The six English Suites, which we may certainly assume to have been put into juxtaposition by Bach himself, stand between the six printed Partiten and the six French Suites, whose combination was only probably, not certainly, due to Bach. They would seem to have been called "English" suites, because they were arranged for some Englishman; the original title was apparently "suites avec prélude." For the English suites, like the Partiten, have each a fairly long introduction, fugal in style, but not conforming to the strictest laws of the fugue. The intermezzi, also, are as numerous as in the case of the Partiten. But that extreme intellectual severity is wanting; they are more graceful and polite. This character is especially noticeable in the introductory fugal movements and the intermediate dance pieces; and one who seeks rather a play of tone than grandeur of soul will perhaps find here a richer yield than in the Partiten. Neat, volkslied-like sarabands, ravishing bourrées, rococo gavottes, ornamental minuets, the exquisitely delicate passepied in E minor —these all lie so thick one on another, that one cannot recall a more sparkling album of dainty dances in the whole eighteenth century. It is true that in the Vienna school (as in the case of the younger [1] Muffat and others) there is in this class of dances a gentle soothing quality, which gives us the first hint of the coming beautiful Viennese dance-music; but they are, like those of Handel, too short in duration and too featureless for us to be able to return to them with the extraordinary affection with which we return to those of Bach. These are so rich in invention that they cannot in many centuries lose their flavour. The dancing underpart of the D major gavotte in the D minor suite, the multiform air of the D minor, E minor, and A minor sarabands, the filigree-counterpoint of the E minor Passepied, the extreme daring of the A minor bourrée, the transport of the A minor prelude, which even grows into a roundelay,—what a depth of originality is there in all these pieces, in which the repetitions so wonderfully satisfy the laws of the mind without becoming mechanical!

How the French Suites came by their name is hard to say. More French than the English suites they are certainly not, for they are quite as Bach-like as the latter. Without Preludes and

[1] August Gottlieb Muffat, of Vienna, 1690-1770, son of Georg Muffat, organist of Strassburg Cathedral.

without too many Intermezzi or "Doubles" (repetitions with variations), they are of astonishing variety. The Allemandes especially, as first movements in every suite, display such a manifoldness of form, that in fact nothing is left in common to them but the four-time beat. The song in the Saraband and the dance in the Intermezzi appear to the same effect as in the English suites, and a light tone runs through the whole. But the tone is lightest of all in the E major suite, which with its rolling allemande and courante, its singing saraband, its stiff and formal gavotte, its characteristic polonaise, its tricksy bourrée, and its cheerful gigue, is a perfect paradise of dainty devices. The flowing courante in it strikes our fancy; for it is precisely in the courantes of these suites with their heavy old-fashioned movements that we shall most often hit on the rare occasions on which we must regard Bach as already obsolete. The ornamentations tend to appear less befitting to us, scattered so profusely as they are in these movements. But to Bach, little as he could as yet succeed in emancipating himself from ornamentations, they were no longer such a matter of course as with the old French clavecinists. If we compare the different manuscripts of his works, we see the uncertainties and alterations. Bischoff, in his excellent critical edition of Bach's clavier-music (Steingräber) has therefore only engraved large those ornamentations which were without doubt always played by Bach. Taste will fill them in in certain places on grounds of symmetry and "thematic"; but they are no longer bewildering in their profusion.

Among the suites which do not belong to these collections, we recollect with great pleasure the dainty dances and intermezzi —for example in the E flat major suite, and especially that in B minor with overture in French style (Largo—Fuga—Largo) which appeared in the second part of the Klavierübung as a piece for two manuals. It presents, among the many intermezzi, a gavotte in the style of the orchestral Partiten, which links itself with the choicest dances, in graceful style, of the preceding century. From the clavier-suites we pass to the clavier-sonatas, which, still in the style of Italian art, mingled with dances, offer free combinations of different movements. The melodious andante of the D minor sonata, and its final allegro-movement rattling off almost in one part, are perfect pearls. A step further we reach the fantasias with fugues ; especially the polyphonic one in A minor, the recitatival "Chromatische" and the concerto-like C minor, fugally treated, but still not a fugue. These three fantasia-pieces were Bach's direct bequests to the future. In the polyphony of the brilliantly rushing fantasia in A minor, rising with endlessly delicate melody, we are reminded of the "Meistersinger"; in the chromatic fantasia, with its broad narration and grandiose concluding pedal point, the clavier seems to us to speak with the freedom of a drama; in the significantly constructed C minor fantasia rests the whole formal talent of the instrumental composers of the expiring eighteenth century.

The three "brilliant" fantasias incline naturally to the concerto style, which partly abandoned counterpoint in favour of a mere accompaniment, and partly subordinated it to the careful elaboration of a single voice-part. The problem of committing a whole concerto to the clavier alone, Bach has solved in his famous "Italian Concerto"—Italian in the conception of the style of execution proper to concertos, which in Italy developed itself specially on the violin—Italian in the form of a slow movement enclosed by two quicker movements, which had emerged as the most practical method for the violin (half in rivalry with the Tutti, half in the interest of solo virtuosity). Bach has in the Italian concerto perfectly attained the object of writing in several movements a clavier piece fit for execution. The grand sonatas of a later time have been able to add nothing essential to it. The first movement is an ingenious combination of pregnant motives, which reminds us of tutti-effects, of running semiquaver figures, and melodious passages on moving quaver accompaniment, which correspond to the second lyrical theme of sonatas. The slow movement is a great recitative song with a berceuse-like accompaniment, of a structure so delicate that we are irresistibly reminded of the contours of old primitive pictures. It has the dainty grace of archaic outline, just like that in the two-part interwoven arioso [1] of the B minor Prelude, or in the crisp melody of the E flat Prelude (Wohltemperiertes Klavier I.). The third movement, which is quicker, unravels the whole into the cheerful linked play of floating parts, unsurpassed in elegant construction by any of the great formalists. Floating passages run up and down among chords, falling like drops of rain, and the voices combine in pleasant unity.

The entire multiformity of music at the beginning of the eighteenth century is expressed in the clavier-works of Bach. As yet the sonata-form with its two themes, and its "free" section in the middle of the movement, has not become the consecrated scheme; [2] and all the forces which had gradually worked towards this form exert themselves unfettered, in order to make themselves effective now in this, now in that combination of movements and parts of movements. "Thematic" is not neglected. To a series of suite-movements similar commencing motives are given, and the motives of earlier parts are taken up in the later. But this tendency to unity does not act as a restraint upon form, and does not reduce everything to one stiff mould. There is a fugue with a prelude, by Bach, that in E flat major (Wohltemp. Kl. i.), which offers perhaps the most delicate example of this unrestrained unity of motive. The Prelude, which is much longer than the fugue, begins with semiquaver figures, whose characteristic is melodious sustained passages advancing by sixths and sevenths; after this introduction, begins in toccata-fashion a kind of slow fugue, which unfolds the just heard motive in a terser form; and finally, in a third part, mingles itself with the former semiquaver figure. The fourth part is so to speak moulded in the fugue

---

[1] This movement is in three parts, and the allusion is to the two upper voices, which maintain a duet in *cantabile* on a gently moving quaver bass.

[2] The idea of the two subjects, and of the "free" section after the central double bar, was already realised incompletely. In the shortest "binary" movements the scheme of *keys* is found to be P, Q. (double bar) || Q, VARIOUS, P.

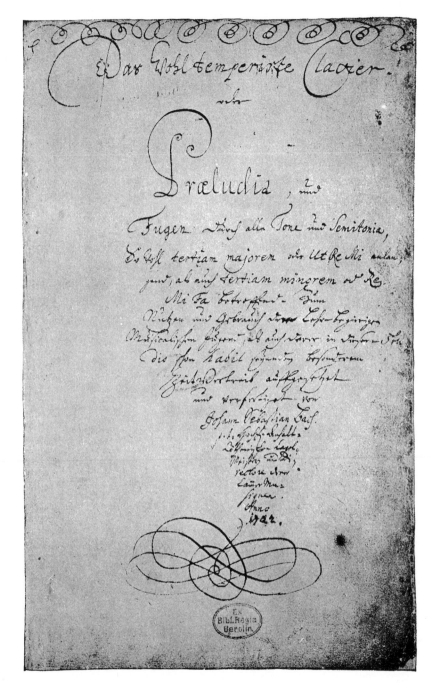

Facsimile of Title-page of Bach's Manuscript of the Wohltemperiertes Klavier.

In the Royal Musikbibliothek, Berlin.

George Frederick Handel.

Engraved by Thomson.

form, which in its "subject" makes use of the characteristic leap of a seventh, found in the Prelude, as a main feature, and brings the play to a conclusion in a busy and lively manner. The relations of motive are only to be *felt*, not seen ; but they are *there*, and give to the formal freedom of this piece a vigour of its own. Thus, in many of Bach's pieces, apart from the direct thematic motives, we shall find this indirect assonance, which, springing from a general feeling of unity, is, in fact, a more dainty framework for the piece than any unity that could be impressed on it from outside.

So also is it with the construction of the pieces. We find everywhere traces of the later sonata-style ; and not less in the dance-forms than in free movements. It was too natural to repeat the beginning of the piece at the end, then to transpose a second theme into the main key, and in the centre to work out the main motive in a kind of free fantasia. But so long as the author held fast to the binary form of the piece, and to the Da capo of each half, as was the case at this time, so long did the parts of the "developments" and repetitions fail to concentrate themselves so completely as not to leave a rich field of varied forms in which fancy could move at ease. Bach's imagination was keen enough to give to every one of these forms, as they developed themselves each moment, a natural and elemental strength. A toccata by him, although they are all very various in form, or a fantasia, like the C minor, which is of sonata-character, is built up so firmly and self-evidently that the later uniformity of the sonata seems rather to betray a weakening than a strengthening of style.

[That the severe forms of Prelude and Fugue are abundantly capable of expressing poetical ideas is easily shown. Turn only to the D minor Prelude and Fugue in the second part of the Wohltemperiertes Klavier. Although the casual reader perceives in the one movement merely an exercise in two parts, in the other, one in three parts, it requires only a slight exercise of imagination to see that the work really pictures some such feelings as the following: In the Prelude, a man suddenly realises himself in the true "out-of-doors" of this life, with the rain and hail of difficulties and troubles sensibly battering him. Bravely, but ineffectually, he tries to push through the tempest, and sinks wearily into half-sleep, is awakened by a renewed riot of the elements around, tries harder than before, and longer too, to impress himself on his circumstances, and be master of things, and succeeds in a sorrowful kind of way, for the storm passes, sighs itself out, and he at last can rest. In the Fugue, he tries to begin his work in the world. His efforts are strong in their intention, but die down as weakly as the devil himself could wish, one after another. But though these messengers of his will return to him empty again and again, he still goes on. "It is the best I can do, and something may come of it in the end," he seems to say. And there is in the final bars, where the subject occurs for the last time, a certain expression of savage pleasure at the thought of not having given in, mingled with the abiding knowledge of an abundant measure of continual failure, such as is no imagination to any man who cares about his work, and has arrived at the sorrowful conviction that most of his walking must be done in the dark.][1]

Perhaps the Bach Preludes show this freedom on the most liberal scale. For the Prelude is not so much a kind of form, like the Toccata, but a mere Piece before a Piece ; it lays down the lines to be followed, but in itself is uncertain, unfixed in form. The Prelude may be a Toccata or a Sonata, a Symphony or an Invention ; it can let its upper part, in arioso style, wander over the continuo, or it may burst forth in fullest polyphony. It may have the rhythm and regularity of beat of the dances, or may speak with the freedom of recitative without thought of a repetition. The abundance of possibilities which Bach found at his disposal in the working out of themes, construction, and style, are mirrored in the Preludes, from the real fugue to the playful

---

[1] This paragraph is suggested by a corresponding one in the author's German edition.

method of the court-musicians.[1] Anyone who undertakes the pleasant task of simply running through the Preludes of the " Wohltemperiertes Klavier " (vol. ii.), will be able to appreciate the full spring-like freshness in which the free music of this time, so rich in promise for the future, lived out its life. And, like the discriminating observer of nature, he will admire, in just these yet unspoilt forms, the great harmony and natural unity which is exhibited by the young life of the creation. The Prelude in E major will always seem to me a blossom of this spring-time (" Wohlt. Kl." i.)—one of the daintiest pieces ever written for the clavier. In an easy $\frac{12}{8}$ time the poem begins with an allegretto theme, ingeniously invented, and playful in style. It is supported by two voices ; but they soon take part canonically in the delightful movement. We have, in the play of cheerful thought, come to the dominant of the dominant [2] (F sharp), and from this F sharp we rest, in a humorous change, a moment on D, and even G, till, just as rapidly, we emerge through a chromatic maze at B natural once more (Bar 8). The repose of the succeeding dominant passage is gently stirred by ravishing transient modulations, on which the very spirit of happiness seems to rest. A beautiful chain of syncopations leads us through F sharp minor, and a jubilant run of semiquavers, built on a dominant chord on E, brings us to the recapitulation of the opening subject in the key of A (Bar 15), starting from which the movement repeats itself accurately (for eight bars) in its eternal cheerfulness, the piece closing with a couple of bars in Schumann's ingenious manner, still sweetly suggesting the spring-song of its earlier strains.

We find, then, that nothing essentially new in " form " has been used by later artists, of which the germ did not already exist in Bach. Nay, even in programme-music (supposed by many to be an invention of modern times) for the clavier, which Kuhnau

[1] The author means such composers as Rameau, Galuppi, Couperin, who wrote for their audience to a great extent.

[2] This expression may be misunderstood unless reference is made to the music. The passage arrives at the key of B (the " dominant " key), but the F sharp mentioned is merely the bass note.

so quaintly worked out in his Biblical Stories,[1] Bach has entered the field in a youthful composition. He is singing the departure of his brother. The first adagio movement in anapæstic rhythms represents the flattery of the friends, who are trying to dissuade the traveller from his journey. It is time for the fugue, and this is the picture of various misfortunes which may befall him in foreign parts. A mournful arioso passage on a ground bass,[2] chromatic in character, is a universal lament of his friends. In a full-chorded Intermezzo they come and bid him good-bye, seeing that it cannot be otherwise. Now the postillion sings his air, broken with octave passages, representing the smacks of his whip; and since a fugue is the end of all good things, we hear one in four parts raise itself above the post-horn, with whip episodes to increase the realism. The young Bach did not go as far as Frohberger, who represented the assaults of robbers, crossings of the Rhine, and even forcible ejectments with violence, on the clavier; or as Kuhnau, who had given the cheating of Laban in "deceptive" cadences,[3] and Hezekiah's doubtings in the rehearsal of a choral; yet this kind of programme-music declined in the eighteenth century precisely as it has grown up again in the nineteenth.

If we believe Spitta, Bach also left behind him one of those anagram-pieces which were so in the taste of his time—the fugue on the letters B A C H. But the composition seems too leathern and insipid for us to be able to express a decided opinion. There is in literary criticism a well-known false method—the wish utterly to deny insipidity to the great. But since Bach's authorship of the "B A C H" fugue is not vouched for, and since he never elsewhere put together so many dull pages, we are not compelled to load his memory with its weight.

---

[1] See above, p. 92.

[2] A "ground" bass is a short passage repeated an indefinite number of times through an extensive movement. In this case it consists of four bars, and is not repeated so strictly as usual, though its general figure is kept up throughout.

[3] This expression, "deceptive" cadence, is a translation of *cadenza d'inganno*, one of the several cadences or closes which had names given to them by the old theorists. The "inganno" cadence was something like the "interrupted" cadence, but was supposed to lead into *another key*, hence the "deception."

As we find in Bach the possibilities of all the great forms of the succeeding centuries, so we find in him also all the germs of future expression, rhythm, harmony, and melody. Nothing is more perverse than to regard this music as academic and expressionless. Expression is never absent from counterpoint except

John Mattheson, at the age of 37.

when it sacrifices impressionism to the mere display of technical mastery. We shall even to-day seek in vain for piano compositions more full of expression than some of the preludes contained in the Wohltemperiertes Klavier. In the remarkably decadent C sharp minor, in the B minor, so full of gentle mournfulness, in the E flat minor with its grandiose solemnity, in the B flat minor with its organ-like seriousness, or in the F major with its Meister-singer melody [1] (in Part II. Wohlt. Kl.), there is an unsurpassed depth of expression. Nowhere is there a greater variety of characters than would be presented by a comparison of the fugal themes in this work. Merely to turn over a few of its pages is to see before us an abundance of content which no other music-book would easily conceal in so narrow a space. It is in the service of expression that the motives for the architecture of the fugues are unfolded ; in the service of expression the rhythms are developed, whose skilful planning is only clearly seen in a piece like the G major Prelude (Wohlt. Kl. i.) ; in the service of expression are formed the harmonies, from their simple successions, as in the C major Prelude (W. Kl. i.) or of the C sharp major Prelude (W. Kl. ii.) to the complicated retardations and tied notes of the B flat minor Prelude (Wohl. Kl. i.), or in the B minor fugue (W. Kl. i.) on a theme so wonderfully sad that no bolder chords can be found in the days of the most furious chords of the seventh. In Bach, says Marpurg, the different talents of a hundred other musicians were united.

Bach played very quietly. In his time technique began to change its principles. The hand was no longer to be held out flat, but curved, so as to provide a series of hammers rather than levers. The passing of the fingers over each other, as practised by Mattheson, a player of distinction almost equal to Bach and Handel, gave way to a systematic *under*-passing ; and the thumb, which Bach had seen applied by former generations only to wide stretches, began its important part as the "linking" finger. The remains of Bach's finger-exercises, and the directions which stand in the lesson-book of his son Philip Emanuel, have been usefully compared [2] by Spitta, who has drawn a picture of the technique of John Sebastian, which in its grandeur well fits with his work. " It was a system of under-moving fingers, worked out by unparalleled

[1] The author possibly refers to the flowing freedom of the counterpoint in the quintet in Wagner's opera. But there is no need nowadays to demonstrate that the Bayreuth master is as necessarily a contrapuntist as he of Weimar.

[2] Meaning, of course, that the fingering methods of the father and son are by no means identical. The former employed the crossing of the fingers over one another freely ; whereas Philip Emanuel's notions of fingering are practically ours. See his " Exempel nebst achtzehn Probe-Stücken, etc.," date 1780.

practice and talent, applying not merely to the thumb but to the middle fingers, and usually so arranged that only a longer finger can pass over a shorter.[1] This produced a technique which, like Bach's work, united past and future in one classic method. Our thumb-technique, which in essentials goes back to Philip Emanuel, is a mere fragment of Bach's method, just as the whole succeeding art was, compared with Bach, but a fragment on a large scale." But it is hard to be clear on these matters. Before the time of "schools" technique was a matter of personality; and reconstruction to us of a later age is utterly out of the question.

Should a diligent scholar try to reconstruct from Bach's pieces his technique, so far as it had influenced musical form, he would soon be brought to a pause. For when we examine this literature, we see that to the master everything was possible, and that he never gave form to a conception for the sake of technique. He is a stupendous genius who does not write for everybody, and therefore his compositions are often difficult ; but the difficulties are never against the genius of the clavier, and can be conquered by anything but idleness. He has, again, written some taking show-pieces, like the Prelude and Fugues in A minor (Steingräber, vii. 29), which, as " paying " salon pieces, sound much harder than they are ; and, alongside of these again, are pieces which spring from the very joy in the abundance of possible techniques and of new conceptions. To this class belongs, if genuine, the Fantasia in A minor (Steingräber, vii. 8), in which pure technical fireworks are let off, of short scale passages for both hands, swinging chords and octaves, running motives with astonishing passage effects, passages of sixths with over and under accompaniments, and melodious phrases with embellishing harmonies. But here the first rank is taken by the famous " Goldberg " variations, already printed by Bach, partly set for two manuals, an album of thirty technical conceptions, in which everything possible in tone-material is contained, from arioso to canon, from

---

[1] This method is still commonly practised. Chopin, Liszt, and others, supply innumerable examples, particularly of the passing of 4 over 5.

grave to *presto;* everything, in fact, which Bach ever adopted for the setting of his ideas. The twenty-ninth variation, which can also be played on one manual, brings before us chords and passages of interwoven beauty which prepare beforehand the way for Liszt. Even in technique, then, the genius of Bach stretches over centuries.

It cannot be exactly maintained that Bach treated the clavier wholly individually, but he nevertheless has helped to individualise it. At the beginning of last century, when the clavier was still for the most part an accompanying instrument, when it sustained in the orchestra the foundation-harmonies, even if at the same time another clavier entered in concerto-wise, genius itself could not release the instrument from this corporate conception without running against the whole spirit of the time. It is remarkable how Bach left it the character of a thorough-bass instrument, and yet allowed it so much independence. It has at one time the divided nature of the unifying organ, as organ-pieces were then regarded still as practically ready for the clavier ; at another the pizzicato and running character of the lute. Bach could entitle his formally interesting E flat major piece, Prelude, Fugue, and Allegro (Steingräber, vii. 30) as Prélude pour le luth *ò cembal*.[1] From the traditions of the lute and organ the peculiar nature of the clavier comes into existence, and it was in the maintenance of the *via media* between these less delicately expressive extremes that its future lay. How *individually* Bach regarded the clavier is seen in the pieces in which it is combined with flute and viol da gamba or violin, or in the concertos with one, two, three, or even four claviers. Among these the C major and D minor concertos with three claviers, now combined, now isolated, represent the highest points of this older form of the concerto, as yet not adapted for solo-virtuosity. But yet plainer is his insight in the direct transcriptions which he has made of violin pieces for the clavier. He interpolates in the freest fashion middle voices, which are kept together by " pedals ; " ornamentations which draw out the air of the melody in clavier-style; or rapid vibrating over-

---

[1] That is, " for the lute *or* clavier."

parts which make up for the loss of the long-drawn violin tones. And by this insight into the peculiar character of the clavier, he makes it more capable not only of speaking with its own voice, but also of spreading over wider circles the literature of other instruments by means of suitable and self-intelligible transcriptions. Bach's extreme love of this instrument, which so often gave him the means of expression for his musical conceptions, contributed not the least to such an interpretative mission. Slowly the world accustomed itself to understand music, not *per chorum*, but *per instrumentum*.

It is at this point that the great need is felt. A mechanical advance is required to bring the expressive capacity of the clavier into a line with the demands of genius upon it. The rivalry between the clavicymbal and the clavichord[1] was not yet quite decided. In Romance lands the former was the favourite ; in Germany the latter. On the former great effects could be better produced ; on the latter the more soulful tone, and the unique embellishment called " Bebung." Bach wrote much, including the Wohltemperiertes Klavier, for the clavichord, which even his son Philip Emanuel still preferred to the clavicymbal. But he was so unable to disguise from himself the counter advantages of the fuller and broader quill-instrument, that he published pieces for " Kiel-flügel "[2], with two manuals and registers for forte and piano. These registers were the only means for giving light and shade to the monotonous note of the " cymbal " ; to give light and shade by turns, as in the organ, so that on the upper manual a melody could be played loud, and on the lower the accompaniment could be played soft. In Kuhnau we see the forte and piano, which he aimed at by simply striking on the clavichord, used as a means of

[1] It is necessary once more to remind the reader of the *essential* difference in " action," power of expression, and strength of tone, between these two instruments ; and of the unfortunate ambiguity which exists in the use of the name " clavichord." *Vide supra*, pp. 21 and 89, note.

[2] Kiel = quill, flügel = wing, *i.e.* a keyed instrument with a plucking " action " of *quill* plectrums, with a case made in the shape of a bird's *wing*. Grand pianofortes are still made in this shape, and therefore are still called " flügel " in Germany. Kiel-flügel is synonymous with clavicymbal (hence " cembalo "), and means " harpsichord."

Pedal-clavichord. Consisting of two manual clavichords, with two strings to each note, of (8 ft. and) 4 ft. tone, and a pedal-clavichord with four strings to each note, two 16 ft. and two 8 ft. Inscribed " Johann David Herstenberg, Organ-builder at Geringswald, made us, 1760." De Wit collection.

expression. In the Biblical Stories Jacob has just been cheated by Laban, in receiving Leah for Rachel. " The bridegroom is contented," as a minuet shows us ; but "his heart prophesies misfortune," and the measure rushes on, becomes piano and più-piano ; suddenly Jacob takes heart again—forte ; after a bar or two he goes to sleep—piano ; he wakes—forte ; falls into deep slumber—piano. In his " Italian Concerto " Bach had made a much more specialised use of this by the register. He had mingled loud and soft parts, and each hand alternately is marked forte or piano. In these, and similarly in the echo-movement of the suite with " Ouverture à la manière française," we are led to think of a splendid clavicymbal, such as the one preserved ostensibly as Bach's in the Berlin Museum of Instruments. In that, everyone of the combinations of four strings can be altered by pulling a register : the manuals admit of coupling, and a soft lute-stop is provided.

We know of a hundred attempts to improve the sound of the clavier, and make it more expressive. Here, too, the eighteenth century is the experimental preparation for the happy successes of the nineteenth. Now the string-choruses were tuned in octaves, now pedals were added for low notes, now the sound-boards were strengthened, now the lower strings were made of copper, and the higher of steel; and throughout a rich experience was acquired as to the best way of constructing the separate parts. Leather plectrums appear everywhere in order to make the tone softer and less metallic. The clavier, in fact, was made to imitate all possible orchestral instruments, and even such natural phenomena as thunder and lightning, by means of register-stops. Or, the forte and piano stops were combined, ever more artistically, into as many as two hundred and fifty permutations, so that an endless number of shades was possible.

The solution of the problem was the modern hammer-clavier or pianoforte, in which the strings are no longer plucked but struck with hammers, so that every *nuance* of touch depends on the fingers. The story of the pianoforte is the usual Story of Inventions. While people were labouring to solve the problem by theoretical calculation, it had long lain solved in an unsuspected fashion before them, and those who were slowly working at the practical realisation were personally forgotten, until a positively sufficient experience made the new invention popular. The beginnings of the pianoforte are therefore, as usual, obscure. The striking of the strings with hammers had long been the method employed in the dulcimer. At the beginning of the last century an artist named Pantaleon Hebenstreit was much talked of, who played the dulcimer so perfectly, that everyone was astounded at the new sound-effects. It is possible that his success gave the impulse : in any case, in the year 1711 there emerges in Italy an instrument called the pianoforte—because it could be played piano as well as forte—elaborated by a certain Bartolommeo Cristofori, who was soon forgotten. This instrument is clearly pictured in writings recently recovered as a hammer-clavier ;

Cristofori, as curator to Ferdinand de' Medici, had a splendid collection of Belgian, French, and Italian Flügel-instruments to look after, the study of which, without doubt, aided him in his invention. His pianoforte, which at first shows a still more primitive technique, gradually draws sensibly nearer to the modern system; yet, on account of its unaccustomed tone and touch, it was unable to gain any appreciable results in the following decades. Cristofori could not have dreamt that an Italian society of our time would build a monument to him as inventor of the world-charming pianoforte, in the national sanctuary, the Santa Croce of Florence.

Whether Hebenstreit built on Cristofori, Cristofori on the French, or the French on the Germans, is unknown. Possibly the pianoforte was invented thrice over, in Italy, France, and Germany. In France appears Marius in the year 1716 as the inventor; in Germany it would seem that a certain Schröter, incited by the success of Hebenstreit, invented it in 1717; at least he himself says so in a writing first published in Freiberg in 1763, ten years after the death of the instrument-maker, Silbermann. But Silbermann had in any case the merit of having, at a more fortunate time than Cristofori, worked so hard at the perfecting of the pianoforte, that from him its increasing spread and the gradual displacement of the clavicymbal and clavichord may be dated. Yet this very Gottlieb Silbermann had constructed a "cimbal d'amour," which by a cleverly devised mechanism heightened the tone of the clavichord—so "lonesome, melancholy, and inexpressibly sweet." But his later renown rests on his exquisitely manipulated pianoforte. He had a good master in this difficult work—John Sebastian Bach. When he brought his first model to Bach the latter found it too weak in the treble and too hard to play. Silbermann was first vexed, then stimulated by this censure. He then sold no more, and went on making improvements in it until the old Bach, as Agricola[1] says, gave him unmixed commendation.

[1] Agricola was a pupil of John Sebastian Bach, and in 1754 helped Bach's son Emanuel to write a biography of his father.

Bach and the Modern Pianoforte

If we play Bach to-day on our extremely refined pianofortes, we are inclined to imagine that his fine effects are solely due to the perfection of the instrument. And this opinion is not wholly false. Though in the cembalo there sounded in his ear something of the accustomed solemnity of the organ, there is yet in his music a cry for a subtle and expressive instrument which he as little possessed as Beethoven possessed an orchestra suited to his ideas. In every great tone-creator lives a superabundance of imaginative form which the instruments of the time cannot embody, and to which the instruments instantly strive to become equal. Because Berlioz was, the modern orchestra is. Because Bach was, the pianoforte is, which knows how to express with justice the subtleties of his soul-music. I think for example of the never-to-be-forgotten theme of the C sharp minor prelude in the first volume of the Wohltemperiertes Klavier. The clavichord could only give this theme in a thin lament ; the spinet in a rigid and unmanageable form. But what features does not the motive show as the piece runs on ! Now it has the slow-breathing rhythm of a noble aspiration, now the opening eyes of an expectant Cecilia, now the heavy oppression of a martyr soul, now the holy rage of a last noble complaint, now the sweet weariness of Christian humility. And with these various tints the piece builds itself up into a broad picture, which leads from renunciations through pain to renunciations ; with these tints every line, every note of the theme is given an active life, as it pursues its course. Composition like this demanded an instrument which should be capable of a new expression in every touch. All that Bach dreamed of, the pianoforte gave, awakening the gentle soul of the clavichord to an unthought-of fulness of existence, and changing the mechanical force of the clavicymbal to a sudden consciousness of personality. The voices of a fugue-passage would now be personally separated from each other ; every line in the great lacework could be brought out at the moment according to the feelings of the performer. What, under the sacred laws of Bach's music, slumbered in the depth of the breast, found in the new instrument its unreserved interpretation.

[1] [It seems at first sight almost tragic that Bach himself can never have realised these effects, which are so familiar to us in connection with his music as it is nowadays interpreted on the pianoforte. But perhaps it is the wisdom of Fate to ordain that the cup of the artist should ever be dashed by a certain bitterness, the conscious falling short of attainment as it appears in complete idea before his mind.

When an artistic form reaches perfection, its active life is

'Bundfrei" Clavichord (*i.e.* with a separate string to each key), by Chr. G. Hubert, Bayreuth, 1772. De Wit collection.

over, and it is a subject of contemplation, no longer a tool to be used.

And just so, when the instrument necessary to the full interpretation of Bach's clavier-music, the pianoforte, had arrived within measurable distance of perfection, then did Bach's own Art reach its highest formal expression, then once more did the fashion of things suffer a change, and his work began to take

[1] Suggested by corresponding paragraphs.

its place as a colossal monument pointing on the road towards the House Beautiful.

Bach is, as it were, the priest of modern music. His congregation sit at his feet daily. Wherever a pianoforte is found, there is his temple. But though the priest cannot utterly control the worship of his hearers (nay, many will bow the knee to Rimmon in the house of the God), still his voice is strong, his words are true, and they may hear if they will.] This is the significance of Bach, and the longer we live, the more we shall believe it.

Philip Emanuel Bach, as he was in his Hamburg period.

The "Galant" School

WHEN Bach died, the musical centre of gravity tended to Germany; but it was doubtful what precise line would be followed. On Bach anything could be built. A great period of counterpoint might rise in which voices might go through a new series of harmonic complexities, similar to, and yet so different from those of the Middle Ages. Or there might come a period of great suites in which the simple dance-forms might grow in many-sided development. A high pathetic style might be introduced, or the details of expression might attract the attention of the amateur. The forms of the various compositions might alter in either direction, of new freedom or new restraint. Counterpoint might be deserted, concerted playing might be improved in the direction of increased grace.

For all or any of these possibilities Bach laid a foundation, and it only remained for the taste of the time to decide on the choice that should be made.

The taste of the time, leaving on one side both the pathetic and the scholarly, went off into the domain of the graceful. The experience of music was similar to that of architecture, which had already gone through the epoch of the " baroque " and " rococo,"[1] by which designers had sought to give variety to the lines of their work. Compared with the energy and manly swing of the Italian Concerto, a sonata of Philip Emanuel Bach is fairly characterised as " rococo." In place of the sober delight in bold outline appears the " galant " appreciation of eccentricities and wayward curvings. Passion is ashamed of confessing itself openly, and offers the amusing spectacle of a natural emotion wilfully covering itself with an incongruous vesture of conventional form.

The newly formed tendency towards simple sensuousness does not obtrude itself; it merely smiles in the graceful oscillations of subtle harmonies.

Caprice is the true ruler, and in improvised outpourings, speaking pauses, piquant leaps, stupefying enharmonic changes, purposed perverseness of motive, she places the same material under the hands of the fair performers, which, a short time before, had taken such a scholarly form.

Where strict canons of the voices used to be carried honestly through, we now observe a pleasant trifling with imitation which becomes coquettish, and the pedantic old Dux and Comes[2] put up very well with the change in their conditions of service. Counterpoint turns into mere accompaniment, and daintiness with humorous ornament is the object of the composer.

The new auditor is the delicate dilettante who listens no longer so much to the inner parts, the ancient severity of which

---

[1] Both these adjectives apply to decorative ornament. The general idea of "baroque" is "odd" or "outrageous." "Rococo" implies an elaborate want of good taste.

[2] "Dux," the *leader*, *i.e.* the "subject" of the fugue; "Comes," the *attendant*, *i.e.* the "answer." So called because the one follows the other as a matter of course, like master and servant.

vanishes and is replaced by chord music. Now we listen to the melody, to the over-part, and we unfold its whole charm, revealing a hundred secrets of melodic pleasure, and disentangling them at ease. And in all this capricious enlivening of music there remains the same delightful contradiction as in the paintings and buildings of the time — the contradiction between inner freedom and the aim at a fixed form. The external form is to replace what was offered by the inner; and yet, from these new free figures, the intention is primarily to gain this form. The aim is not at collections of suites, but at the type of the free movement, of the piece, of the sonata. It is the same spectacle as when we see Hogarth and Greuze expressing a definite moral lesson in their pictures, or architectural principles conveyed in the play of childhood. In music, however, that exclusive predominance of form, which the French Revolution caused to prevail in the representative art, has never been quite attained. It is important to notice that this was only possible since music had emancipated itself from French influence. It was only in Germany that a Beethoven could arise.

The distinction between " professional " and "amateur" is one to which our attention is always more and more drawn. "Tablatures" and apparatus for the scholar vanish gradually, and titles meant to attract the amateur become more frequent. Bach's inscription—" for the delight of amateurs "—over suites and concertos, appears on more than one title-page. We read " Cecilia playing on the clavier and satisfying the hearing," or " Manipulus musices, a Handful of Pastime at the Clavier," or again, "the Busy Muse Clio," or even " Clavier-practice for the delight of mind and ear, in six easy *galanterie parties* adapted to modern taste, composed chiefly for young ladies." A certain Tischer has put it very shortly on some suites—" The Contented Ear and the Quickened Soul." As the most complete refiner of this taste, relying on the public at large, appears Philip Emanuel Bach, who inscribes his sonatas " easy " or " for ladies," and thus openly confessed, much as he was censured therefor by the pedants, that he had systematically introduced the light *genre* as a music for the future.

Like the princes in the seventeenth century, or the middle classes in the nineteenth, it was the nobles in the eighteenth who played the part of Maecenas; and under their patronage appears, for the first time, a precisely marked musical society. Here too, in music, the nobility became an invaluable link between the artistic court and that public interest in art which, it would seem, is the necessary condition of all future advance. Even in the didactic musical romance which old Kuhnau wrote in 1700 under the title of "The Musical Quack," we miss the type of the amateur Maecenas. In the background, invisible, stands the prince who keeps the chapel; in the foreground there are only musicians and quacks. The amateur who is not a quack, the genuine dilettante, first attains importance in the beginning of the century; but very shortly the concerts which are given in the salons of the Fürnbergs, Esterhazys, and Schwarzenbergs, do more for the beneficial advancement of art than even the devotion of a keenly musical court such as that of Frederick the Great at first was. The greater courts, like Dresden and Munich, begin somewhat to decline, while the smaller advance, and in England, Italy, and elsewhere, the nobility, who are not unlike small sovereign princes, aid the spread and development of music. The nobility are soon followed by the gentry; but it was not till the Revolution had shattered the nobles that the bourgeois Maecenas steps upon the scene. In this displacement of old relations it was inevitable that the clavier should play its important part; in accordance with its social nature it advanced more and more from an accompanying or supplementary instrument into an independent centre of drawing-room existence, as well as of bourgeois evening parties. Thus, in the attractive and successful pieces of the generation from 1750 to 1800, its popularity was for the first time established. Old Bach had as yet been the most serious professional musician who had yielded to "galant" impulses; and his concessions to the popular taste were only by

F. W. Marpurg, Theoretician and Clavier
Teacher. 1718-1795.

the way. The distinction between public improvisation on
set themes, and public interpretation of written works, was
not yet sharply defined. The
player was at his highest when
he extemporised variations or
fugues on a given subject. Such
had been the improvisations of
Sebastian Bach; but the spirit
of improvisation, as it lives in
the works of Philip Emanuel,
is something quite different. In
him the hand directly follows
the inner feeling, constructs
easily and simply, and plays for
the sake of the playing, not for the sake of the art. Before the clavier
had become a social instrument, this division of labour between
composers and players had become imperative; reproduction was
bound to diverge into a separate branch. The amateur, on whom
more and more the art depends, is incapable of composing, but
he will, on his clavier, hear the works of the masters, which are
now so numerous, or even play them himself. He desires to
have acts of operas, arrangements of concertos, or many dainty
short pieces. The old clavier-books, which we can trace from
the Elizabethan Virginal Book to the volumes of Bach's children,
now gradually disappear. Instead of copying with its personal
character, the press is more and more in requisition, and the
musical treasury is more and more thrown open to the public.
The engraving of notes, during the eighteenth century, rapidly
improves, and the clefs and types become more simple. The
ornamental devices become constantly more fixed, and the player
has less and less liberty in his use of them. And whereas, in
earlier times, the instruction-books did not always distinguish
between composition and playing, now, since Couperin's time,

the instruction-book of pure playing became constantly more common ; while Philip Emanuel, to whom, perhaps with justice, we trace the systematisation of the principles of modern clavier-playing, wrote a book on playing, and then waited eight years before publishing a second part on the thorough bass.

The extension of musical interest led further to such a multitude of musical magazines as even to-day is not to be found. For the most part they disappear after a few years, but we have, as a matter of fact, in a year's issue of such a paper, a very fair picture of musical tendencies. I have before me a volume of the last of these, published in 1762, by George Ludewig Winter, in Berlin. It is well printed, with dainty rococo borders. Very amusing and characteristic is the sanguine Preface, in which also is to be discerned the inability of the German tongue to restrain itself while talking of our classics. " Music," says the publisher, " serves either to delight with its mere art the professor, whether he be such by nature or by cultivation—as a well-built house, or a well-laid out garden, satisfies the connoisseur ; or, on the other hand, it is the language of emotion. Then roar forth tones teeming with revenge, sorrow glides over the strings, passion frantically beats the air, joy revels in the blue æther, friendship and love sigh forth on the delicate notes, praise and thankfulness well from a full heart on the vigorous melody, or rise, cleaving the clouds on the tongues of men, to the very throne of the Almighty."

The good man, with his fearful fluency, declares that he is going to bring forward much of the lighter kind—meaning what we call the dilettante class of music. The numbers appeared week by week, and the continuation was always postponed for the next, often at the most thrilling passages—in the approved style of the clever magazine. The authors' names are only given when they are very well known. Among these distinguished men are many whose names have not remained in the memory of history—fashionable composers, such as every epoch has in plenty. But there are also Philip Emanuel Bach, Kirnberger, and many others of the great Bach School. Most of it is clavier-music.

Operatic airs, which occasionally appear, are so arranged that the voice part, under which the words are printed, is played by the right hand, and the completing orchestral notes are written small in the upper staves. There are also popular songs in abundance. A French spirit breathes through these pages ; a fashionable spirit of enjoyment. The short character-pieces, which the French loved so dearly to introduce with significant titles, are mingled plentifully with sonatas and rondos, arranged in the Italian manner. Under the character-pieces, in the appropriate places, as in the biblical stories of Kuhnau, the explanatory programme-text is printed. Thus in a piece called "La Spinoza,"[1] the developments are marked as being philosophic reflections on a certain theme. Two pieces, called "Wonderment" and "Youthful Joy," easily explain themselves. In one piece entitled, "Two friends grumbling over their wine," by the arrangement and form of the two voices, in right and left hands, is represented how they converse, console each other, gain courage, and wait for a friendly glance of fortune. The most humorous is a short clavier-piece, "A Compliment," which, usually in two voices, exhibits the following spirited contents : "If you are well, I am charmed." "Rather I am glad that I see you so well" (Repeated). "I have heard that you have been poorly : I am sorry to hear it." "Heaven be praised I am recovered." "But I am ashamed "—"allow me "—— They quarrel who shall bring the chair, and finally sit down. "I recommend myself"—"and *I* recommend *myself*" — "to your friendship."

It was precisely at this period, when the clavier first became truly popular, that its construction was rapidly and constantly improved. It was then that the separation of the two systems of mechanism—the so-called English, and the Viennese—took place. The names mean nothing, for both systems alike arose in Germany proper. The distinction lies in the fact that in

---

[1] Meaning "The Philosophy of Spinoza," *i.e.* an illustration of Spinoza's method, given in musical notes.

the English the hammer rests on a separate bracket from which the key strikes it, while in the Viennese the hammer rests directly, though loose, on the end of the key-lever.[1]

Although Germany was so partial to the clavichord with its intimate intellectuality—a quality which even to-day we can only reproduce in its fulness by reproducing the clavichord—yet it was the German pianoforte which for a long time took the lead. It was one of the first triumphs of German manufacture, and perhaps precisely because so little manufacture lay in it. In Italy the invention of Cristofori had vanished without leaving a trace. So utterly indeed was it forgotten, that when Italy decided, though very tardily, to replace the Gravicembalo by the pianoforte, instruments of this construction were preferably brought out there with the notice, "built in the Prussian manner." Alongside of the Silbermann pianofortes, those of Friederici of Gera—which were known as "Fort Bien" and were still built largely on the clavichord model—and those of Spath of Regensburg, enjoyed a great renown in the second half of the century. But soon, chiefly through emigration, the best manufactories were transported to foreign parts, and it is only in the latest advance of German industry, especially by the labours of Bechstein and Blüthner, that pianos built in Germany itself have again achieved a world-wide repute.

The great French, English, American, and Austrian pianofactories can almost all be traced back to Germans. The three great Parisian houses, those of Erard, Pleyel, and Pape, were founded by Germans. Steinway emigrated from Brunswick to build in America those pianos which are to-day regarded as the best. Johann Zumpe carried the hammer-clavier to England,[2] where it was played by German executants, and brought into repute. It was, however, English houses, with that of Broadwood at their head, that effected the improvements which have resulted in the

---

[1] It is impossible to describe this action in words. See the diagrams in Grove's "Dictionary of Music," vol. ii. pp. 716 and 718.

[2] I possess a Zumpe pianoforte, date 1766, which is apparently the earliest surviving made by him in England. E. W. N.

appropriation of the name "English" to the mechanism of Silbermann.

Factories alone, however, would never have brought about the final victory of the piano if there had been no virtuosos to play them. Clementi in England, Mozart in Germany and Austria, were the workers who won the decisive triumph of the piano. Even Philip Emanuel Bach had much preferred the clavichord to the newer instrument. But Mozart, the first world-virtuoso, the idol of the concert hall, thinking solely of sound-effects in the great halls, never hesitated for a moment between clavicymbal and piano. In 1777, at the age of twenty-one, he made, at Augsburg, the acquaintance of Silbermann's disciple, Stein, the inventor of the Viennese mechanism. This received the name of "Viennese" when Stein's children came to Vienna, and there, along with Streicher, the well-known friend of Schiller, established the world-renowned business. Here in this family for the first time appears a new phenomenon in musical society. Round the king of clavier-builders and his musical wife, young Streicher and Nanette Stein, there moves a brisk circle of musical spirits. It is a type which in our time has further gained in importance. With the greater popularity of the art, the social standing of the piano manufacturer has risen ; and nothing contributed more to the introduction of the piano into middle-class houses than the reputation of this much-envied Viennese coterie.

Old Stein and young Streicher are two clearly-marked types. The latter is a romantic spirit, raves over the just-played "Robbers" of his school-fellow Schiller, forms the plan of going to Hamburg to perfect himself in clavier-playing under Philip Emanuel Bach, but never gets there, since he spends all his time running from town to town with the restless Schiller. Then he gives music lessons ; next he meets Nanette Stein, marries her, goes to Vienna, becomes manager of the factory, and makes the invention associated with his name, in which the hammers strike from above. Finally, he becomes a centre of Viennese musical life. What a contrast is this modern industrial prince to the old Stein, working like a mediæval crafts-master there in Augsburg at his claviers, and giving equal devotion to every single part! He has been sketched by Mozart in a well-known letter; and I reprint this picture of the last of the old patriarchal clavier-builders, because it is not less interesting as showing the type than as showing the condition of technique at that time.

"I must now," writes Mozart, "begin at once with Stein's pianoforte. Before I saw anything of Stein's work I liked Spath's

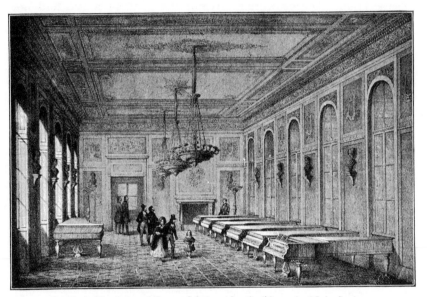

Streicher's Pianoforte and Concert Saloon. After the lithograph of Lahn-Sandmann.

best; but now I must give the preference to Stein's, for they damp much better than the Regensburg instruments. If I strike hard, whether I let the fingers lie on the keys or lift them up, the sound is over and done with the very instant I lift my hand. I may come down on the keys as I like, the tone will always be the same; it never hangs fire; it doesn't get weaker, or grow stronger, or stay on; it's just all *one*. It's true you can't get a pianoforte like that under three hundred florins, but the trouble and diligence he shows is not to be repaid. His instruments have this point that makes them better than others : they are made with an escapement which there isn't a man in a thousand knows anything of; and without this it is just impossible for a pianoforte to help blocking or sounding again.   His hammers, when the piano is played, fall back again the very moment they touch the strings, whether you hold the key down or let it go.   When he has finished a piano, so he says, he sits down to it and tests all kinds of passages, runs and leaps, and works and scrapes until the piano 'll do anything ; for he works only for the good of music, and not his own merely, or he would be done long before.   He often says : ' If I myself didn't love music so passionately, or couldn't do a little on the piano, I should long ago have lost all patience in my work ; but I'm just a lover of instruments which don't try the player and will last.'   His pianos *do* last, too.   He guarantees that the sounding-board won't warp or break.   When he has got a sounding-board ready for a piano, he puts it in the air, rain, snow, sun, or any beastly thing, to warp it, and then he glues crossbars in until it is strong and firm.   He's quite glad when it warps, for you're about certain nothing more can happen to it.   He often cuts into it himself, and glues it again, and so makes it strong. He has three of these pianos ready, and I have played to-day on them for the first time.

"The machine which you move with the knee is also made better by him than by others.   I scarcely touch it, when off it goes ;   and as soon as I take my knee the least bit away, you can't hear the slightest after-sound."

We see from this letter of Mozart's that in 1777 the "escapement," which lets the hammers fall back immediately after the strings are struck, was as yet by no means universal, but that the pedal, which was pressed at the side by the knee and raised the dampers, was already a usual feature.   What numberless small modifications and improvements must have been introduced before the developed mechanism exhibited by the key-levers, the hammers, the dampers, the escapements, the pedals, the sounding-boards, could have advanced to the self-evident simplicity which made possible the meteoric splendours of piano-technique about the middle of this century! Prices for pianos were still fairly high. The younger Ruckers obtained three thousand francs for a clavier, but it had painted on it those rich pictures with which the spinet, when it began to take its place among household furniture, was so captivatingly adorned. We hear also that the Parisian pianos with leather-plectrums (jeu de buffle) fetched, in their finest specimens, as much as three thousand francs. A Wagner clavicymbal from Dresden, which was a so-called *Deckenclavier*, in which the tone could be softened or strengthened by fan-shaped dislocations of the inner lid, fetched six hundred and sixty thalers; and Frederick the Great actually gave seven hundred thalers to Silbermann for the first hammer-claviers. If Stein, with his three hundred florins, seems to fall off from this price, we must remember the difference in the purchasing power of money. But, to-day, two thousand marks for a good pianoforte is cheap in comparison with the prices of those days. It is only through the growth of popularity that the greater demand and the lower price have become possible.

I turn to the works themselves. Our step falls very heavy, and our judgment may easily be unduly harsh, when we have just parted with old Bach. This meeting with genius, which we celebrate in every bar—this earnest greatness which meets us at every turn, has made us very exacting in our demands for the higher beauty. In the first moment the "Galant" School seems to us a school of pigmies, until the sight has again adjusted itself, and the vision has again become awake to the miniature beauties of this smaller art. A good transition is provided by Handel, for, against Handel, Philip Emanuel Bach appears an astonishing genius.

The tendency of the public, to group celebrities in pairs, has brought not merely Goethe and Schiller, but Bach and Handel, into juxtaposition. How little the scholarly hermit had in

common with the grandiose world-musician—who first followed
the wise prescription, glory in Italy, gain in England—would be
seen from a comparison of their clavier-writings, which are a fair
average of their general work.   Handel is the negation of the
classic.   He gets his results from materials close at hand ; brings
them into plastic clearness, and writes from the point of view of
the vulgar herd ; he is never troubled by an exacting inward conception, or overwhelmed by his own imagination, as are all true
classic artists.[1]

Handel's clavier-pieces are written in an extravagantly
popular style.   His suites, which moreover embrace not dance-
forms only ; his capriccios, variations and fantasias, flow like
futile "water-music."   They are brilliant without being difficult,
and entertaining without being suggestive.   There is no colour
on the sky of their landscapes ; no tempest lashes their trees.
We roll in our coaches on well-macadamised roads, the melody
of the wheels reminding us meanwhile of this or that well-worn
turn in the operas or oratorios.   Seldom is a halt necessary in
order to look at the view.   Perhaps we may stop a moment
longer than usual at those frequent singing sarabands in the
popular style, at the charming salon-gigues (especially the long
one in G minor), the genuine virtuoso's Tarantella, or at the
better F sharp minor suite with its short free prelude, staccato
largo, insinuating fugue and dramatic gigue.   Perhaps, also, the
fugue with its *three beats* from the E minor Prelude may please
us ; but there is a something which the whole fails to give us.
It is an acquaintance—not a personal intimacy.

Quite other is the impression produced by the "galant"
music of Philip Emanuel Bach.   While his elder brother Friedemann stands somewhat nearer to Sebastian in kind, and actually
wrote pieces, like the C minor fugue, of which the old man need
not have been ashamed, Philip Emanuel, with greater decision and

---

[1] Such a judgment of Handel, which would be ungracious in the mouth of an
Englishman, is not unfitting in a German.   England alone, apparently, knows and
cares about Handel, the athlete in *choral* music.

also with greater significance, pursued a different path. It is as if fate had marked out this difference. Sebastian Bach held Friedemann as the cleverer musician ; but he frittered his life away. Philip was first set to study jurisprudence, and out of the painstaking lawyer grew the sober and energetic composer. The life of Philip was as simple as his father's. In 1740, at the age of twenty-six, he went to the court of Frederick the Great, where he worked as royal cembalist and accompanist. In 1767 he went to Hamburg, and died there in 1788. He does not seem to have been able to agree with the King ; and it is likely enough that he felt and worked more freely in Hamburg. Berlin was always having trouble with its people. Had Philip Emanuel stayed there, Berlin would have been the greatest centre of piano-playing in Germany, and its walls would have been associated with lasting memories of the ancestors of modern musical forms. Had Mozart, in later years, accepted the offer of Frederick William II. of a position as chief Kapellmeister with the extraordinary salary of three thousand thalers, Berlin would have been enabled to absorb a little of the musical life of Vienna. Or, later still, if the Academy of Singing had been given to Mendelssohn (who was a candidate), rather than to Rungenhagen, the intoxicating glory of Leipzig, which lasted for a time, would have been transferred to the banks of the Spree. But the spirit of Zelter remained over Berlin.

In 1753 Philip Emanuel published at his own expense his "Essay on the true Method of playing the Clavier." This was the most copious work on clavier technique that had yet appeared. It was at the same time the sufficient apology for the technique of the thumb, which has become the ground-work of our fingering. When the extreme importance of the thumb had at last been recognised, it was not hard to investigate systematically the places of its application. The main rules were necessarily that, in ascending, the thumb of the right hand is put *after* one or more black keys, and the thumb of the left hand in descending, and *vice versa*. The setting of the thumb on the black keys themselves must be avoided, and the passing over of one finger by another, which earlier had been the main feature in scale passages, was now abandoned. The whole art was built on the thumb, which passed under in the right place. This work of Philip Emanuel, which gives special attention to the legato, may be called a panegyric on the thumb. In this clear insight, as well as in the arrangement of his exercises, which begin with scales and chords, preferring the unison practice of the two hands, and advancing slowly to easy pieces, his work is still one of our most modern exercise-books. We might guess that in this diligent application of his thumb-technique to scales and broken chords, Philip Emanuel places in the forefront of his exercises certain scale figures which to-day could not correspond to the most pressing necessities of the piano-player. We should expect them to be a mere training of the hand, and no preparation for the real difficulties which appear in actual literature. A glance at the works of any great master will show us, however, that such is not the case. These very scales, chain-passages, and broken chords, which are the material of teaching, are also the figures of free composition. Some fashionable composers may have employed them extravagantly, because they were at the fingers' ends of the players, but the most independent writers must use them, because they are, from the very nature of the clavier, the most fruitful in effect and most harmonious in sound. The old disruption of musical material into short passages of four or five notes was now antiquated. Performers practised the whole scale and the chord. And since Philip Emanuel carried through this natural training with methodical clearness, his teaching has been fruitful, and has not run merely *alongside* of the literature. In his book we can clearly see how the clavier has contributed not least to the formation of modern secular musical perception. In this its equal temperament, which was so urgently necessary, and its complete presentation of the tone-material, which so to speak we have only to read off, have largely aided.

The case is dissimilar with his treatment of the "manieren."[1] On their employment he writes as follows: "No man, assuredly,

---

[1] *i.e.* the ornamentations, turns, appoggiaturas, etc.

hath doubted concerning the necessity of 'manieren.' We can observe it herefrom, that we meet them everywhere in great abundance. Everywhere are they indispensable, if one considers their use. They hang the notes together, and give them life ; they give them, if it be necessary, a particular energy and weight ; they make them pleasing and therefore awaken a peculiar attention ; they assist to make clear what is their meaning, which may be sorrowful or glad or otherwise disposed, as it pleaseth, yet do they contribute of their own thereto ; they give a notable part of opportunity and material to the true execution ; a moderate composition can by them be aided, as without them the best air is empty and monotonous, and the plainest meaning must appear throughout obscure." This is a judgment which surprises us in a man so intelligent and advanced as Philip Emanuel. He has not yet perceived that ornamentations were in his time only the relics of an earlier style. An appoggiatura, which takes away half or two-thirds of its note, and thus becomes a mere melodious retardation, or a double-shake which completely disintegrates its note, and requires to be expressed by an antiquated stenographic mark, is already a mere fossil in a period which gives such independence to the melody. It is not the notes which then appear which are fossil, but their arrangement as decorations. What had originally been truly decoration, in the heyday of figuration, had, in the course of the eighteenth century, long become an emancipated melodic phrase. The idea of the retardation, which earlier veiled itself under the name of appoggiatura with suspended main-note, was not allowed to step in openly ; and the doppelschlag [1] or the trill could say plainly what they were, without masquerading as modest satellites of some main-note or other. Had Philip Emanuel but had the courage to discard the old signs, and to hear the customary ornamentations as independent music, he would have been able to spare himself much dead weight, to avoid much confusion, and to get rid of the trammels of many dead traditions, which have come down even to

---

[1] The doppelschlag was the "turn," beginning with the *note above*.

our day. He has in his book exhibited a stirring knowledge and an individual treatment of the "manners"; yet he was forced to maintain an arbitrary distinction between the "manners" and the other figurations, although between the turn and any other melodious line-curve there is no longer any essential difference whatever. He has not been able to introduce any system into the relation of the appoggiatura with its note; and, because he saw that the effect of the appoggiatura could be produced equally well without the little note, he has been obliged to take refuge in the sentence: "The appoggiaturas are partly written like other notes and thrown into the bar, and partly specially indicated by small notes; while the larger ones keep their full value to the eye, although in practice they lose something of it." At this point he should have been able to see that a system of "manieren" as such was no longer possible.

From indications given by Philip Emanuel, it would seem that in these matters he was deliberately behind his time. He bemoans that the well-known marks in clavier-pieces were already beginning to be strange, and points to the careful way in which the French had always put in their marks. He delights as a rule in setting up the French as the masters of the clavier-exercise, and is vexed that people had an "evil prejudice" against their pieces, "which yet," he says, "have always been a good school for clavier-players, forasmuch as this nation, by the smoothness and neatness of its playing, hath marked itself off specially from others." Philip Emanuel's love for the French is a very important point to keep in mind in appraising his works. Not only did he find in them the only great precedents for his "galant" style; he has also expressly continued the method of Couperin and Rameau by transcriptions, in the French manner and the French language. Nay, his endeavour, in his sonatas and rondos, to construct stiffer forms with *reprises*, appears as a mere continuation of the French rondo; and, however Italian the musical form may be, in more than one of his pieces, we inevitably think of the "Cyclopes" of Rameau. Possibly his whole book was suggested by Couperin's "L'Art de toucher le clavecin," and respect for this French tradition has hindered him from revolutionising the "manieren," which still had their justification in France, so thoroughly as he did revolutionise the finger-exercise. It is thus very amusing to see how he himself challenges comparison with Couperin. He calls him " a teacher formerly so profound," referring of course to the "manieren." The "formerly," of course, implies that Couperin had not yet learnt the thumb method, and had been too fond of changing the fingers on one note. In point of ornamentation it was *he* that was conventional; and in point of fingering—why, old Sebastian, lately dead, stood between him and Couperin.

"Fantasia-making without strict tempo," says Philip Emanuel in one place of the Essay, "seems in the main to be specially adapted for the expression of the emotions, because every kind of barring brings with it a certain constraint." In this verdict and in its application lies for us to-day, viewed externally, the greatest surprise which Philip Emanuel offers us. He has, as a matter of fact, written many fantasias which are almost designed without bars, and thus very logically give expression to the character of improvisation which they bear. They are great recitatives full of reflective melodies, of linked staccati, of sounding broken chords, which the player, when moved, knows how to unfold. They were the last free specimens of the unfettered forms of the older time.

Not only in these fantasias, but as a rule in his whole creative energy, especially in the Hamburg period, Philip Emanuel exhibits that extempore humour and freedom, which has at all times given to clavier-pieces their greatest charm. He has sufficient invention to be rarely at a loss; and the pieces from his earlier "Württemberger Sonaten," which are still more contrapuntal than the later, or from the later six volumes "Für Kenner und Liebhaber,"[1] have all that variety and multiplicity in unity which was also a feature of the collections of John Sebastian. But the desire for caprice works in him more strongly than the fulness

---

[1] " For professors and amateurs."

of invention.   He is untiring in pulling a melody humorously to pieces, in surprises of pause or in remarkable transitions.   Occasionally his language positively dances, and it is hard to be certain whether it is intentional distortion—a cloak for poverty—or the genuine caprice of the moment which leads him after the charms of eccentricity.   In any case he belongs to those rare and subtle natures which in a moment give us the genuine artistic touch of brotherhood.

Even in his harmonies his freedom is clearly noticeable.   He does not object to write separate movements in different keys, which he often connects by direct transitions.   The third Sonata in the " Kenner und Liebhaber " stands in the first movement in B minor, in the second in G minor, and in the third in B minor once more.   The fifth Sonata, which is set in F major, begins quietly with a phrase in C minor.   In the first Rondo of volume V. we find the chord of the seventh (G, E, B, C sharp), set at the key-deciding place, *in B minor ;* a chord at which some of our best memories of Wagner are revived.   For such things he was severely censured by his comrades in the profession.

As to his melody, it is as delightful as is to be expected from " galant " music, and from that only.   At one time it shows a charming sentimentalism, in which the stronger use of retardations has its share, now it is frisky and playful, toying with itself ; in both cases anticipating Mozart.   Specially characteristic of the author are numerous melodic phrases, the like of which have played an important part down to our own time.   Philip Emanuel used them with the greatest depth and penetration in the F sharp minor movement of the A major sonata (No. IV. in Kenner und Liebhaber, vol. i).   In all these points he manifests his independence ; and in spite of his study of the French, it is but seldom that, as in the " Siciliana " of one of his sonatas in the " Musikalisches Allerley," we catch an echo of a phrase from Couperin.

Like all the "galants," he wrote much.   A considerable number of his works were printed in his own time in the magazines or separately.   Among these the sonatas to Frederick the

Great to Charles Eugene of Württemberg, to Amalie of Prussia, and the "Kenner und Liebhaber," take the first place. But yet more remained unprinted. Prosniz has counted four hundred and twenty of his clavier pieces, of which two hundred and fifty were printed. There is no modern comprehensive edition of his works, but the "Kenner und Liebhaber" has been very beautifully reissued by Krebs in the Berlin Academy collection of original editions. Apart from the first volume these are written exclusively for pianoforte.

The name of Philip Emanuel generally rises to our lips when we speak of the origins of the modern forms of chamber-music and symphony. This is correct enough if we are content to establish his claims as an agent in the crystallisation of the two main forms of classical composition—the Sonata and the Rondo. But the creator of these forms he was not; he found them very far advanced in France and Italy, and on the other hand he handles them so freely that their regulation cannot be said to have been completed till the days of Haydn and Mozart. Thus he is in these points also but an intermediary.

The strict sonata introduces first a main subject, then in an allied key an allied subject; next the middle section [1] in which these subjects are developed and completed; and lastly it repeats the exposition, transposing the subordinate subject, however, with a view to the finale, into the main key.

In the Rondo, on the contrary, there is *one* main theme and many subordinate motives. The main theme is chiefly melodious; the by-themes alternate in all kinds of forms among the repetitions of the melodic strophe.

To the Sonata and the Rondo all older dance and fantasia forms gradually gravitated. The Sonata is the more dramatic, the Rondo the more lyrical. The Rondo, considered as to logical content, is the more organic; but advance and climax are wanting

---

[1] Various names have been used for this "middle section" of the "sonata form," *e.g.*—"Development," "Fantasia," "Free part," "*Durchführung*, carrying through," "Working-out."

to it.   The Sonata on the other hand, is, because of its *reprises*, less intellectual than architectural ; but it has the sobriety of greatness.   Usually, in thinking of the forms of this musical age,

Mary Coswey with the Orphica, a portable clavier, which at
the beginning of this century had a certain vogue.

our thoughts dwell on the Sonata—in which form as a rule the first movement was cast.   But the Rondo was equally important, and is equally often used in the second or last movement.   Purer dance-forms were always in use as intermezzos between the movements.

In Philip Emanuel, then, we see a preference for the types

of the sonata and the rondo which prepares the way for their sole supremacy. He only needed to proceed eclectically. Not only the French Rondo but the Italian Sonata had led to the *reprise* form. Philip Emanuel did not advance far beyond these models. A second theme is not universal in his works ; and only the modulation of the keys within the first half, to the dominant or relative major, is strongly stamped on them. The Sonata movement with him still admits of all *tempi*. In the third of the " Kenner und Liebhaber " Sonatas the peculiar sonata-form is not on the whole adhered to, but allegretto, andante, cantabile, follow each other in free fashion. On the other hand, in the following piece, the first and the last movements both show the sonata-form ; but in the first of the "Württembergers" only the last movement has the stricter sonata-style. The third sonata of Volume II. of the " Kenner und Liebhaber " is actually written in a single movement. On the other hand the second Württemberger begins with a genuine sonata with double subject ; and in the Kenner und Liebhaber, Vol. III. No. 2, the type of the modern sonata appears in full development. We see then from these examples that while Philip Emanuel uses the *reprise* of the first part almost universally, he is yet far removed from the classical model of the sonata. In a word, we shall find in him nothing that is not already to be found in Rameau, Scarlatti, or above all, his great father.

The Rondo was more in accordance with his genius. Here, where he had fully developed French models, it cannot be denied that with all his freedom in detail he has brought the form appreciably nearer to the classic type. Even Beethoven was often unable to improve on his alternations of intermediate movements, or the grace with which he returns to the air and makes his theme gently rock to and fro. He loves those simple popular rondo airs, which, as we listen, we all seem to have heard before. As couplets[1] he

[1] The word " couplet " is here used as in Couperin, and other old French composers. It means the subsidiary themes or sections which alternate with the main subject in these ancient rondos. Call the main theme A, the subsidiary ones B, C, D, etc. Then the course of the movement is—A, B, A, C, A, D, A, etc., and B, C, D, etc., are called " couplets."

prefers to use technically brilliant figures, which in their turn offer a good contrast to the air. He is untiring in toying with the theme. He makes it now break off in the middle, now become sentimental; now it becomes questioning. As time goes on he develops his whole power of expression, so that he is far removed from a stiff alternation of theme with couplet. In a fantasia (K. and L. v.; last piece), which is perhaps his most charming composition, he blends the rondo-form most skilfully with the free style of an improvisation, and thus shows himself on his best side. Hardly less delightful is the last piece in Volume VI., a Fantasia-Rondo whose main theme is a kind of hunting-call. In this movement the hunt is interrupted by a beautiful romantic *andante*, then by emotional reveries in *larghetto sostenuto*, and in the conclusion the reflective style gains the upper hand.

The Rondo was so attractive to him because by its means he was able the more easily to bring his beloved "affettuoso" into expression. And his inner genius was not so much formal as lyrical. In his music there is even to-day a strong spiritual charm, to which the slight archaism adds a pleasant flavour. In his Rondos he comes very near to us, and not less in those little characteristic pieces which, written in dance-form, followed French models in the very style of the inscriptions. He uses for titles proper names, such as Hermann, Buchholz, Böhmer, Stahl; and such more general appellations as La Xenophone, La Sibylle, La Complaisante, La Capricieuse, L'Irrésolue, La Journalière, and Les Langueurs Tendres—names, it will be remembered, used also by Couperin. La Sibylle has a wonderfully beautiful melody; and Les Langueurs Tendres is such an unsurpassable air in two mournful voices, that it bears endless repetition. Nothing has ever been written to surpass this tender clavichord-sadness.

The great counterpoint of Bach is now forgotten with extraordinary rapidity. The ancestor of the following generation is Philip Emanuel. Wherever we look, to the London Bach, Johann Christian, to the Austrians—anywhere—we find the work influenced by his style. " He is the father and we the boys," said Mozart.

Joseph Haydn.

Engraved by Quenedey.

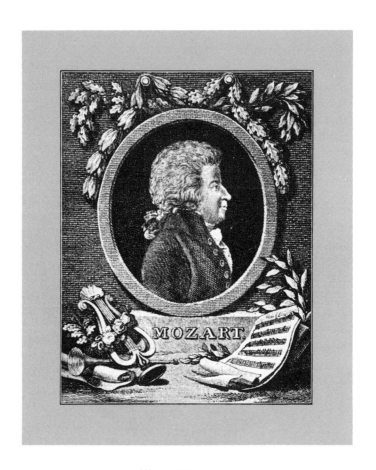

W. A. Mozart.

Engraved in 1793 by C. Kohl (1754-1807).

Haydn knew well what he owed to Philip Emanuel, and was as little chary to acknowledge it as Mozart. In actual essentials Haydn made no advance in clavier-music. The stream is perhaps a little clouded, and it is not till Mozart's time that it again becomes çlear. Haydn's genius lay in composing for the orchestra, not for the piano. He has of course written clavier sonatas—they number thirty-five—and other pieces in which the clavier takes part; as numerous and light as the works of all these "galant" musicians. But his trios are to be preferred to the sonatas for piano only; there is more depth in them; and the ideas are lit up more brightly by the instrumental combination. Only in the sonatas after 1790, as in the first in E flat major (Br. and H.) does something more noteworthy emerge— but by that time Haydn had studied Mozart.

Still further, in his pieces, Haydn is no great virtuoso. In his Trios he knows well how to make the most of the character of the clavier, by contrasting it with the strings, by means of arpeggios, all kinds of passages, full chords, and the beloved octave-melodies. But a more interesting virtuoso performance, such as that in the F minor variations, appears very rarely. The ornamental work is still extensive, but within limits; and much of it is written out in full, just as the cadenzas, which used to appear in small notes, are now preferably printed in the usual type. At the end of the century everything was taken away from the caprice of the player, except the great cadenzas at the conclusion of the concerto-movements. Philip Emanuel had taken a last important step, when, in his Sonata dedicated to the Prussian Princess Amalie, he wrote out exactly for the second time the ornamentations and alterations in the frequent repetitions of musical phrases of a few bars, instead of leaving them to the pleasure of the players. To judge by his preface, caprice in these matters must have flourished like a green bay-tree; and he takes great credit to himself for having been the first to offer accurately formulated "alternative *reprises*," which run no risk of spoiling the whole aim and meaning of the piece. His point of view is interesting. It is, he says, not possible to avoid altering a musical phrase in repeating it. This conception is endorsed by all his contemporaries and successors in style, in their works: Haydn and Mozart cannot be conceived apart from this mannerism of altering a musical idea in repetition by slight turns and adornments. This method is the fixed law of movement of their musical ideas, and dictates their progress through long stretches in advance. Deep founded in the general delight in variation so characteristic of the time, it enables us to understand that great development which forms a whole branch of musical history—the development, namely, of improvised "manieren" into strict and firm melodies.

As far as *form* is concerned, the work already begun is continued by Haydn. The Sonata-form tends to limit itself more and more to the first movement; more and more clearly does the "second theme" crystallise itself; slow-drawn movements are preferred more and more in the second place, and graceful rondo-like movements in the third—without, however, any appearance of compulsion. The only relic of the traditional "suite" of dances, which Haydn retains in his sonatas or symphonies, is the "Minuet" which he is so fond of using as an intermezzo.[1] The old dance-forms, *as* dances, were so speedily forgotten, that in a certain trio a delicate slow waltz is marked as "allemande"— whereas the old allemande is not even written in the time of a waltz, apart from the difference in style.[2]

Haydn received more from the clavier than he gave to it. He transferred to the orchestra the clavier-forms of the time, and thus pointed out to it the path to the symphony. Without doubt the modern symphony, in the first instance, is to be traced to the clavier pieces of Philip Emanuel Bach; and Haydn, to whom fell the task of the intermediary, was the first to put the rich development of this chamber-music to practical use. Clavier and orchestra always advance in mutual rivalry, treading on each

---

[1] See, for instance, Haydn's earliest string quartets, where he commonly has *two* minuets, one on each side of the "slow" movement.

[2] Does not "allemande" here simply mean "German" waltz?

other's heels. In Haydn it was the clavier that aided the orchestra; in Beethoven the orchestra aided the clavier; Mozart, standing between, gives to each its own.

Thus it is that Mozart has given much, and much of its special character, to the clavier. This equilibrium—and Mozart is always the very personification of equilibrium—is most striking in his piano-concertos, which justly enjoy the renown of having created an epoch in this class. Especially remarkable is the C minor concerto, in which the piano experienced one of its chief emancipations. On one side stood the orchestra, on the other the instrument, and yet neither of these two great rivals loses anything of its essential nature; rather, they owe to this very rivalry many of their best effects. When clavier and orchestra address and answer each other; when the clavier intertwines itself with the strings and the wood, and they in turn blend with the clavier; when in the running strife each sounds in its own style and gives birth to a natural variation of phrases and to delicate alterations of the constituent forms; all proceeds in accordance with that self-evident logic which, at such critical points in artistic history, naturally dispenses with internal laws.

Mozart is the great virtuoso who, even as a boy, was the astonishment of Europe. It is not to be expected that he should content himself with the intimate reflectiveness of the pianoforte; he drags it out into the great world; he needs the concerto-form just as he needs great concert halls. The new pianoforte, with its fuller and more subtly expressive tones, is precisely adapted to his aims, and he is the first to launch the pianoforte on its decisive career. With his triumphal progresses the popularity of the new instrument was not likely to decline. The great enchanter leaves the tiny victories of the spinet far behind; his public recitals in hired halls, which henceforward become more and more popular, demand new feats. He has to work on bold lines; he has to bring into use the special features of the instrument he adopted; the rippling scale-passage, the variety of tone, the *forte*, the *pianissimo*, the hundred gradations between these extremes, the altogether new possibilities of senti-mental expression which were now at the disposal of the public performer. But amid all the intoxication of the concert hall, the virtuoso remains an artist ; the idol of the hour retains his deeper feeling. As he was only truly himself when, after the furore of publicity, he touched the notes in solitude or before a few friends, so in his concertos, behind the external glitter, a romantic soul lies hidden. In the beautiful Romance in the D minor Concerto, for example, the soul looks out on us with a wonderful and never-to-be-forgotten intensity.

In almost all his pieces Mozart composes according to the bidding of the moment. He is an " occasional " composer. In the concertos the occasion was his own appearance on the stage. In the duets and double pianoforte pieces he found the occasion in his association with his sister. From this species of performance he drew new effects. The D major sonata for two pianos stands alone in the skilful and effective blending of the two instruments. His four-handed sonatas are astonishingly successful in the individualisation of the hands, and started a numerous class of clavier-pieces which have been too often mis-used. We shall not appreciate such duets, if we take the clavier as a diminutive orchestra.[1] But here again Mozart has been unwilling utterly to sacrifice combined effects to individual demands.

Through the ravishing chamber-music in which, especially in the quintett for oboe, clarinet, horn, fagotto and pianoforte, the splendid treatment of the pianoforte with regard to the wind deserves notice ; through all the melodious pieces for piano and violin, the trios, the quartetts ; to the numerous smaller clavier-pieces, the fashionable variations, the relics of the suites,

---

[1] It is a great pity, and a great loss in every way, that the careful *artistic* playing of duets on one pianoforte has largely ceased. What Moscheles and Mendelssohn were not ashamed to do in public, surely is not an unworthy employment. It should be revived, if only to popularise Schubert's beautiful works for four hands, the widespread ignorance of which is a simple disgrace to us all.

Beginning of Mozart's A minor Sonata. Royal Musikbibliothek, Berlin.

the scattered fugues, the fantasies so rich in variety; we follow Mozart to the eighteen pure piano sonatas, which are the very miniature mirror of his unfailing musical invention. We shall treat them in chronological order, for here for the first time we perceive a distinct development which renders such treatment the most natural and advantageous.

At first we meet the daring harmonies and enharmonic changes by which every innovator makes himself notorious, and which draw on him the first severe criticisms. But there is not yet the concentration of later works. A light counterpoint runs through the whole, a conscientious treatment of the themes, which bears witness to sound training. A striking feature is the unforced inventiveness in motives, which succeed one another in unfailing profusion. Intellectual themes, as for example in the B flat major, remind us of Philip Emanuel. The form becomes more distinct, the rules of sonata-arrangement more rigid. But it is not till we reach the A minor (1778) that the full brilliancy of form is seen. This piece has all that wonderful proportion and balance even in the smallest parts, which was, and remained, Mozart's most peculiar characteristic. Proportion in the well-balanced opposition of themes in all three divisions, in the liveliness of the piquant semiquaver runs, which already leave Scarlatti far behind, in the brilliant and yet simple execution of the last movement—proportion, indeed, is everywhere.

After 1778 our impressions deepen. The D major is the creation of Mozart's indestructible caprice. The motives become ever more tuneful, more *speaking:* in the C major we hear the phrases as though sung; we seem to hear words with pauses for breath, as from a distant exquisite opera. The melodies run after each other, and—what is so typical a feature of Mozart —it is by this that our attention is held rather than by any inner development of the themes.

The A major sonata is an excellent example of this melodic regularity. Its contours are of an unimagined loveliness, and its airs of a magic delicacy. The Turkish March stands out in

Mozart at the age of seven, with his Father and Sister.

Engraved 1764, by J. B. Delafosse (b. 1721) after L. C. de Carmontelle (? about 1790).

Lithograph by C. Fischer, after the original portrait of 1817, by A. Kloeber (1793-1864).

variegated national colours, far removed from every triviality—
if only we give to the Janissary rhythm its full due.

The airs become broader, the piquancies more daring, until
the allegretto of the B flat major with its jubilant sevenths
stands before us as a new peak of Philip Emanuel's Rondo forms.
Here is that bright laughter, which from Mozart's lips has the
most delightful of sounds.

This was in 1779. In 1784 Mozart has entered upon the
second half of his life, the unhappy half, and the C minor sonata
appears. New tones now strike upon our ear, harsh, strong,
broad, intense. But all is still in proportion. The hand is
freer, rushing more boldly from the heights of the piano to its
depths; bolder also are the episodes which are the pivots of the
thoughts. In all is the sweet intoxication in the bewildering sound
of the pianoforte, and the air so full of soul, growing richer in
retardations, and more and more taking the lines which Mozart
decisively fixed for the beautifully-formed melody. A strange
reserve, the reserve of maturity, characterises the last movement,
otherwise so flowing; its expressive raggedness forbodes new things,
the victory of matter over form—in a word, Beethoven; and then,
in this period of Figaro and Don Giovanni, we meet the F major,
the most sombre in content of all his writings (1788). With its
two movements we are accustomed, not improperly, to connect
the Rondo written in 1786. Counterpoint has slowly advanced to
its old position—the sign of the mature man, who is seeking his
fixed abode. This it is which stiffens the weft into what at times
is a solidity worthy of Bach. The dominion over the world of
tone is now absolute, the melodies sing heavenward, as for
example in the theme of this andante, which came spontaneously
from his soul.

We have reached the limit of the " galant," over whose fields
dark clouds are already gathering. But we are also at its highest
point. In Mozart the ideal of popular music was more fully
realised than its father, Philip Emanuel, could ever have dreamed.
Mozart's well-balanced nature preserved the clavier from super-

ficiality; and he himself was saved by an early death from sacrificing this balance to the sombre thought of a new time. His sense for form brought the sonata into more typical shape, but the endless melody and the free intelligence of his music took all sharpness from the forms. No music can be less easily described in words than his; and therefore, as a great beautiful sound, it was the best content which the forms of the galant popular epoch could find. It is not till we have left youth behind that we see proportion and equilibrium in this repose; and it is then, as Otto Jahn says, that we are amazed at the wonderful wealth of this art and at ourselves for being so slow to feel it.

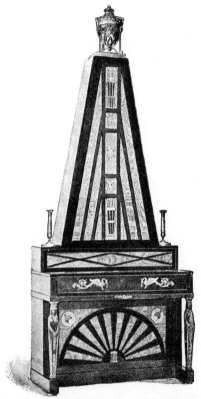

Upright Hammer-clavier (pianoforte), about 1800, called the "Giraffe." Mahogany and bronze, with open work in green moiré. Three pedals, *forte*, *piano*, and "fagotto." By Joseph Wachtl, Vienna. De Wit collection.

Beethoven at age of 31.

Beethoven

WHEN a great scheme was started in Berlin for a common
monument to Haydn, Mozart, and Beethoven, it was plain to
see that the artists felt themselves in the presence of a very
mixed task ; but it was not so clear where the incongruity lay.
They stood under the influence of the popular opinion, which
binds these three heroes under a single yoke, and they were
the victims of this influence.   Nations have an instinct of
symmetry in the classification of their great men.   The ancients

had their seven sages; to-day we are content with two or three; but even so the combinations are none the less strained. The false ideas due to the pairing of Bach and Handel, or of Goethe and Schiller, are hardly to be numbered. The triumvirate of Haydn, Mozart, and Beethoven, is the very acme of perversity. Haydn and Mozart, though two fundamentally different natures, have yet in common the similar features of the age. But Beethoven is as little like them as Goethe is like Racine. We have only to glance round a salon in the Vienna of the last century. The old Haydn and the old Salieri sit smiling and friendly on a sofa; they move in the stilted fashion of the eighteenth century; they retain in their carriage all the features of the " Zopf und Schopf"[1] period; and in every judgment, in every gesture, they show their antagonism to unrestrained emotion. Over against them a young man is leaning on the piano. His demeanour is modish though untidy, and smacks of the Rhine; his movements natural but wooden; his hair is loose and disordered; his compliments are few; he accepts strangers only on compulsion; his playing is perhaps too vigorous, too full of feeling; and the ideas which he incorporates in his works are in their originality half revolutionary, half romantic. This new-comer is Beethoven, a man so different from the settled type, from the old "composers of the Empire," as he himself calls them, that it is easy to anticipate the future which he himself is conjuring up. He is the first of the Titans, the first of the great fragmentary natures, the first tone-artist who breaks the forms of music to pieces on the iron of his emotions. A strange Providence closes his outward ears, and thus gaining a clearer vision, he receives from Nature herself unheard-of inspirations. How this strange new man, this romantic raver, could be coupled with Haydn and Mozart is a wonder; but popular opinion accounts for it. Beethoven came to Vienna just as Mozart began to be missed. The world gave him the honour of attaching him to the classic school.

---

[1] *Pigtail and Tuft*, a combination of " Bigwig " and " High and Mighty," with " Sir Oracle."

But it is a mere blunder to treat him as the end of an epoch —he is the beginning of a new one.

It must be observed at this point that the world had meanwhile become really musical—or perhaps less truly musical than music-loving. Nay, more ; political events, as formerly church ceremonies, could now be celebrated in music. The famous concerto which Beethoven gave in honour of the Vienna Congress was perhaps the first great occasion on which music lent itself in festal manner to the adornment of public events. It was now no longer a mere incident in a commemorative display, but to a great extent pure music ; and the rapid and vigorous education of men to instrumental music by the classical masters was the necessary precedent condition of the attainment of this point. In these matters the clavier played its important part as an intermediary and a teacher ; it made the innovations into current coin, scattered them among people in their homes, and accustomed their ears to understand better and better the absolute language of music, as it dealt in wider and wider abstractions. The publishers were more active, the issues more frequent, the popular settings more numerous and artistic. Even the great men themselves take a share in the work. A frequent phenomenon in the music-trade is that composers like Clementi, Dussek, and Pleyel, themselves open publishing houses — and secure the advertisement of their wares, oftener perhaps than was really necessary.

International exchange became more active year by year. If we look to London, we see Johann Christian Bach at work, helping to give form to the Sonata ; we observe Haydn and Pleyel in vigorous rivalry for the favour of the public ; we see the virtuoso Clementi from Italy setting up a clavier-school. In Petersburg meanwhile lives the Englishman, Field, one of the chief nocturne-romancists, and Klengel and Berger, the Germans, all three brought out by Clementi. Next we see there also J. W. Hässler, the ex-hatter, who has left behind such agreeable works that Bülow regarded him as a good intermediary between Mozart and

Beethoven. In Paris the opera is the favourite agent of musical pleasure. With Gluck the old quarrel between the Italian and the northern manner is renewed. Chamber-music retreats into the back-ground. Schobert and Eckard, decorative musicians, are hardly known beyond the border; and Adam and Kalkbrenner, who restore the fame of French clavier-technique, leave productive art on one side.

In Vienna there is a swarm of prominent figures. Gradually the city is preparing itself for the state of things which in 1820 W. C. Müller thus describes in one of his " Letters to German Friends " : " It is incredible how far the enthusiasm for music, and especially for skill on the piano, is now being carried. Every house has a good instrument. The banker Gaymüller has five by different makers ; and the girls especially play a great deal." Indeed, a glance at the society of Vienna at that time shows us innumerable ladies, ranging from the merest amateurs to the maturest artistic performers, thronging round the great and the mediocre alike. Even Beethoven, the misanthrope, sees himself surrounded by them ; he cannot keep from them, nay, he often does not choose to do so. The Baroness Ertmann, Julia Guicciardi, Nanette Streicher, are some of the actual persons of the fair sex, who, amid innumerable legendary beings, hovered about the Master. As usual where social life forms the basis of culture, the ladies come to the front. Invitations fly in bewildering profusion ; the great houses exchange their guests ; new compositions are made known in the salons before they find a publisher ; and when they are published, old acquaintances become subscribers. This narrow circle gives a great opportunity for the advance of chamber-music. An accurate observer will notice how the modern international musical public slowly develops itself from this old-fashioned, close corporation.

The names of the best teachers are in every mouth. Czerny, who was destined to raise Vienna technique to its height, and to become the teacher of a Liszt, tells us in his Memoirs who were known as the best teachers in Vienna at the commencement of the century: "Wölffl, distinguished by his bravura-playing.; Gelinek, universally popular for his brilliant and elegant execution; Lipawsky, a great sight-player, renowned for his performance of Bach's fugues. I still remember how Gelinek once told my father that he was invited out for an evening to break a lance with a foreign player. 'We mean to hew him in pieces,' said Gelinek. Next day my father asked Gelinek how the fight of yesterday had gone. 'Oh,' said he, 'I shall remember yesterday's fight. The young man has a devil. I never heard such playing. He improvised fantasias on an air I gave him, as I never heard even Mozart improvise. Then he played compositions of his own, which are in the highest degree wonderful and grand, and he brings out of the piano effects the like of which we never heard of!' 'Ah,' said my father, astonished, 'what is this man called?' 'He is,' said Gelinek, 'a little, gloomy, dark, and stubborn-looking young fellow, and he is called Beethoven.'"

Beethoven was discontented. He knew what lay within him, and yet could not help seeing how the crowd preferred to shout itself hoarse over the brilliant exponents of technique, then beginning to swarm over Vienna. He was brought into a contest not only with Gelinek, but with Wölffl, who was renowned for his abnormally long fingers. Such contests are a mark of the times. As yet the division of labour between composers and interpreters had not been introduced. Playing and invention had a more intimate association. The following is the programme of the "Academy," which Mozart performed in 1770 at Mantua: "First, a symphony of his own composition; secondly, a pianoforte concerto, which he will play at sight; thirdly, a sonata just placed before him, which he will provide with variations and afterwards repeat in another key. Then he will compose an aria to words given to him, sing it himself, and accompany it on the clavier. Next, a sonata for the cembalo on a motive supplied him by the first violin[1]; a

---

[1] Meaning the "leader" of the band, practically the conductor in those days.

strict fugue on a theme to be selected, which he will improvise on the piano ; a trio, in which he will take the violin part *all' improviso* ; and, finally, the last symphony of his own composition." No sharper contrast can be conceived than this performance offers to the modern concert. Almost all is here arranged for sight-playing and improvisation, or for the instantaneous exertion of inventive or executant skill. There is in this still a good deal of the earlier notion of music, in which the conception and visible development of a theme was preferred to the performance of a completed work. Later, the demand for such instantaneous performances gradually disappears. In Mozart the cadenza at the conclusion of the concerto-movements remained as the last refuge of the improviser in the written-out piece. Beethoven insisted that his E flat major concerto should be performed without an improvised cadenza.

At a period in which instantaneous performances were so popular, contests of the kind mentioned above were not misplaced. But Beethoven had more to suffer in them than others, since his genius had already outgrown them. He was a poet who loved to live apart and to offer his gifts in a more intimate fashion. How wonderfully did that very deafness, which turned his genius inward, preserve him in later years from public playing and conducting! But, before, he had been forced to enter the lists not only with Wölffl, with Gelinek, with the renowned technist Hummel, but actually with so contemptible an artist as Steibelt. This Steibelt was one of the disgraces of the age. Bespattered with praise, he rushed through Europe with his trashy compositions, his battles, thunder-storms, Bacchanals, which he played *ad libitum*, while his wife struck the tambourine in concert with him. The populace was enraptured, for Steibelt and Madame tickled their nerves with sparkling shakes and tremolos. At the house of the Count von Fries he fell in with Beethoven. A quintett of Steibelt's and the B flat major trio of Beethoven's (Op. 11) were played. In the latter occur the variations on a theme of Weigl, from the opera L'Amor

Marinaro. Beethoven was out of humour and would not play. A week later the same company met again. On this occasion a quintett by Steibelt is again played, and to it Steibelt adds a series of wild clattering variations on the same theme of Weigl. Such "Leit-motive" attacks are familiar in these contests. It is well known that underlying Mozart's Zauberflöte overture is a theme which Clementi had already used in his B flat major Sonata. Clementi had played it in a contest with Mozart, who did not care much for the Italian "mechanical" artist. But Beethoven this time avenged himself bitterly on Steibelt. After a long persuasion from his friends he stepped negligently to the piano, struck with one finger a few notes from the just-played quintett, and twisted it in and out until he had produced a fantasia; but Steibelt, before the conclusion of the piece, left the room and never came near him again.

Thus Beethoven lived in a world with which he had no sympathy. It is true that there were some houses in which the higher class of music was openly cultivated. Such a house was that of Van Swietens, where Beethoven often played to a late hour from Bach's Wohltemperiertes Klavier. But the multitude, whose musical horizon was bounded by the Italian opera, occupied itself with the glitter and splash of the executants. In such a city old Diogenes might have sought long for a man. A composer of the best class, Friedrich Wilhelm Rust, who in the midst of his capriccios in the style of Philip Emanuel often showed features reminding us of Beethoven, died at Dessau in 1796 alone and inglorious. A Franz Schubert lived close by Beethoven, but no one knew of his existence. Those who are heard of are virtuosos and writers for the pianoforte. Dussek, however, is of importance not only from the technical point of view, but from that of true *art*. He is noteworthy also as the first musician to compose almost wholly for the piano, with or without accompaniment. How distant are the times when we could feel surprise when a piece appeared written for piano alone! And this man, within the limits of his genius, made the poetry of the piano into a life-work. It is as if for the first time an anticipation of Chopin rose before us; but the likeness is after all only in externals. Dussek is the bourgeois romancist, when he spends his whole year in the country with his lady-love; but he is the true son of the eighteenth century when he in turn attaches himself to successive princely patrons. Especially devoted was he to the musical Prussian Prince Louis Ferdinand, on whose death at Saalfeld he wrote a suitable composition. His style would seem to have been noble and full, and his pieces are more charming than was usual at the time. Unlike Hummel he was very partial to the pedal; and it is in his pages, perhaps, that we find it for the first time accurately employed. His works themselves are of all kinds and degrees of merit. When, led by his national temperament (he was a Czech), he gives full play to the dance forms in the last movement, he strikes a fine and fresh note. He was one of the first to use syncopations effectively. But he has also written a final movement, that of the E flat major sonata in $\frac{6}{8}$ time, which has a true and solid worth over and above its dance-form. He is less attentive to his first movements, and his most famous sonata, that in A flat major, which he entitled " Retour à Paris," disappoints in this regard our expectations. In his second movements he is quicker to light on tones which, by their tender character, linger in the memory; as above all in the slow movement of the D major in $\frac{2}{4}$ time.

After all, if Dussek does not stand among the immortals, he yet, in intellect and power of invention, ranks among the lesser stars[1] to whom we owe the full elaboration of the popular forms. His style is soon grasped. We know one of his sonatas already as soon as we hear the first bars. A broad first theme gives us a good tune; then it goes smoothly flowing through grateful pas-

---

[1] The author here uses a term to describe Dussek, which I remove to the foot of the page, viz. *Epigonus*, which means "one born after," in the sense of a descendant who merely continues his father's work. Often it is equivalent to our "decadent."

sages to the second theme in
the dominant or relative key.
Other runs give the fingers
some further opportunity for
bravura ; perhaps a third scrap
of melody peeps out, and we
are at the landmark of the first
double bar. Next some suitable free fantasia is arranged,
which sounds more scholastic
than it is ; we pass with it
through a series of related
keys—until a motive already
known, the first theme, brings
us back again with a smooth
glide to the beginning, from

Dussek.

which point the movement practically repeats itself. In the
following movements there is a longer melody adorned with
variations. In the third a seductively familiar theme tickles
our fancy, which at times spreads itself out in bravuras, or gives
itself effect in a very poor imitation of a fugue.

In company such as this Beethoven stands absolutely alone.
It is true he has not yet wholly cast off the garment of his time.
In many a harmonic phrase, in many a formal turn, he is a child
of the period ; above all in many a *naiveté*. And he not seldom
exerts himself about passages which are utterly unworthy of him.
He, the composer of the A major symphony, wrote at the same
time the incredible " Battle of Vittoria." Conscious advance, such
as Wagner set before himself, is to him unknown ; and we find
among his later works various things that remind us of an earlier
period, as, for example, the wonderfully Mozart-like C major
Rondo for the pianoforte. But his *naiveté* was strangely warped ;
and thus arose noteworthy mixtures of style, such as we so often
observe in men who stand on the borders of two ages. His
character was the most complicated that ever musician had ; and

only investigators who know not the demon of the great soul, can seriously ascribe the paltry avarice of the master to humane goodwill for the notorious nephew whom he supported. A soul like Beethoven's is a mystery into which we can only penetrate slowly and with difficulty ; and who knows—even if perhaps the deepest secrets of his "last style" should become common and familiar, whether even then the last word would have been said on this strangely complicated and distorted character? But Beethoven composed from the soul outward. This was the great novelty. And we must penetrate into his soul if we will rightly apprehend him.

The enthusiastic compiler, Thayer, who died while writing Beethoven's biography—musical history has often been the death of its authors!—remarks very excellently how differently from others Beethoven already sketches out his work. The motives stand there in hasty cursive—applications of motives—tone-ideas in words—as a painter sketches or a poet notes down his observations or inspirations. It bubbles up not like Bach's steady stream of self-restraint, but in a torrent of unmeasured passion, which regards self-restraint as a weak concession and the correctness of the "galants" as a lie. In this man music spoke in words, not in pictures. He had the unparalleled boldness to tear out his secret feelings, all bleeding as they were, and hold them up before his own gaze. It was the boldness of a Zarathustra-nature. He belonged to those who worship Bacchus, not to those who follow Buddha. In Thayer's possession was a note from Beethoven to his friend Zmeskall of Domanovecz. "For the future I bid farewell to the cheerfulness which I sometimes enjoy ; for yesterday, through your Zmeskallic chatter, I became quite gloomy. The devil take them—I don't want to know anything of their universal morality. Might is the morality of men who distinguish themselves above others. It is my morality, anyhow. If you start on me again, I shall pester you until you find everything I do noble and praiseworthy."

We shall then only understand Beethoven thoroughly when we leave form on one side and take music as a speech. It is no feeble paradox to say that the reason why Beethoven, in his operas and songs, paid so little attention to the words, was because the music was to him words enough. To this greatest of instrumental geniuses was revealed the great secret of pure music, which, precisely because it has no speech or language, speaks infinitely the more profoundly. Words obstruct it. When Beethoven, at the end of the Ninth Symphony, has recourse to the human voice,

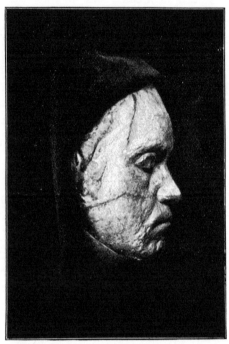

Cast of Beethoven's living face, 1812.

everyone feels that it was to him only the highest of all instruments, with which he can do yet more than with trombone or contrabass. It is the utmost triumph of the pure musician who can draw even the voice under his sway.

Music is to him a speech, because it is full of associations of ideas, which bring tones into relation with the outer world, and make them reverberate with a thousand inner meanings. In his orchestra we hear nature, as in his pianoforte we hear the orchestra.

Not without reason has Bülow, in his edition of Beethoven, in more than one place translated the piano-piece for the reader into score, in order to make its content clearer. These are things which did not exist in Bach. The world of tone has sacrificed her great unity for the great fragmentariness of unveiled speech, and a never dreamt-of height was thus reached in that absolute tone speech, which formerly in Venice and in England had taken the place of the mediæval vocal music.

What a Gabrieli, a Bull, a Bird, a Couperin, each in his own way, had begun, was by Beethoven brought to full completion. Here was the perfect opposition to the Middle Ages. Here was the Michael Angelo who could stand alone against the ancients. The abstractions were perfected, the relations more general, the language more intelligible. If Beethoven began his first Symphony with a chord of the seventh, it was possible to understand what he meant by it. To this man, who completed one epoch in beginning another; to this symphonist and chamber-musician, the clavier must become a daily necessity. His life has been written in his works. Words, which could only fetter him, are kept at a distance ; the notes tell the story by themselves.

If we would understand Beethoven's language we must study the way in which he works out his motives. His peculiarities are the peculiarities of the naturalistic school. The melody mounts or falls as his emotion mounts or falls. He takes a motive and narrows it until its parts curve upon each other, and then again makes it greater and broader, until it lies open before us. This is a deep and mysterious language, which deals with the tones as a word, an expression ; which looks on us, shall I say ? like the eye of certain animals—we understand them through and through, and yet their speech is not ours. But the most powerful agent in stirring our emotion is the rhythm, that soul of all expression. It is the absolute pulse of things, which only the finer ears can hear in the outer world ; it lies here before us in its artistic purity. The pauses, the leaps, the syncopations, the gigantic parallelisms of structure, the dynamic surprises, leave but a thin wall of partition between the phenomenal and the transcendental of music. There is no longer any reserve in the language. There are some movements in which Beethoven's music stands at the very doors of verbal speech : such, for example, as the allegretto in Op. 14, 1 and the first movement of Op. 90. The words appear to tremble on the lips ; but it would be the disappearance of the apparition were we to utter them.

Over Beethoven's realm broods a deep tragedy. A constraining seriousness speaks to us—the dark abyss of passionate emotion : a total pitilessness, a gloomy brooding, accents of misery, a unison of terror. Beethoven began his piano publications with the three sonatas (Op. 2.) dedicated to Haydn ; works full of inexhaustible inspirations, of the ravishing freshness of youth. The second is introduced by sharp accents and those broad extensions of chords by means of octaves, which remained to the end characteristic of the author. Another man would have begun the piece *after* this tragic cry, with the contrapuntally-rocking motive. But the first of his greater tragic outbreaks was the mighty Sonata in C minor, the so-called Pathétique, which he dedicated to his patron Lichnowsky. Upon the heavy, slow introductory passage follows the stormy First Movement, whose themes are, first, a tempest of rage, secondly, an utter despair ; and the Grave intrudes its monitory remembrances in the midst. Unity of colouring is preserved. Over the second singing movement, and the third with its rondo-like passages, lies the same sombre tone ; and the conclusion is sharply cut short.

Beethoven revels in the gloomy. He buries himself in deep tones, as in the Andante of the Pathétique or in Op. 22, its cheerfulness notwithstanding. Later, on the magnificent Broadwood, which he received from England as a present, he goes with delight into the regions of the deep. A mystic tremolo attracts him ; and the "trios" of his scherzi are full of the sonorous murmuring of billowy chords.[1]

---

[1] The author may perhaps refer to the Scherzi of Op. 2, No. 3, in C, or Op. 7 in E flat.

A new and grand expression of pain is the last movement of the Moonlight Sonata (Op. 27, 2), which is as full of hopelessness as the last movement of the other Sonata of this great pair (Op. 27, 1) is full of invigoration. The threatening strokes of the quaver chords which sharply define each repetition of the stormy motive-passages, the quivering secondary theme, the unrestful rests, the melodies, which seek to calm down the seething bass ; all this was a world of seriousness which the clavier had not yet learned to know.

But this was still a *composition*, compared with the naturalistic chaos of the Recitative Sonata (Op. 31, 2). This first movement is a remarkable embodiment of gloomy brooding, which is continually being disturbed by despairing cries, until it finally loses itself in that resignation of utter indifference, which is a typical form of Beethoven's tragic finales.

It seems to me beyond question that the impulse which drove Beethoven to compose great piano-pieces was supplied by the concerto-form. The concerto, in its secular character, had not remained without its advantages ; it was broader and freer than the regular sonata. It avoids *reprises* in the first movement, and arranges the divisions with more circumspection. In order to give the clavier-player a chance to rest, the orchestra must take over some independent parts. It begins with a broadly planned section, which so to say arouses curiosity, in which various themes are treated ; and portions of this introduction are then inserted between the successive entries of the pianoforte, or even simultaneously with them. The piano itself appears usually three times. In the first and last of these the music is to some extent repetition, the intermediate section is a kind of free fantasia. Even in Mozart a strict unity of theme between the orchestral and the solo sections is not always to be observed ; it was Beethoven who first carried it thoroughly out. He it was who with visible affection fashioned the concerto form. It is no accident that the two last of his pianoforte concertos, the G major and E flat major, to-day enjoy an exuberant popularity. What Mozart had promised

in his C minor concerto, these perform to admiration.   They are
built entirely on that plastic sensuousness which is the essence and
the aim of the concerto.   Their themes are remarkably adapted
for a polyphonous orchestral development, for a delicate imitation on the piano, or for the storm of the fullest harmonies.

The technique, whether of the piano or of the orchestral
colouring, though joyous, is yet severe.   Far from all coquetry and
all mere show—the technique stands, especially in the cheerful
E flat major, on a height of extraordinary purity.   The form is
clear, but not so precise as not to admit of modifications in single
sections, especially those devoted to the solo instrument.   The
intellectual G major, the technical E flat major, represented an
extreme of happy sympathetic innovation.

We only need to compare the great Waldstein Sonata in C
major (Op. 53) with the Concertos, in order at once to see that the
latter have stood godfather to the former.   There are not merely
external likenesses, as when the piano figures a theme which
might have been played already on the orchestra, or when more
important divisions close with a long shake, as in all concertos
the piano sections usually do on the re-entrance of the tutti ; or
when with passages played pianissimo, and hurrying ghostlike, or
in octaves, an effect is introduced which in Beethoven's concertos
the delicate piano is generally used to play out in contrast with
the orchestra.   Rather the important likeness lies in the whole
broad outline.   The themes appear as a rule twice, as is naturally
the case in the concerto ; the exposition is done leisurely and
cheerfully ; a cadenza, such as Beethoven had already used (*e.g.*,
in Opp. 2, 3, and 27, 2), gives to the conclusion of the first movement a specially concerto-like quality.   The second slow movement is a short emotional transition, such as Beethoven has written
so exquisitely in the G major and E flat major concertos ; and
the last movement, far from being a " concession " to the " light-
robed " muse, is a spirited rondo, in brilliant style it is true, but
in its augmentations and diminutions, its *stretto* and the trill-
conclusion, a genuine Beethoven—as no other could be.

As thus the dependence on the broad effects to which the concerto style had accustomed the hearer, gave to the first movement of the sonata a new form and extent which it had hitherto not known, it was possible for Beethoven to infuse into it a tragic content which soars far above the general coloration of the " Pathétique" and the brooding naturalism of the " Recitative " Sonata. Here for the first time we hear those trumpet-calls to the battle with Fate, those heavy rolling waves at the return to the first theme, which later in Op. 111 found so concentrated an expression. A monumental epic develops itself about the conflict, which usually forms the content of first movements. This mighty form represents a mighty picture.

What was thus given in the Waldstein was deepened and unified in the Appassionata (Op. 57). The uniform colouring of the Pathétique is here deepened by hints taken from the concerto. A sublime and rhythmical theme, based upon the simplest harmony, a solemn unison, dominates the first movement. The second theme, lyrical as it appears, is really only fashioned out of the first. As the movement progresses, we seem to hear mysterious winds, stormy seas, convulsions of nature. A cadenza, straight from the heart, leads to the most colossal *stretto* ever written : a wild upheaving, a sudden down-sinking and extinction. Its spiritual connection with the choral-like andante con moto is obvious. The note of aspiration is heard throughout, first by pauses, then by a clearer and clearer expression in those deeply-felt variations, which finally repeat their theme. The despair of the final movement is the last act—a giant melody, uttered in piercing cries, sinking down panting in the middle, and at the end breaking out into Bacchanalian revelry, in which laughter and ruin are inextricably mingled.

This was the most comprehensive tragic picture ever drawn by Beethoven on the piano ; and it has therefore remained a unique composition. His works tell us that he outgrew the epoch in which misery is enjoyed. His tragic art leads us beyond despair not to Nirvana, but to the Elysian fields. Hymns of

joy sound around him. Strong joy, Dionysian strength, was the
aim of this Faust. What he once depicted in the wonderful mono-
logue of Op. 27, 1, becomes his life. In the Elysian Fields the
fugue of adolescence returns to him, giving him repose and safety.
In it he allows the tragedy of Op. 106 to tower heavenwards. Or,
ethereal, world-dissolving glories shine around him—these are the
bright, cheerful phrases of the E major or A flat major Sonatas, in

From Beethoven's A flat major Sonata, Op. 26.   Royal Musikbibliothek.

which they now give the theme, now the figuration, or in the
scherzo, grow up in flowery profusion.   Into this serenity he allows
the tragedy of the last Sonata (Op. 111) to pass at last.   After
a movement of wild outcry come the simply resigned variations,
which finally mount from dull earthly devotion to angelic harmonies, to end in the glitter of their smile, in the bright sphere of
their unearthliness.

   To understand the joyous Beethoven of later years we must
remember the capricious Beethoven of youth.   A strong leaven of

cheerfulness lay in him, a healthy will, which knew how to be humorous.

The sportive Beethoven lies in the lap of Nature. There he hears the entrancing imitations of his Haydn Sonatas, the hurrying ghost-like scherzo with its Schubert-like romantic middle movement (Op. 10, 2), the sparkling Rondo of the Variation Sonata. This we must hear played by Risler in order to appreciate its inimitable humour and poetry, which is based entirely on the soft touch of the contrary motions. The most perfect of Nature prayers, a Pastoral Symphony on the pianoforte, is the *Pastorale* (Op. 28). Not only the second movement with its bird-like middle part ; nor only the third with its extreme cheerfulness, nor the fourth with its outlook on the woods, its delight in the chase, its joyous conclusion ; but also, and in the highest degree, the first movement, are confessions of Beethoven's natural symbolism. This work stands on that indefinable border-line between the comic and the tragic, which is the unfailing mark of the intensest poetry. It is a complete picture of the world. Beethoven's scherzi, his most peculiar form of art, which in the Sonata take the place of the old minuets, stand on this ground, and might be termed "secular," in comparison with the dramatic embodiments of his first movements, or the complete picturings of the last.

The Rondos exhibit a similar process of alteration. In them first, so early as the time of Philip Emanuel Bach, had the capacity of tonic art to " let a theme speak," been exercised. They allowed a theme its full expressive value. To Beethoven, accordingly, in his first period, such rondos appealed with the strongest effect, and their charming melodies throng in his earlier sonatas. But he was able to give this form a still deeper meaning. In place of the melodies he adopts genuine motives of pregnant brevity, which, as in Op. 10, 3, he develops with characteristic reserve. These pieces, as contrasted with the old melodic rondo, show a convincing naturalism. To the old rondo they are related as his scherzo to the minuet. Equally significant is his love for certain diatonically moving accompaniment figures, as in Op. 14, 1, or Op. 28 ; he thus avoids the impression of a regularly harmonised theme, and allows the naturalistic motive to predominate over the formal melody.

In the treatment of form in general, the sonatas exhibit a series of different experiments, which are of emotional interest. His other chamber music—the Violin Sonatas, the Trios, and all the rest, to which I now only allude—could not accomplish the suppression of form like the free, pure piano-pieces. The great Fantasia for chorus, orchestra, and piano (the latter treated in concerto fashion), which we value as an anticipation of the Ninth Symphony, was unique in its disregard of rule. Psychologically viewed, the sonata-form is much richer in content, and unravels the most wonderful mazes. Here is the history of the re-constituted sonata-form ; a history which is too complicated to run in a straight line.

Down to Op. 10 on the whole we stand on the classical ground of the sonata. In the three Sonatas, Op. 10, appear the first important irregularities. Both in the first and in the second Sonatas there is, in the "free" part, a quite new theme introduced, which points to a definite design ; and in the third we find that wonderful D minor movement, with its utter abandonment to melancholy, which by means of a stretto [1] in the Largo raises itself absolutely out of the contemporary style. Yet all this was new only in tone ; it was no more absolutely new in idea than the Grave of the Pathétique or the Variation Sonata with its Marcia Funebre, where the middle section is introduced by means of realistic drum-reverberations.

An essential change is to be observed in the two sonatas Op. 27. We are at the beginning of the nineteenth century, not far from the time of the composition of the Eroica Symphony. Beethoven was fully conscious of the freedom of these sonatas (E flat major and C sharp minor): he inscribed both "Sonata quasi una fantasia." In the E flat major a dainty andante movement meets us, whose voices are strongly interwoven. It develops itself slightly,

---

[1] The student is not likely to find the passage marked with this word, but the author is none the less correct in his description, for it must be played so.

Lyser's Sketch of Beethoven.

in variation manner, but it is interrupted, once by a sustained melody, again by a stormy episode in C major. What has become of the rondo with its couplets? There follows the apparition of a rolling, beating, gigantic scherzo, beginning in C minor and ending in C major. The C (always *attacca subito*) prepares us for the bright A flat major adagio, which gently takes us up till the whole idea is exhausted. Finally we have the wholesome, powerful, and busy E flat major movement, arranged in free rondo-form, with its stirring reminiscences of the adagio. The twin sonata in C sharp minor is the so-called Moonlight, with its classical first movement, which was a unique expression of melancholy; and which, only slightly interrupted by the episodic allegretto, breaks out again into the despair of the presto agitato, which we have learnt to know as one of the most deeply tragical of Beethoven's outbursts. Of a sonata as a regular composition there was here no further idea. These were transcripts from experiences.

The experiences of Beethoven's life in the following period, so far as they are recorded in the diary of the piano-sonatas, exhibit a certain archaic character. In this period from 1803-4 (the period of Op. 31) to 1811 (Op. 81 a) lie the most varied tendencies in confusion. It is a mighty attempt in all possible paths, but the reader will soon see that every path leads to a definite goal. In all the paths there is an attempt to grasp certain great elementary principles, which lie outside the direct development, and which are made subservient to the new spirit.

This archaism of form appears first as an application of old forms to modern purposes. In the G major (Op. 31, 1) we are surprised by strange retrogressions — which yet are not mere retrogressions. The rosy coloration of the adagio draws past recollections into new life. The third movement shows us Bach's application of the pedal bass, transfigured by passing through the mind of Beethoven. In Op. 31, 3 the minuet returns again, and in other passages, with their simply-cut melodies on "Alberti" basses[1] we seem to have gone back a generation. In the "easy" sonata (Op. 49) and the "Ländler" (Op. 79) this tendency reaches its height. It is a return to nature; a growth of simplicity, in all points, however trifling; the reaction experienced by every mature genius. Beethoven never wholly lost this tendency to reaction. He became in his later days more Mozartian than he had been even in his youth, and more of a Bach than Bach himself.

The second path leads us back not to the form but to the essential nature of Beethoven's youthful period. The delicate work of the porcelain age lives again in him; above all in the charming F sharp major Sonata, of which he himself was so fond. It is quite extraordinary how in Beethoven the spirit of a past time receives life under astonishingly new forms. This graceful filigree-work, with its sweeping unearthly conclusion in the first

---

[1] See Op. 31, No. 3, first movement in E flat, bar 46 and ff.

section,[1] built entirely on delicate inspirations, piquant harmonies, dainty modulations—has wonderfully shot up in such colour, as autumn blossoms only can offer. Take next the famous Les Adieux, dedicated to his pupil, the Archduke Rudolf (E flat major). It shows a delight in the minute and the intimate, such as we meet in old Dutch pictures. There is not a passing-note, not a modulation, which was not worked under the magnifying glass. I should myself not like to omit the last movement, known as the " Wiedersehen."

The beautiful characteristics of the "Absence" Sonata are well known; the various metamorphoses of the three descending notes, more or less obvious, but always helping to enlarge the meaning of the first idea [see, for instance, in the first Adagio, bar 7; also the bass of each phrase from bar 10 (third quaver) to the first double bar; then in the Allegro, bars 19-21, in the bass, and the semibreves just before the repeat; also in the " free " part after the repeat mark; and 13 bars from the end of the movement, left hand, etc.], the meaning of a dreary longing, which Beethoven tries to portray in the " Lebewohl " movements. The tender expression of the Andante, the trembling joy and almost over-powering delight of the " Wiedersehen," the sweet charm of the delicate prolongation of this movement at the *Poco andante* near the close, all these cannot but deserve mention here. Of course there was nothing new in having three movements labelled with such names as these. What *was* new was the inner unity which was attained in this piece, and which was only equalled by the delicacy of the workmanship itself. To this (so to speak) archaic and delicate style was added the world-embracing Art which found its proper field in the C major (Waldstein, Op. 53) and the F minor (Appassionata, Op. 57) sonatas. Thus was the proper foundation laid for the grandiose poems of the last six Sonatas, which lead the three streams into one course.

The first of these (Op. 90) is in two movements, like the last :

---

[1] Apparently the passage referred to is the 10 bars which precede the second subject, in the first movement of the F sharp major sonata.

the first, a thoughtful and restful movement without reprise, with a new motive in its development; the second, a slow rondo, embracing the parts of the theme fugally. It is a work which, like all these last sonatas, is never thought of as a "piece," but stands before us in one transparency, laying bare the inmost fibres of the man.

In Op. 101 an unparalleled height of thematic development is attained. Rhythmical motives are plentiful; the smoothly flowing six-eight time; the same with accent completely displaced (as in bar 29, etc.); the vigorous dotted quaver and semiquaver of the Vivace; the prominent formula of the section in B flat in the same movement, etc. As before in the Appassionata, the boundaries between first and second themes fade away before the consciousness of their unity. The Sonata exhibits thematic in all its forms. The fugue half changes into the rondo, free in expression, lively in character. An unearthly sweep of music, born tone by tone, rolls over us; the *e a* of the motive is its air-built scaffolding. It is the streaming forth of the most inward intuition of tone; a special kind of absolute naturalism, which yet enfolds in itself the future of music. We think of the "Bagatelles," which Beethoven wrote and published at this time, cabinet-pieces of remarkably genuine character.

Then suddenly rises before us the "Grand Sonata" (Op. 106). We recognise no longer the old well-known features. It has assumed the forms of the giant-world; it laughs in its greatness, in its childlikeness. Will it really permit itself to be played by human hands? We are at the mysterious limits of piano-music. Rhythms marked by sharp blows, modulations in thirds, enharmonics, narrow-cut successions of chords[1]—these are the very hand of Beethoven. The first movement works with its three themes—an Olympian poem—as far as the *stretto*. Its development rests on a fugal foundation. The scherzo is all rhythm; in the trio, it is all unrhythmical; mystical colours, sliding

---

[1] Things corresponding to these expressions, which convey scarcely anything in themselves, will be found in this order in bars 1-3; bars 5, 6, 9, 10; bars 25, 26; bar 18, et cetera, of the first movement; and will illustrate the author's system of description.

passages from B flat minor to D flat major, as in the Ninth Symphony from D minor to B flat major. The Adagio is so to speak the last possibility of the old form, wide as life itself, Michael Angelo-like in its strenuous longing for F sharp major. The transitional passage, the Largo, which introduces the last movement, like an old Toccata, tries this and that, prelude-wise, and striving after fixed forms. The three-voiced giant-fugue is the deliverance, in whose retardations the old storm, how-ever, still conceals itself. But there is a joy in the mighty strain-ing of these dissonances, which Bülow ought not to have tried to soften. Theme and counter-theme, "cancrizans" canon,[1] lyrical episodes, dainty counter-motives, inversions, new canonic motives, tied up again with the fugue, contrary motions, diminutions. This old lofty tone speech remained serious; it is the refuge of the anchorite who turns back to the powers of Nature, and finds rest in the wise observation of the stars. It is the utmost of art for art. Who is there whom it troubles?

Three flowers bloom in this late garden, three unique docu-ments of a pure masterdom: the "playing" sonata, the "land-scape" sonata, the "life" sonata. The first is on the heights of pure technique, the second is a clarified objective picture, the third is pure subjective inwardness.

Op. 109 opens with a graceful impromptu-like harp-play of broken chords, which twice thicken themselves in recitative songs. A somewhat hard sounding scherzo stands in the midst. It is closed by the variations on that never-to-be-forgotten melody in E major, which, through reflective romance, cheerful étude-like activity, sober fugues, bright trill-heights, lead back to the capti-vating simplicity of their theme. The freedom of the first move-ment and the confinement of the second are both made use of by the third.

---

1 "Cancrizans" (*cancer*, a crab), is an adjective applied to a tune that is the *same* whether you play it from the beginning to the end, or the reverse way. Here it is used to characterise some rather mild reversions of the theme, *e.g.*—first section with two sharps, bars 15-17.

We have a landscape in the A flat major (Op. 110). Over the sward rises the tender song. Butterflies and sun-glitter are the accompaniment. A wholesome strength mounts up and cheerfully wings its way. In a pause of meditation it comes to rest; and from the contemplation rises the old eternal lamentation of man. From its last breathed tones ascends the fugue, the great law of nature. Once again the lament, broken, helpless, dashing itself blindly against fate—and all the more dazzling is the fugue, embracing all, Truth with its disregard of the individual.[1] Thus does Beethoven express his pantheism.

But even this sonata seems feeble in comparison with the unheard-of intensity and greatness of Op. 111. The master sits at the piano, and his hands run preluding over the keys, in broad, piercing, dashing chords, which become closer and intenser round the node-point of the dominant. From the dominant grows a theme of savage grandeur, of Titanic power, all-embracing in its widening grasp, its Medusa-locks flying in the air, crushing out all sweetness and softness, till, as it came, it sinks terribly to earth, in those helpless *diminuendo* chords,[2] with no *ritardando*, such as Beethoven alone experienced. In the elemental song of the Adagio comes the release. In its variations it spreads itself out into a world-embracing grandeur, till its wisdom attains the two extremes of deep internal ardour and ethereal brightness, whose opposition is developed in the last pages in broad lines. The earth remains below; the minor conclusions are forgotten; the forms have become a twilight dream; only when *our* soul meets the Master-Soul does man attain to these realms.

At this time the inventive composer-publisher Diabelli had a good idea. He composed a childish waltz in C major, and invited fifty of the most distinguished composers and virtuosos of Vienna and the Austrian states to be kind enough to set variations to it.

---

[1] This appears to be a subtle reference to the "inversion" of the subject when the fugue is resumed. The "individual" must learn to see things right side up, knowing they are upside down !

[2] Thirteen bars from the end of the movement. *N.B.*—A curious instance of "cribbing" on the part of Chopin stands confessed in the following passage.

Beethoven sent him thirty-three variations, which appeared as Op. 120. Diabelli may well have been astonished. He had perhaps some dread of the "last" Beethoven who was then so full of youth. But he had not expected anything of this kind. Perhaps he did not quite know whether it was all done in earnest. Even the name of Beethoven did not aid the venture much. The world during many years troubled itself little about it, and let the strange colossus alone. It was reserved for Bülow, who had the keenest sense for the last efforts of Beethoven's genius, to penetrate deeply into the great mass. He observed that the thirty-three variations are no co-ordinated series; they are an inner drama, like one of the later sonatas. They rise from the explanatory sections which lay out the theme, through a gentle minor group, by a double fugue, into calmer regions; a minuet concludes, which is no minuet, but one of those wonderful resurrections which were the old Master's special love. The variations are a testament, as the Goldberg variations were those of Bach. From melody to canon, from gloom to parody, from archaism to anticipations of the future, from popularity to the philosophy of the hermit, from mysticism to dance, from technical glitter to the mystery of enharmonics, they lead us along three and thirty paths to different realms.

Beethoven's last Grand Piano, by Graf, Vienna, with four strings to each note, on account of his deafness.

Viennese pianoforte players about 1800.

Eberl.   Gelinek.   Wölffl.

The Virtuosos

BEETHOVEN'S playing was naturalistic. In him there were no tricks of technique to be admired, no mere virtuosity to praise; but the hearers were stirred to their hearts. In this storm and stress, this whispering and listening, this awakening of the soul, they recognised an original naturalism of piano-playing, standing by the side of the naturalism of his creative art. Rhythm was the life of his playing. He thought out all technique with a view to rhythm. In the Berlin Library is a collection of Cramer's Études, containing a series of annotations by Schindler, the well-known biographer of Beethoven. The expressions are so remarkable that the spirit of Beethoven has not unjustly been detected in them. Shedlock, in fact, has published them simply as Beethoven's elucidations of Cramer, whose Études the Master is known to have prized exceedingly. In every Étude the *melos*, or latent melodic air, which lies at the base of the figurations, is brought into prominence, and the rhythmical presentation of these figurations is made as accurate as possible. The rest is for the most part left to the time, the diligence, and the ability of the player. Thus could a great creator look at Études. Of necessity he looked at them from a totally different point of view from the virtuoso pure and simple. He cared chiefly for the presentation of the idea, for the inwardness of the piece. Everything that was written down in concrete notes served to him but as a means for that expression, the mastery of which was the mastery of interpretation. From this point of view Beethoven would have written his " Klavierschule," of which he often spoke in his latter years. With mere fingering and wrist action he would have had little indeed to do.

This great task was undertaken by a band of artists who must not be undervalued. They stood in the first rank of virtuosos. It is precisely at this time that technique first properly arises as an art ; and their zeal in the attempt to solve the new problem was great indeed. They discover new possibilities of expression, they disclose new effects in the capacities of the pianoforte, and they reveal an inventive power in these new paths which offers the most surprising beauties. We must consider them from the right side, and never forget that the development of the piano could never have taken place so naturally and organically unless its technical advance had gone on in parallel lines with its spiritual progress.

I have here no other aim than to view things under a certain *species aeternitatis*. What was done by Bird, Bull, Couperin, or Pasquini, though to-day perhaps only one in a thousand piano-players knows their names, was of more importance than a Polacca of Kalkbrenner or an Étude of Ludwig Berger. We have a fixed horizon ; what is not within it remains outside it. Lives of entire and rich content, sorrows and joys of extreme intensity, may sink into oblivion ; they are in history a mere grain in the quicksand. It is useless to look up in my index the name of everybody who has composed a Rondo or given piano-lessons in Moscow. We must content ourselves with those who, by the great halting-places, have deserved a monument on the way : those only without whom history would offer a distinct blank.

A very great work is represented by the theoretical piano-schools, which followed one another at this time in close succession. If in the little book of Philip Emanuel Bach there was the beginning of a unifying system, on which the following age had only to build, yet, in the face of the most varying theories of the first half of our century, we can but recognise that piano-teaching, from mere excess of zeal, never succeeded in developing a genuine system. It has always been the tendency of the piano-teacher to keep in the past an ideal to worship, while with the present he has such a poor understanding that every new method of instruction makes a *tabula rasa* of the preceding method, begins all afresh, and allows the pupil salvation only according to its private judgment. Piano-study has never enjoyed the advantage possessed by other sciences, of building up from century to century, each upon the last. In theory it has remained a mere mosaic ; and it has been saved only by practice.

It is practice also that gives a certain systematisation, not to the teaching, but to the history of teaching. All the separate workers at the great task, little as they admit the possibility of salvation outside their own creed, are yet driven forward by the stream of time and by the results of experience ; and the law of averages brings about a clear advance apart from their personal agency. If we compare the systems of the eighteenth century, the schools of Philip Emanuel, of Marpurg, and that of Daniel Gottlob Türk, which closes this series, with the works of the epoch on which we have now entered, we see clearly how practice has marked out the path for theory, always reflecting upon itself, itself inducing its decomposition into its constituent *à priori* and empirical parts, and finally limiting itself to a mere application of experience.

The Pianoforte School which was written by Adam was a kind of pronunciamento of the Paris Conservatoire. This Conservatoire, founded in the midst of the troubles of the Revolution, ultimately gave French technique a position to which for a long time it had been a stranger. Adam's principle is to put the "manieren" more on one side, and to avoid that too eager devotion to the teaching of general composition with which the books of the eighteenth century had been occupied. In its place he brings the study of touch more prominently forward. The day of the spinet is over; the hammer-clavier now dominates the world, and leads theorists to attempt methods of touch which may correspond to its possibilities of delicate expression. The pedals also begin to play their part. Adam recognises four pedals, of which one is our damper-raiser, and three serve for soft effects. Gradually they have been reduced to two, the damper-raiser and the so-called "soft" pedal.

A great opponent of all use of the pedal was Hummel. In our time it is no longer necessary to point out that the pedal, an integral part of the hammer-clavier, deserves not to be rejected, but simply to be treated on its own artistic lines. But Hummel stands, in his theoretic relations, so strongly on the foundations of tradition, that his attitude can excite no surprise. His "Ausführliche theoretisch-praktische Anweisung zum Pianofortespiel," which appeared in 1828, is the crown of the united exertions of piano theory. This voluminous work, which gained with difficulty a circulation that it soon lost for ever, is a system, carried out into the minutest details, of all the technical capacities of the piano; so systematic, indeed, that here theory, by deductive methods, discovered effects which practice could not have attained alone. It is an unparalleled example of theoretic speculation, and yet really nothing more than the extension of Marpurg's or Türk's old-fashioned methods. These countless headings in capital letters, each describing a different class of "passage," these numbered possibilities of fingering, these pedantic elucidations, beginning always from the first over again, are nothing but, as he calls them, an "Anweisung," mere directions, abstraction from reflection outward. Any one who has mastered the first part has the second already at his fingers' ends, but this master of dissection troubles himself not a whit on that point, and knows no economy in pupilage. He is opposed to learning by heart, since the fingers, he says, ought to find the keys without sight : so far is he from the modern view that only a complete mastery of a piece renders adequate interpretation possible. He troubles himself little about a science of touch. He introduces the " manieren " ; but, contrary to the method of the eighteenth century, he makes the trill begin on the upper note. So far is a system of execution from his purpose that he can actually write as follows : " Runs

The Brothers Pixis. 1800.
Engraved by Sintzenich after Schröder.

and notes going upwards are executed crescendo, downwards diminuendo; but there are cases in which the composer intends the reverse, or that they should be played with even strength." Hummel's book is to-day a monument of misguided diligence, great in its patient calculation of permutations, but a dead curiosity.

If, on the other hand, we look at Kalkbrenner's Paris Pianoforte School, which he dedicated "to all the conservatoriums in Europe," we see—with no heavy artillery—advances of all kinds which in part fill up the perspective of Adam. Where Hummel has ten main classes of fingered passages, he has only six ; five-finger exercises for the unmoving hand ; scales in all forms ; thirds, sixths, and chord-forms ; octaves with the wrist ; trills ; over-lapping of the hands. In this there is more thrift, while there is no talk of absolute completeness. The " manieren " slowly cease to occupy important chapters ; the pedals again come by their own ; for Kalkbrenner as a Parisian hates the dry tone of the Vienna pianoforte. Execution also begins to receive a systematic treatment. Interesting references are made to punctuation in order to illustrate musical phraseology ; conclusions on the tonic are a full stop ; on the dominant a semicolon ; while interrupted cadences are a note of exclamation. This is naive enough, but it is at any rate a beginning.

We are thus already standing at the point at which clavier theory decomposes itself into its elements. If Hummel was the great theoretician, Czerny was the great man of practice ; a quite unique person, the hero of all piano-teachers, whose practical eye runs equally over all the possibilities of playing, and works them out in separate parts ; the genius of the Étude. He it was who discovered the great secret that no separation of methods of fingering is of any avail in practice, but that the perfection of the fingers must be carried out solely on the basis of their mechanical gymnastic. It is useless to try to apply my five fingers to so many theoretically possible permutations ; the im-portant question is what practical use can be made of my fingers according to their physical structure. Czerny has no obsolete rules of practice, but a science of mechanism ; thus taking the very opposite pole to Hummel. Piano-study, which with Couperin and Philip Emanuel was still a part of a musical training with just the necessary amount of mechanics, became with him primarily the gymnastic of the fingers with the addition of instruction in touch and execution. Long past are the times when the good old clavier was only used to " fill " the song, which was after all the essence of music. From music we have come to the fingers. A science of the fingers is constructed, and the fingers are trained as earlier only the throat was trained. Technique has remembered her own ways, and made the last first. The emancipation of finger-gymnastic was an epoch-marking point in the treatment of the piano, the desired answer of theory to practice, which for a long time had recognised the specific art of the piano. It was perhaps the last important stride in its emancipation when the results of practice were made the groundwork of instruction. Czerny, in his great Pianoforte School, his Opus 500, is almost entirely free from the *à priori* theory. He transfers mechanics to music. With good results he treats individual cases, as for example, when he appends to the beginning of passages a finger-exercise not given in the scale ; he designs immediately to return to the usual fingering in order to arrive duly at the extreme notes with the extreme fingers, and to avoid unnecessary underpassing. It was reserved for a later time not merely to bring the note-material lying before us into harmony with economic fingering, but also to make execution, which with Czerny has but a loose dependence on the finger-exercise, re-act upon the fingers. Bülow, for example, is fond of unusual fingering, in which the execution forbids any too easy playing, and a too loose rendering is prevented by irregularities in the succession of the fingers.

The mechanics of the fingers formed the first part of piano-instruction ; touch and execution were the second. Their importance as means to the mechanism of music was fully seen ; and in the " Technical Studies " of Plaidy, or in Köhler's " Methode für Klavierspiel und Musik " (1857), they are as exhaustively handled as before had been the " manieren " or the thorough-bass. The former contents himself with the simple terms, Legato, Staccato, Legatissimo, and Portamento ; the latter gives a more mechanical division, always according to the use of the fore-arm, the finger-joints, the wrist, or the elbow. Neither is complete, neither supplies a systematic advance on the lines of his predecessors ; and we should be astonished at these divergences if we set the numerous schools of these times, from a theoretical point of view, over against one another. Practically considered, however, they agree well enough. The holding of the hand as enjoined by Philip Emanuel Bach has remained on the whole unaltered down to the present day. With trifling differences, which concern the relation of the extreme fingers to the middle finger, and the profile of the back of the hand, Bach, Türk, Müller, Hummel, Logier, Kalkbrenner and the rest, are at one as to the support of the arm which carries the hand, and of the hand which carries the fingers as they descend. In Paris Logier constructed an instrument to hold the hand in practice, in shape like a bracket, which he named "chiroplast." Kalkbrenner, in his "Guide-mains," introduced some modifications on the chiroplast; but such mechanical contrivances gained no general acceptance. Logier's speciality was his prefatory note that the finger must remain in continual touch with the key. With this was allied that special kind of sensuously charming touch which differentiated the Parisian school from the brilliant playing of the Viennese and the emotional style of the English. That *carezzando*, or stroking of the keys, was a favourite practice of Kalkbrenner and Kontski in Paris. To-day Risler remains perhaps alone in this school with his pure sensuous charm of touch.

If, in the whole great group of technical artists, which is bounded on the one side by Wölffl, Wanhal, Kozeluch, Eberl, in Mozart's generation, and on the other by Thalberg and Liszt in ours, we should look for truly pre-eminent spirits, then we should have remaining Clementi, the father of all technique; Hummel, the inventor of the modern piano-exercise; and Czerny, the genius of teaching. But if we ask for the lines of the motion which runs through this epoch, we observe the victory of a virtuoso impulse, which goes back to Hummel, over a plainer and more intellectual tendency which has its rise in Clementi. The school of Clementi prefers the English pianoforte with its heavier but richer touch; that of Hummel the Viennese, with its lighter tone, which lends itself more easily to effects.

But it is not possible to
draw a sharp line between the
two groups. A Moscheles
serves not less the spirit of
Clementi than that of Hummel. The simplicity of Cramer,
the counterpoint of Klengel,
the plainness of Ludwig Berger,
the intensity of Field, belong
to the circle of Clementi's influence. Berger's pupils, Greu-
lich, Heinrich Dorn, Wilhelm
Taubert, Albert Löschhorn,

Ludwig Berger. Pupil of Clementi ; founder
of a widely influential piano-school at
Berlin. Lithograph by Wildt.

whose studies still live, carry this style down to our own time.
The teaching of Hummel lived on in Ferdinand Hiller, Benedict,
Wilmers, Baake, Ernst Pauer, the Viennese Pixis. While Beeth-
oven left behind him as actual pupils only the Archduke Rudolf
and Ferdinand Ries, a respectable imitator, his temporary pupil
Czerny passed over into the wake of Hummel, and brought the
Viennese style to a final victory. Kalkbrenner, Moscheles, Weber,
Liszt, Thalberg, Döhler, Madame Oury, Madame Pleyel, Theodore
Kullak, Pollini, of whom many belong externally to Clementi's
school, passed as apostles of Viennese technique to all lands from
St Petersburg to London, from Paris to Milan.

Certain traditions of musical coteries and centres of instruction exhibit with this international character some more or less
important local groups. In Prague men adored Tomaschek, the
composer of Eclogues and Rhapsodies ; Dionysius Weber, the first
director of a Conservatorium there ; and his successor Kittl.
From Tomaschek's school proceeded Alexander Dreyschock, the
specialist of the left hand ; Ignaz Tedesco, the "Hannibal of
octaves"; and Schulhoff, the fashionable composer. In the middle
of the century the Prague tradition was upheld by Proksch.

In Frankfort lived Vollweiler, who enjoyed a widespread
renown as a teacher, and later went to St Petersburg ; and Aloys

Schmitt, whose delicate Études have been taken up by Bülow into his great collection of educational pieces.

Vienna alternates, but never loses in wealth. Berlin and St Petersburg as yet produced no fixed or permanent school. Leipzig takes its colour from the foundation of the Conservatorium with Mendelssohn and Moscheles and their fellow-citizen Schumann. England, from Clementi to Moscheles, imported a constant succession of Continental artists. The influence of the Conservatorium runs far and wide. A Strassburger named Hüllmandel, who took up his abode in Paris in 1776, had started clavier-instruction there. His pupil Jadin was director of the piano at the new Conservatoire. For forty-six years after 1797, Adam, whose name we remember because of his improved piano-school, carried on his labours in Paris. He was a tasteful professor, and brought the Parisian renown to its height. Kalkbrenner, the acrobat, succeeded him. Adam's colleague, Pradher, was the teacher of those worst of fashionable composers, Herz, Hünten, Rosellen, shallowest and emptiest of musicians. Within the same walls was a Chopin !

The life of the great virtuosos is a reflection of the unrest inseparable from their calling. It is indeed no longer a life of adventure, as with Marchand and Froberger; there is method in the madness. The life of the executant, no less than the execution, has found its form. The concert-campaigns are the foundation ; the warrior returns to his home at greater and greater intervals ; until at last, when delight in recitals has waned along with the pliancy of the fingers, some resting-place or other is found—a share in a piano-manufactory or a steady round of instruction. During the campaigns instruction also takes a kind of locomotive form ; devoted pupils follow the master, and leave him at fitting places, to pitch their tents there and make room for other peregrinating pupils. Or, on the other hand, pupils swarm from all parts of the earth to a place which the Master is always leaving, but to which he constantly returns—like the summer students of German universities—a type of professional existence of which Liszt's Weimar period gives perhaps the most famous exemplification.

John Field, 1782-1837.
Steel engraving by C. Mayer.

Muzio Clementi (1752 - 1832) was the first to exhibit this form of virtuoso-life on the great scale. Born in Italy, he found a home in London through the support of a wealthy Englishman; but he was far from showing the sedentary character of a Bach, a Couperin, or a Beethoven. Virtuosity impels to travel, as composition keeps a man at home. The difference which we observed between the sensitive anchorite Bach and the cosmopolitan popularity-hunter Handel, appears again between Beethoven and these executants. Mozart was too many-sided, and besides he died too young, to become a universal teacher of the piano; but Clementi lived almost three generations, during which half Europe grouped itself round him and his pupils. Down to 1780 he was still "cembalist" at the London Italian opera; during the next ten years he undertook two great tours, one to Vienna, the other to Paris. Meanwhile he became partner in an English piano-firm, which failed, whereupon he founded one of his own along with Collard. He set out for St Petersburg with his pupil Field; left him there; but on the way gained two new pupils, Berger and Klengel, whom also he established in St Petersburg. On one of his tours at Berlin he married, only to lose his wife shortly after. In 1810 he made another circular tour through Vienna and Italy. He spent another whole winter in Leipzig, and married a second time. His last years, when the world had outgrown him, he spent quietly in London.

In the life of Hummel (1778-1837), the favourite pupil of Mozart, posts as kapellmeister with Esterhazy, in Stuttgart and in Weimar, with a longer, unattached residence at Vienna, regulated the varying domiciles at which he lived. Weimar, as a great resting place, enjoyed through him its first musical renown, which reached half through the period of Goethe. In the intervals he took his concert-tours to Dresden, Paris, Holland, Berlin, Belgium, England, Scotland, and St Petersburg. These, as far as the furloughs of a kapellmeister permitted, recurred with a certain regularity, till they gradually ceased entirely.

Cramer (1771-1858) had two long stays in London, in the midst of which a sojourn at Paris occupied the years from 1832 to

Marcelline Czartoryska, *née* Princess Radziwill, pupil of Czerny.
Engraved by Marchi.

1845. He found a secondary occupation in a London musical house, in which he was a partner from 1828 to 1842. Kalk-brenner (1784-1849), on the contrary, lived in Paris, but his residence there was interrupted by a nine years' stay in London (1814-1823). He too had secondary interests. He was concerned with Logier in a company for the exploitation of the "Chiroplast," and he had also a share in a piano-factory. Moscheles (1794-1870) had no business. His external life was made up of his youthful time in Vienna with Beethoven and Meyerbeer, his sensational Parisian recitals of 1820, his glorious stay in London from 1821 to 1846, and his professoriate at the Leipzig Conservatorium. At intervals, of course, he made Continental concert-tours.

Among all the great virtuosos and teachers only Czerny had a really fixed abode (1791-1857). As a boy of fifteen he was already a teacher in Vienna, and as such he died there ; his tours also being few and far between.

Prince Louis Ferdinand.
Engraved by Geiger after Grassy.

But Czerny is in this respect an exception. Otherwise the international play of virtuosity led to an exchange and co-operation, to the mutual curiosity and desire to learn, which mark the concert-life of that age. Duet-playing by great executants, in private or in the concert-hall, is nothing unusual throughout this time. But the genuine interpreter does not as yet exist. The player has mostly a personal interest in the piece performed, and the friends assist at the christening. It is the time of the Hexameron. Exchange is often even too self-abnegatory. Moscheles

composed for Cramer (with whom, as also with Ries and Kalkbrenner, he often played duets) a last movement for Cramer's own
sonata for two pianofortes. Later on he took the piece back again
and tacked it on to his well-known piece, " Hommage à Haendel! "
We need not then be surprised at such gruesome pasticcios
as the programme of a London Philharmonic concert under
Weber,[1] when were played the C sharp minor concerto of Ries,
the E flat major of Beethoven, and the Hungarian Rondo of
Pixis.

The two volumes of " Recollections of the life of Moscheles,"
which his wife compiled from diaries and letters, give a clear view
of the rich international concert-life of this age. Year by year we
follow the kaleidoscopic existence of these artists, who see each
other constantly and constantly part. Triumphs of virtuosity fill
the winter seasons, followed by recreation in the country and pre-
parations for an enlarged repertoire. The halls echo with jubilation and applause ; and the audiences, especially the easily-kindled
Viennese, are enthusiastic in their cheers. Music has become so
popular and the compositions are so extraordinarily banal that it
certainly did not often occur that they were rejected for shallowness—although, on the other hand, Kalkbrenner's experience with
a Beethoven symphony at a Paris Conservatoire concert was a sad
warning to those who try to improve the public taste. The dilet-
tantes push forward the more, the circle of instruction widens the
cheaper and better the pianos become. They push themselves
into rivalry with the artists in great concerts ; as Moscheles relates
of the celloist Sir William Curtis and the pianists Oom and Mrs
Fleming. " I have to hear so much insipid music." " Musique
mise à la portée de tout le monde." From professional piano-
playing—and they often played at two places in an evening—
the artists took recreation with the good temper which never failed
in those years. The great singer Malibran would sit down to the
piano and sing the Rataplan and the Spanish songs, to which
she would imitate the guitar on the keyboard. Then she would

[1] Weber conducted the Philharmonic in 1826, in which year he died.

imitate famous colleagues, and a Duchess greeting her, and a Lady
So-and-so singing " Home Sweet Home " with the most cracked
and nasal voice in the world. Thalberg would then take his seat
and play Viennese songs and waltzes with " obligato snaps."
Moscheles himself would play with hand turned round, or with
the fist ; perhaps under the fist disguising the thumb, which in

Marie Charlotte Antoine Josephe, Countess of Questenberg.

Moscheles' peculiar way of playing used to take the thirds under
the palm of the hand.

These players preferred to play their own compositions. The
separation between composer and virtuoso was not yet complete.
Of course, when Ferdinand Hiller in his " Life of an Artist " says
that he had never heard either Hummel or Chopin, Thalberg or
Moscheles, play a piece by another composer, his experience was
at least unique. Moscheles, for example, even played Scarlatti on

the old harpsichord. But, as a rule, they abode by the old custom, so far at least as amateurs were not concerned. These latter were in their instruction-books liberally provided with historical material.

Improvisation also flourished in concerts and soirées; and playing and composing, which in improvisation form a true union, can only with difficulty be severed in an age of creative virtuosos. Kalkbrenner composed while playing, and played while composing, so that no one could tell the difference between the two; and Czerny used to invent the necessary étude in the midst of the lesson. Thus it happened—a state of things unparalleled to-day —that the beloved duet-playing could be combined with the equally beloved improvisation—mutually contradictory as they appear. Moscheles speaks of an improvised duet with Mendelssohn. The latter played in the bass some English songs in ballad-style; the former interwove in the treble the scherzo of his friend's A minor symphony.

Slight as was the advance yet made in division of labour between player and composer, there was equally little comprehensive division between the species of music. We do not hear of chamber-music evenings, pianoforte evenings, orchestral concerts. All was mingled in one; and chamber-music finds the same audience as the symphony. A piano-recital without orchestra was a rarity; and the concerto-form is almost *de règle* in all the greater performances. This is seen in the compositions of this period, which, as a rule, so far as they are specially adapted to public performance, were written for orchestral accompaniment. By their side were editions for private use, including the important orchestral portions. This concerto-piece could not greatly or permanently aid in the advance of a delicate or intimate piano-music. Through the rarity of special piano recitals it was not so easy to get pianos when they were wanted. In Frankfort there lived a well-known old lady who had absolutely the only piano store in the city. People had to praise her playing, to blow the trumpet of advertisement for her wares (they were Streicher's), to court her and cringe to her in order to get an instrument for a concert.[1]

In 1837 Moscheles ventured to introduce piano-evenings without orchestra. This was an important step. But even yet the evening was not wholly devoted to the piano. A soprano or contralto filled the gap between one performance and the next. How long was it before the serious nature of a concert was universally acknowledged! Possibly here the production of dubious works of the performer's own led to a low, acrobatic conception of the true state of affairs; and it was only the interpretation of good works by others, which were more serious, that saved taste from complete degeneration. The public gradually became quiet, and felt itself turned from educator into educated. The court ceases to take its supper during the playing;[2] the cantatrice no longer concludes her *roulades* with a smile worthy of the circus; and a singer is no longer hissed off the stage if he forgets to give his hand by way of thanks to his fair partner. Slowly it is realised that the concert is not a place for showing off, nor a mere form of social amusement, but a religious service.

This composite structure of virtuosity carried to the extent of vapidity, and of interpretation carried into historical research, is reflected in the compositions of the period. On the one side the tradition was exactly carried on; people began to view the existing classical works—Mozart's and Beethoven's Sonatas, or all kinds of pieces by Scarlatti, Bach, and Handel, as material for study; they republished half-forgotten or badly edited authors like Scarlatti; they even wrote sonatas "in the style of Scarlatti"; they arranged for the piano great quantities of the most various chamber or orchestral music. Alongside of the historical tendency stands, as so often, the international. Spanish, Irish, Russian, Italian, Polish national airs and rhythms are taken *en*

[1] This sort of thing is by no means without example in our own time. The difficulty is very commonly solved in English towns even of the size of Frankfort, by having pianos sent from London.

[2] But the best bred evening party still (in London at least) shouts at the top of its voice when it "hears a master play." See "Punch," and Du Maurier, *passim*. A striking illustration of the vulgarity of modern manners.

masse into the circle of salon music; the air swarms with Polonaises, Boleros, Gipsy airs, Ecossaises, Tarantelles. But this quite cosmopolitan music was stamped by a *fade* enthusiasm for beauty; and there is bound up with the pieces an empty sentimental greeting or a hypocritical reminiscence. The mythological titles of the seventeenth century, and the realistic ones of the eighteenth, yield to the sentimental ones[1] of the bourgeois empire. But never was this system of naming pieces on a lower level; and never did it so corrupt the taste of the believing multitude. Even to-day we are not yet freed from its traces. Then there are the "Hommages à Beethoven" or "à Händel" corresponding to the old "Tombeaux," but with less sincerity of intention. Then there are the "Fire pieces"—a whole collection of dedications to fire brigades— the "Burning of Mariazell," and the "Ruins of Wien Neustadt," figure among the salon-music of Czerny. Then follow the geographical recollections—the innumerable souvenirs of all possible towns, rivers, mountains, and people, such as the "Souvenir de mon premier voyage," "les Charmes de Paris," "le Retour à Londres," etc. By their side are genuine characteristic titles chiefly employed to gild the pill of the "study." Most objectionable of all are the favourite opera-fantasias, which are specially in vogue in the Parisian school. These tear the airs almost from the very mouths of the singers, and the composer's completed melodies from his work, and stuff the *pot pourri* with passages, figurations, and fragments of études, with spurious slow introductions and sentimental passages, so that finally absolutely nothing of the essence of the original airs is left. These are perhaps the worst examples of want of style and taste to be found in the history of art. Here the curse of popularity came home to roost; here was reached the extreme point, in the publicity of the concert and of society, which the clavier had to pass through since the development of the hammer-mechanism. Any harshness in an artistic work was sufficient to condemn it; invention was tabooed; smooth-

---

[1] The author means "Pearls of the Ocean," "Fairy Revels," "Convent Bells," and such like.

ness and the tickling of the ear were the only law. What in Paris was done by Herz, Hünten, Karr, Rosellen, Kontski, and their fellows, made a great sensation, and quickly vanished. Hünten received for a moderate-sized work from fifteen hundred to two thousand francs; to-day he is banished even from the salon. Karr wrote to order hundreds of pieces; to-day no amateur knows a single one out of the huge mass. And the days in which Kontski's "Reveil du lion" was put in the hands of pupils appear to be past for ever.

The interdependence of piano and opera was not merely external. In Paris the opera, with its world-ruling influence, not merely forms a musical centre to which everything gravitates; it is itself subjected to the great law of this period—the law of mosaic work and of the aim to please. In the thirties and forties the world had thus reached hollow ostentation in the grand opera, and in the comic opera mere ballet-dancing. "Where," wrote Wagner at that time, "where has the grace of Méhul, of Isouard, of Boieldieu, and of the young Auber gone, chased out of sight by the abject quadrille rhythms, which to-day rattle through the theatre of the opera comique and keep everything else out?" What was seen there was like what was heard on the pianoforte—pointless situations, introduced for the sake of the "business," tirades which seem to be closed with the smile of the acrobat when he has finished his trick—technique, and nothing but technique. A librettist like Scribe is loaded with commissions, surrounded by Parisian or foreign composers—even Wagner in his youth having once written to him. He understands how to manufacture the proper substratum for the musical triflings. Read from this point of view Auber's later operas, as the "La Part du Diable," or those overtures whose whole structure depends on the fact that they are skilfully adapted to dances; or that daub-work in the musical setting with the jaundiced transition passages, where a proper modulation would be almost out of place; or those boleros, which people sing in circumstances of the utmost grief, without being able to raise themselves to the height of the irony; or those étude colourations, introduced in the most indifferent places provided they pay, and developing themselves vigorously about a single vowel; or those scores, which are so miserably transparent that one can see the author first rapidly composing them at the piano and then putting in the instrumentation slap-dash. It is the first, and let us hope, the last time, that the piano reaches its hand to the opera—a most unfruitful elective affinity. Opera and piano are necessarily and essentially hostile. In the Paris of that day, when absolute music, as well that of Berlioz as that of Chopin, is still a modest retiring flower, the crowd ran after the gentle titillation of the opera, and the mass of piano music moves in the operatic humdrum path. Among the Parisians as among the Italians there was assuredly not an operatic composer who did not invent at the piano and transfer his inventions from the piano to the opera. Donizetti has left an interesting letter to his brother-in-law Vesselli, which was fastened as an inscription on his piano: " Do not sell this piano at any price, for it contains my whole artistic life from 1822 onwards. Its tone lingers in my ears. In it murmur Anna, Maria, Fausta, Lucia. Let it live as long as I live! I lived with it my years of hope, of wedded happiness, of loneliness. It heard my cries of joy, it saw my tears, my disenchantments, my honours. It shared with me my toils and the sweat of my brow. In it dwells my genius, every section of my path. It saw your father, your brother, all of us ; we all have tortured it ; it was a true comrade to us all, and may it always be a comrade to your daughter as a dowry of a thousand sad and happy thoughts."

There seems so much that is contemptible in this technical school that it would almost appear, at least from the artistic point of view, to have lived in vain. And yet it was at this time that a form sprang into existence which, born from technical necessities, became a custom, and from a custom a style, and so emphatically a style that it was able to enter into effective rivalry with the older styles—the contrapuntal, the thematic, the *leit-motif*. We are still under its dominion. This form is the *Étude*.

The Étude was not the invention of the technists.   It existed in germ in Bach ; it half grew out of thematic ; only the visual angle altered with time.   In an invention or symphony of Bach a motive is treated according to the free laws of imitation ; it is used up in all the voices, for all fingers.   In a Prelude on some thematic ground-subject, in a fugue with its stern code of canonic succession, the same is the case : the motive is expended on itself. But between the broken chords of Bach's C sharp Prelude and those of Chopin's C sharp Étude there is a vast difference in the treatment.   What in the one is used with a view to the motive is here expended with a view to the technique.   Bach sets before him the artistic possibilities of the theme : Chopin the mechanical.   Bach wrote many of his preludes with educational purposes ; but he did not compose them with a sole view to their full practical value.   As in theory the musical and the mechanical cannot be sharply severed, so the pieces are half for the purpose of supplying music, half means of instruction.   The mechanical part was obliged first to emancipate itself before the conception of the Étude could be fully grasped.   On the straight line leading from the old thematic to the Étude style, the conception of the motive altered itself.   Motives were now found which could be arranged according to their technical productiveness.   We see perhaps even the same motive, considered first contrapuntally or as a fixed idea, but afterwards according to its mechanical value.

There are motives whose interest lies in the size of the hand ; or in the playing of a legato passage simultaneously with the chords in the same hand ;[1] or again, contrary motion of chords in both hands has to be carried out ; or, yet further, attention is paid to an easy gliding of the hand over great stretches ; or finger-changing on the same key is the ground-idea.   The piece may aim at *cantabile* or at the perfect legato in a *fugato* movement, or at the practice of octaves, pearl-like scales, pianissimo touch, the freedom of the left hand, a double melody, or any of the hundred technical

---

[1] It is convenient to refer these descriptions to Chopin's Studies, though of course they can be paralleled elsewhere.   Cf. Chopin's Studies in C, in A minor, in F, etc.

possibilities. There are dry and insipid methods of thus working out academically a technical idea ; but it is also possible to see in delicate and ingenious ways, slumbering germs of great fruitfulness in the technical motive, and to develop powers of unexpected beauty. The one way sees in a broken chord only the means of using it in major or minor modes, or in the seventh, or in some unusual successions, first for the right hand, then for the left, then for both, and perhaps finally with sustained notes. Theory is satisfied, a practical object provided, the academic conscience laid to rest. But the other way sees in the broken chords their elementary character, the germ of the Rheingold or of the Götterdämmerung. It permits them first to sound slightly, then to grow further and further, to assume a daemonic grandeur ; like eternal signs, to stretch over the heavens and embrace the worlds. Thus, no less than the other, it presents all the *nuances* of major, minor, seventh, right, left, up and down ; but it covers these technical variations so perfectly with the sense of the inner meaning that they become identified, and can never be separated : the technical and the characteristic content have, in the mind of a genius like this, involuntarily become a unity. Such a master, for example, takes the neat finger-changing on one note as the means for a rococo-sketch, the pianissimo leaps for a dance of the elves, the rolling passages in the left hand for the roar of the sea with elemental upper parts ; the rhythmical varieties in left and right for graceful fetters of the dance ; the scurrying glide over the black keys for a picture of homely pleasures. Here reveals itself the entire fruitfulness of the technical setting, which —who could believe it ?—precisely by the limitation of the motive, approaches very near to characteristic art and realism of presentation. Here is a rich field opened to technical subjectivity. Personality is very variously displayed in the setting of a technical idea. Contrast with Clementi, who scarcely ever shows any specific sense of character in a motive, such a man as Hummel, who on theoretic grounds calculates out the utmost technical possibilities of a motive ; or Czerny, who in a practical manner attains the same many-sidedness ; or Cramer, who was the first to find his way back to music from technique ; or Moscheles, Chopin, Schumann, who cannot think technique without feeling character.

Deep and mysterious is this connection between the Étude and its musical setting. Like the fugue the simplest Étude goes back to those elemental foundations which cannot fail of their impression, even if practically nothing is composed upon them. I hear some simple scale-étude of Bertini played, with the smooth harmonies on which it is built. There is nothing in the piece, no soul reveals itself to me, and yet there is a weird charm in these eternal ground-motives of all music, and in their tonics and dominants which are so to speak anchored in eternity. The dull man is soon wearied by them, but the sensitive man instantly responds. At this point the Étude sinks down to the great mother of all music : like the fugue it springs directly out of Nature. With the consciousness of character the Étude grows tuneful. In the studies of Moscheles, in the Symphonic Études of Schumann, in Chopin's studies, art creates what Nature created. From the technical theme rises a certain spiritual aroma, reminding us of a tune, a scene, a land-scape ; the tune condenses itself in the return of the technical motive ; it collects itself all the more narrowly and closely, in pro-portion as all contrasts and secondary tunes keep their distance. It is a spiritual melody, set in a firm frame, as condensed as neither the free fantasia form, nor the thematic sonata, nor the canonic fugue, had ever presented it. The tune is so concentrated that it cannot dispense with the frame, or it would fly to pieces. It has no capacity of transference ; it prefers to exist as a fragment ready-made.

It is thus that the Étude fixes the form. It favours fixed and limited technical models, which fit mosaic-wise into each other. It is opposed to huge, Beethoven-like emotions and their expression ; its horizon does not pass beyond two pages. It is still further removed from Bach's method, which depended on plain thematic development ; it loves the speedy and the limited, and confines itself entirely to the practical. It penetrates into all works in which technical brilliance gives a false impression of the contents, or in which the greatness of the contents only finds its last expression by technique.

The technical setting of the form, and the technical expression, pass over entirely into the consciousness of the time, and create new works in chamber-music, opera, and orchestra.

Compare the development of a sonata by Weber with that of one by Beethoven; for example, Weber's fourth in E minor with Beethoven's Op. 28—two sonatas which in original idea, a soft melodic tune, were not so unlike as they turned out to be. In Beethoven the first melody develops itself on a $\frac{3}{4}$ rhythm, which begins and ends naturally; the second theme is an unforced contrast to the first; gradually figurations attach themselves, which are natural offshoots of them, intertwining themselves without losing their original dependence; all grows logically out of itself; the end is given in the beginning, and the progress in the variation. In Weber, on the contrary, each piece is carried through by itself: the whole is no organism but a mere pasticcio. The sensitive first subject is treated in its naked melodic beauty; a semiquaver passage is attached to it; a bald enharmonic study leads on to the second theme, which treats its soothing character from many sides; and only the " free " section brings the whole a little closer together. And we know how even in the best men of this period the great creative organism, in which every part conditions its own subordinate part, gives place to a mere isolation and to total want of system. In the concertos, after the traditional mutual compliments of orchestra and piano, the solo instrument starts, with surprising suddenness, on its passages, which are strung together from étude-pieces, selected haphazard. At the conventional places the curtain is withdrawn, and the whole glitter of technique is displayed. The harsh transitions, the quick returns, the jostling fugues, are not only a peculiarity, say, of Schumann—they are the style of the time. They are the *framing* style of a time which does not care for the want of restraint that attends great emotions.

Its preference is for constructive logic in detail. More genuine piano music than the Étude there cannot be. The essence of the piano has in it become music. Matter and aim here alone determine the form, which no longer speaks merely in a universal musical language.

The piano follows the lines of the time, which pursues technical purity in all things. In the representative arts certain styles were long seen to predominate, which for limited periods were indifferently transferred to all objects without respect to matter or aim. Renaissance, Gothic, antique, exhibit their churches, their tombs, their doors, their tables, their cupboards, their keys, whether they are bosses or reliefs, marbles or bronzes. In our century technique begins to speak its first word: a chair is to be a chair; a carpet shall be constructed with a view to the aim of carpets; a vase must speak in accordance with the material of vases; and painting must in the first instance be painting. A cupboard is not an entrance to a temple; a table leg not a statue. These are intrusions which art has not often experienced in its history. With music the case was not dissimilar. The fugal style ruled once so mightily that it drew church, dance, salon, fantasia, tune, all indifferently, under its sway. The good fugue was a good tune, and the best tune could only be expressed in contrapuntal form. Now, however, the emancipation had taken place. The organ no longer worked necessarily along with the piano, nor the song with the violin; and the orchestra became conscious of its power as a totality. What the Venetians had once timidly begun was now carried into actual fact; and the artistic form of the étude was the seal of this individualising process. The much-praised Paganini had no longer, like Corelli, to prompt the piano, as far as its content was concerned, from the violin outwardly. Paganini-études, by Schumann, were strict piano-pieces, which as far as form went borrowed nothing from Paganini, and in matter only a groundwork of notes. They strive towards the brilliancy of Paganini's execution—that astonishing, spiritual technique, which aroused so wonderfully the emulation of a Liszt.

Clementi. Engraved by Neidl
after Hardy.

And in turn there passed from the piano the brilliancy of a technique which inspired the orchestra to its own special triumphs. The "Queen Mab," the "Mephistopheles," the "Feuer-Zauber," and the "Valkyries' Ride" did not need to envy the piano. Yet without the fame of the Étude they would never have been so brilliant.

We are now coming nearer the personalities themselves. It is no long stride from the virtuosos to the romantic writers; the latter are only to be explained by reference to the former. We pass slowly from the domain of pure virtuosity to that of compositions of deeper meaning; from the realm of the teacher to that of the poet; from piano purism to the longing after poetic interdependence; from the noise of concerts to the intimate retirement of the home.

In Clementi these signs appeared first. What he had to say was little; but what he had to teach was only the more in consequence. He collected, he tested, he drew out his experiences, and never willingly abandoned the historical attitude. This was the first recoil on the classical period. Clementi's Studies were so fruitful that even a Beethoven was not unmoved by them; although of course there were many who opposed themselves to his speciality, the passages in thirds and sixths for one hand. Mozart hated this unrest; he aimed at a graceful and easy style. But the growth of technique soon shook off this old-fashioned rococo method; it aimed at universal conquest.

As Clementi still lives in what we may call his *"grand-pupils,"* so his Gradus ad Parnassum has remained the father of all Étude-works, often reprinted, often re-edited. It is easy to recognise in it its antiquated constituent parts. No principle of distinction is adopted between the fingering of diatonic and chromatic scales. In his directions Clementi begins his chromatics with *E*. The Études move in a peculiar middle region between compositions and exercises. Single Études, like the splendid Presto in F sharp minor, reach the heights of a Cramer (Simrock, 24). He even provides genuine fugues in order that the fugal style may also be practised. In one Étude (Simrock, 38) cantabile and triplets are mingled as exercises. Often again three pieces appear together as a suite — a patriarchal retention of old customs. Others again are mere dry and insipid instruction-exercises. We follow with pleasure the process by which fixed technical problems gained in content as time went on. For example, the change of finger on one key is in Clementi a mere tedious motive with three notes only (Simrock, 20). In Cramer (Pauer, 41 ff) is already perceived the charm which short held notes may introduce into this monotonous exercise ; and the drollery which a change of fingers as the characteristic motive carries concealed in itself, gives the character to the piece. Chopin, in his well-known C major study (Op. 10, 7), gives us a good example of this scheme of fingering, which is carried out strictly, the alternation of thumb and first finger never being interfered with, even on the black keys, in spite of the various awkward chords that occur. Thus he gives perfect freedom to the piquant turns and droll character of the piece without to any extent spoiling its effectiveness as an Étude.

Over against the Gradus of Clementi, as a remarkable collection of the most varied pieces, stand certain smaller studies of a more defined physiognomy. The well-known "Préludes et Exercices" are written in all the keys, and keep on the whole to the scale-motive. The "Méthode du Pianoforte," with its fifty lessons, collects all kinds of airs and old pieces, provided with marks of fingering—which, however, are very much behind those of Czerny. The book is noteworthy as one of the first important attempts to make use of already existing pieces, not the work of the collector, as material for studies. Very soon the sonatas of Beethoven appear in these collections, where they are arranged according to their difficulty. Here are Handel, Corelli, Mozart, Couperin, Scarlatti, Pleyel, Dussek, Haydn, Paradies, and the Bachs.

Clementi sowed his wild oats in a series of preludes and cadenzas which he published (Op. 19) under the title of " Characteristic Music." These were written in the styles of certain masters and other famous clavier-teachers, such as Haydn, Kozeluch, Vanhall, Mozart, Sterkel, and Clementi himself. It was half a jest, and a very moderately successful one ; but it is worth noticing as a sign of an interpretative and compiling tendency.

Among the hundred sonatas and sonatinas, for one or two players, which Clementi left behind, there is not a single one without interest or utility from the standpoint of instruction ; but from that of content there is at most only one which can to-day attract us by its originality or genius. This is the so-called Dido sonata, dedicated to Cherubini ; and even in it the genius is cold. In the other sonatas we see the body of a Beethoven without the soul. It is Scarlatti once again—trivial and soul-less ; but unlike Scarlatti, who cut short what had a short life, it is pretentious in its eternal repetitions. It is a manufacture of music, nourished by the didactic spirit : compared with the full effects of Hummel it is an empty style.

The index to Cramer's works does not look promising. The Variations, Impromptus, Rondos, Divertissements ; the Victory of Kutusoff ; the Two Styles, ancient and modern ; the Rendezvous à la Chasse ; un jour de Printemps ; Hors d'œuvre, grande sonate dans le style de Clementi ; or the combined composition, in the fashion of the time, by Cramer, Hummel, Kalkbrenner and Moscheles, of variations on Rule Britannia—all these are equally unattractive. The hundred and five sonatas are almost unknown. Cramer's importance lies entirely in his Études, which have been frequently reprinted and arranged. Of the various editions the finest is Pauer's English " édition de luxe," which is adorned with a fine engraving of Cramer. Here he is all genius and sensibility. The somewhat highly-coloured nose, on which he himself used to jest, attracts no notice in the portrait. " It was Bacchus

J. N. Hummel.

Engraved by Fr. Wrenk (1766-1830), after the portrait by Catherine von Escherich
(beginning of 19th century).

Lithograph of 1846, by J. Kriehuber (1801-1876).

who put his thumb there," he would say ; " ce diable de Bacchus ! "
The whole delicate spirit of Cramer breathes in these Études, which
to-day are unforgotten and unsurpassed in their kind. Their instructive value lies in the isolation of the technical exercise, which
is made less exacting by skilful introduction of contrary motion at
the proper point, while the most noble musical forms mount up
from them. They are pieces full of character, and without titles,
to be heartily reverenced. On the other hand " Cramer's Pianoforte School," which went through countless editions in his own
time, has now become useless. The most noteworthy thing we
find in it is a preface on preludes and codas, which, unlike
Clementi's, does not simply copy the approved models, but sets
forth theoretically a series of " styles " in such improvisations, from
the simplest chords to melodic development. In the period of
public improvisations such instructions were not without their use.
Preluding is still a " style " with us ; codas we excuse ourselves.
But in those days a player saw nothing out of place in the direct
connection of such free inventions with the piece before him. And
Cramer was still old-fashioned enough not to object to interweave
with pieces of Mozart all kinds of flourishes—often, as Moscheles
assures us, trivial indeed.

Over against Clementi, the genius of teaching, and Cramer,
the genius of technique, stands Hummel as the inventor of the
modern piano-exercise. Dussek had already, by his unusually
full collection of exercises, accustomed the public ear to the new
state of things ; but Hummel brought the charm of the pianoforte
and the effects of the seven octaves within the reach of all. What
our amateurs, from the days of Chopin, know so well, that full and
satisfying tone, that blazing colouration, is all in Hummel.

In his huge Piano School a combination in Hummel of the
old master and the modern player is very visible. He systematises
fingering into the following divisions : (1) advancing with simple
finger-order in easy figure-successions ; (2) passing the thumb
under other fingers or other fingers over the thumb ; (3) leaving
out one or more fingers ; (4) changing a finger with another on the

same key; (5) stretches and leaps; (6) thumb and fourth finger on the black notes; (7) the passing of a long finger over a shorter, or of a short under a long; (8) change of different fingers on a key, with repeated or not repeated touch, and often the repeated use of the same finger on several keys; (9) alternation, interweaving, or crossing of the hands; and, finally (10), the legato style. A stupendous work indeed; and for every head of the fingering, for every technical possibility, a number of examples are introduced, with the completest calculation of permutations ever seen. There are in all two thousand two hundred examples, and more than a hundred exercises develop the possibilities of playing between C and G. Before every exercise stand the harmonic ground-chords. And thus comes to pass the great miracle, that by means of the utmost conceivable combinations, by means of the hundred chromatic subtleties, musical figures are formed which no composer had previously invented, and which lead on to sound-effects never before suspected. In the examples of an exercise-book lay undreamed-of novelties in piano-composition.

Hummel himself had a very modest opinion of his own compositions. He knew that he had made no advance in the path of Beethoven; and that no greatness was possible outside of it. "It was a serious moment for me," he said once at Weimar to Ferdinand Hiller, "when Beethoven appeared. Was I to try to follow in the footsteps of such a genius? For a while I did not know what I stood on; but finally I said to myself that it was best to remain true to myself and my own nature." With this determination Hummel founded the new, rich school of piano-playing, delighting in sound, and revelling in execution, in which even seriousness and passion are expressed with pomp and circumstance. Brilliancy has expelled grace, and the pompous the lightness of the dance.

Like most of his contemporaries he composed at the piano, making pencil-notes the while. But he heard it as though he were his own audience. "When I sit at the piano," he said, "I am standing at the same time in yonder corner as a listener, and what does not

Hummel in his later years.
From a steel engraving by C. Mayer.

appeal to me there is not written." This was not Beethoven's method. Such a conscious striving after effect was not consistent with absolute sincerity. The concerto was the mainspring of Hummel's creativeness. The innumerable concertos and concert-fantasias take the first rank among Hummel's works. They appeared also with quartet-accompaniment, and also with a second piano, or arranged for one piano. He wrote, unlike Clementi, far more concerto-pieces than sonatas. All kinds of Variations, Rondos, Capriccios, and "Amusements," gratified his publishers. He wrote dances in the profusion characteristic of the time. The Sonata in A flat for two pianos is precisely in harmony with the age. It is only in the second half of the century that original works of this kind begin to lose vogue, while the duet confines itself to the drawing-room. The Duet attained its highest point in Schubert.

Hummel's works bristle with sound-effects. We observe many full chords, as in the orchestra, when all the groups of single instruments are employed in full harmony. The treble of the instrument is for the first time properly used in the grand style, a noble contrast to the melodic, burlesque, dæmonic, firework style of Steibelt and the rest. We meet the genuine pianoforte charm of sharp chromatic successions, where a Bacchanalian tumult of colour appears to sound a rattling fire of sensuous effects.   Even modulations are conceived from the side of technical effectiveness ; and chromatic insertions or sudden third-passages, charming us in the vigorous voice of the piano, are of common occurrence.   The various registers of the piano, the bass, the middle, and the treble, are applied to surprising effects ; a note of one register suddenly thrown into the other gives a colour of its own.   Passages rapidly gliding through the various registers give a glittering spectrum. Take, for example, such a development as that of the second solo conclusion in the last movement of the A minor concerto. Here, starting at the *con dolcezza*, we find the pianoforte bringing into play most of the effective methods of the concerto style.   The simply-harmonised cantabile, for the solo instrument alone ; the repetition of the melodic phrases by the clarinet, etc., with an arpeggio accompaniment on the pianoforte ; the ornamentation of the phrase by delicate scale-passages ; the closing lines of bravura for the right hand ; the showy chromatic scales, accented by superimposed thirds on the first of every group of four semiquavers ; the sequences of semiquavers descending chromatically ; the string of shakes for both hands which introduce the final *point d'orgue* (four bars in strict tempo) ; all these are commonplaces of Hummel's style, and are of interest as an illustration of the fashionable music of the time.

The concerto pieces of Hummel stand in respect of intrinsic value below the solo pieces.   His great concerto fantasia, " Oberon's Magic Horn," is a banal piece of bravura with artistic references to Oberon.   The part of it demanding most execution is the great storm with its thunder and lightning on the piano—a somewhat different performance from the tame storm in the Fitzwilliam Virginal Book.   But the solo pieces also are of unequal merit.   Fashionable compositions, like the Polonaise " La Bella Capricciosa," which was then eagerly heard, are no longer tolerated. Hummel at his best, as we know him in his immortal Sextet, lives

A Canonic Impromptu, by J. N. Hummel, from the original edition of his
Pianoforte School.

in certain delicate turns, such as are common enough in Wagner's
earlier operas, but were then a style of the time, making use of the
melody both of Mozart and of modern days. The better Hummel
is also seen in certain Schumann-like movements, full of fire and
feeling, such as the fresh pulsating Scherzo "all' antico" of Sonata
Op. 106, or the concluding movement of Fantasia Op. 18. Perhaps
the Bagatelles (Op. 107) are his most interesting clavier-piece.
Even to-day they show no sign of age; there is not a dead note in

them. In them the pupil of Mozart is seen in the dainty melodic lines, such as an Audran has revived in our day; but the fore-runner of Liszt is equally visible. In the last Bagatelle, the "Rondo all' Ongarese," he stands precisely between the two epochs. The true spirit of nationality, as Dussek so happily applied it in his sonatas, mingles with classical reminiscences, as the concluding phrase clearly shows. Fugato episodes, derived from tradition, are interwoven with surprising anticipations of that method of variation which works by diatonic movement—a method very familiar to us from Liszt's Rhapsodies. Hummel then is a kind of Janus.

Much more simple was Czerny, king among teachers, whose life and work were taken up with the enforcement of one great principle. Every piece must be played in that manner which is most natural and applicable to the case in hand, and which is fixed partly by the notes before us and partly by the execution. His genius for teaching was so cultivated that in a moment he could de-vise the right study for a student who exhibited any defect. How precisely he worked in such matters a glance at his "Higher Steps in Virtuosity" will show. The themes of the Études in the third volume are called : (1) seven notes against two or three; (2) five against three; (3) five against three in another manner; (4) pass-ing of the fingers over the thumb; (5) passing under of the thumb with a quick alternation of the stretching and retraction of the fingers; (6) motion of certain fingers while the others remain stationary; (7) broken octaves legato. This is not the gram-mar of Hummel with its theoretical chess-play of possibilities; it is the method of Toussaint-Langenscheidt, which invents its exercises from the data of experience. In the great Piano School the exercises are always continued in the course of the instruction. The scales are recommended for daily preliminary practice, and duet-playing is drawn into the circle of regular exercise. It is, of course, impossible to review the whole enormous crowd of his works. In addition to the numerous general practice-pieces, which appeared in manifold combinations, there are the special pieces also: the school of velocity, of legato and staccato, of ornaments, of the left hand, of fugue-playing, of virtuoso-performance; the art of pre-luding, the introduction to fantasia playing, octave-studies, the practice of the full common chord and of the chord of the seventh in broken figures; and everything be-sides. It is a mighty arsenal of mechanical appliances. His works are numbered up to Op. 856; but all except the Studies are lost in oblivion; they are mere hack-work. Even the

Czerny. Lithograph by Kriehuber, 1833.

greater Studies are, in musical value, inferior to Cramer's. Czerny's great collections from previous masters are the work of a practical historian. Such are the arrangement of the Wohl-temperiertes Klavier, the edition of Scarlatti, the arrangements of Beethoven, Mozart, or Mendelssohn for two or four hands; and the innumerable selections of the most brilliant passages from the works of masters from Scarlatti and Bach to Thalberg and Liszt. His practical History of Piano-playing — the first that ever appeared—was thrown into a didactic form and appended to the great "Art of Execution." Every composer is treated from the point of view of playing, under six heads. Clementi is to be played with a steady hand, firm touch and tone, distinct and flowing execution, precise declamation; Cramer and Dussek *cantabilmente*, without glaring effects, with gentle legato and the due use of the pedal; Mozart with less pedal, clearly, staccato, with spirit and vigour; Beethoven and Ries characteristic-ally, passionately, melodiously, with a view to the *tout ensemble;* Hummel, Meyerbeer, and Moscheles brilliantly, rapidly, and gracefully, with definition in the proper parts, and intelligent but elegant declamation. Thalberg, Liszt, and Chopin, the great innovators, form a class apart. Czerny's astonishing genius for instruction embraces the whole field of the clavier, with a many-sided capacity that seems almost more than human. A greater teacher there never was than he. He gathers all into his net, even the works of his own pupils; he practises everything, even setting it for three or four pianos; he arranges everything, even isolated passages of great masters; he composes everything, even penny variations and Chinese rondos.

In Kalkbrenner we see the lowest type of the time. Externally a fine gentleman and artistic man of the world, he is inwardly hollow and vapid. It is hard even to give an idea of this extreme emptiness; but it is well illustrated in such a piece as the "Charmes de Berlin." This great virtuoso won his triumphs in the worst kinds of salon-music as well as with all sorts of Études, Concertos, and Sonatas. Le Rêve, Le Fou, La Solitude, Dernières Pensées Musicales, La Mélancolie et La Gaité, La Brigantine, are some of these detestable compositions. But his opera fantasias touch the very nadir. Here a sort of sanction is given to an utter want of taste. After largo introductions, full of feeling, he slices favourite melodies into passages, till the contour of the air is utterly destroyed, and the commonest cadenzas are flung higgledy-piggledy into their artistic forms, and so we rush off into a sweep-dance. The fantasia, once the freest outcome of the musical soul, becomes a wretched conglomeration of fragments of Études. Kalkbrenner once remarked, as Ferdinand Hiller tells us, "Ze Tance is a tream, a referie; it begins with lofe, *passion*, despair, and it ends wid a military march." The story is true enough.

To imagine that with Weber we already pass over into the fairy-land of romance is, alas, a mistake. He would doubtless have made the transit had not an early death overtaken him in the midst of the uprising of genius that began in 1820. But, as it is, his piano music belongs to the technically rich but spiritually empty style of the time. If he did not still live as operatic

composer and orchestral poet, his piano-compositions would be
forgotten. His technique, successful as it was, is never so rich
as that of the majority of the virtuosos of his time. It is not
hard to perceive that he recurs again and again to certain
motives. The ornamentation which was earlier called " Anschlag "
—the preparatory striking of the under and over note before the
main note, which is seen brilliantly exemplified in the Rondo in

Lithograph by Eichens, after Vogel, 1825.

E flat major—the S-curves of the melody, which are a simple
re-arrangement of this "anschlag"—the "pizzicato" notes over
embellishing or broken accompaniments—held notes over struck
chords—broken combinations of three notes, ranging themselves
chain-like after one another—these are his somewhat limited
repertoire. In the Polonaises in E flat major and in E major, in
numerous operatic variations, in Écossaises and popular national
dances, he pays his tribute to the time. But there is no local

Moscheles in his youth.

colouring in the variations on the Russian "Schöne Minka," or on a Gipsy song. Dussek and Hummel were in this point his superiors. The intellectual themes, like the second of the C major concerto, show the greatness of Weber as behind a mask. The favourite concerto Op. 79, if judged by a severe standard, is only a fashionable if very clever and successful mosaic of neat Études with the requisite melody. The daintiest mosaic piece, the March, is given to orchestra alone, as if Weber had felt compelled to enter his proper abode. Liszt perceived this when he played in the concerto, and played the *tutti* brilliantly with the instruments, and thus exhibited a remarkable *tour de force*. The four sonatas, often utterly trivial, are in the main a congeries which perishes by its eclecticism. As with all his contemporaries, the first movements, those touchstones of the inner meaning, are the weakest. The subjects are thin, the framework is that of the drawing-room; and the other movements have a higher stylistic value. The powerful rhythm of the second movement in the C major, the excellent minuet-scherzo, the stirring perpetuum mobile as last movement are admirable single ideas. But the importance rises only slowly; the fourth sonata has, not inner meaning, but a certain majesty. Yet what is this romance, this octave-scherzo with its rapid waltz-trio, this masquerade of elves, to Chopin, to Schumann, or even to Mendelssohn? Weber's most popular piece is also his purest—the Invitation to the Dance. It is a *pot-pourri*, such as the age loved; and the very title is *à la mode*. But the conception of forming the introductory adagio as a dialogue, the brilliant advance from the ravishing waltz to Bacchanalian tumult the pure and not virtuoso-like colouring, which rests on this happy invention, raise the work far above all that is merely fashionable.

Moscheles

The true man of the transition is Moscheles — double-souled, with his concessions to modishness on the one side, and on the other his wealth of invention and his musical intensity. He was born out of due time. He ought to have left virtuosity behind him, in order to be able to give full play to his characteristic, not undramatic, and broad-lined art. To-day he is almost forgotten; no opera, as in Weber's case, preserved his fame to our times. But his works more than repay study; if our pianists would once again take up his C major concerto, they would be amazed.

Moscheles, later, 1859.

In his youth he composed Variations on the Alexander March, with which he was compelled, much against his will, when a ripe composer, to dazzle the world. It was one of the most popular of concert pieces. It is not true that in later years he altered his style and wrote more soberly. His very sober Melancholy Sonata (Op. 49), written fairly early, in one movement, with its charming accompaniment figure, reminds us of the Parsifal tremoli. And on the other hand, a later work, the Danish, Scotch, and Irish Fantasias (this latter on the Last Rose of Summer), are *pot-pourris* in full modish style. What would the Virginal Book composers of English and Scotch folk-songs have said to these variations? In order to avoid the fashionable appearance, several movements are even written in various tempi, as in a sonata. In his A flat minor Ballade, on the contrary, he has with astonishing dramatic force struck the legendary tone in a free and genuine manner, in a sort of romantic rondo.

Moscheles, who was the first master to arrange for piano an orchestral score by another writer (that of the Fidelio, by commission from Beethoven), was unable to escape the operatic rechauffées of the time. His speciality was the putting together of different operatic airs, which formed the favourite repertoire of a singer. He wrote such fantasias on the favourite pieces of Pasta, Henriette Sonntag, Jenny Lind, and Malibran. They are commonplace enough. Yet this same Malibran, after her sudden death, he honoured in an " Hommage," which was one of his finest pieces. There is in it an unearthly power of invention, a dramatic life, as if drawn from the stage ; spirit breathes in every bar ; and the interest is sustained to the final sorrowfully rising cross-passages, which strangely forebode the longings of Tristan for the sea.

He wrote many drawing-room pieces, which bore the usual significant titles—Charmes de Paris, La Tenerezza, Jadis et aujourd'hui, la Petite Babillarde. Similar titles he superscribed to his Études, such as his three Allegri di Bravura and his characteristic Studies (Op. 95). Among the former are La Forza and Il Capriccio ; among the latter are Juno, Terpsichore, Moonlight at Sea, Dream, and Anguish. In these the seeker after mode will be disappointed. They are pieces worthy of Schumann in power of form; half exercises, half characteristic pieces, reaching that height of technique where air and étude unite in the closest bonds. The work which Cramer began has reached the height of artistic achievement. For here, where meet knowledge, technical sense of form, and poetic conception, the peculiar musical vein of the age is found. The fugal " Widerspruch " [contradiction] is an artistic construction that stands alone ; "Anguish" is a penetrating tuneful picture, which once more reminds us of Wagner; it is a foretaste of Siegmund's flight or of the Valkyrie Prologue.

The untitled Études Op. 70, which rank as his best work, stand out as the forerunners of the Studies Op. 95. There is the same delicate characteristic sense ; they are a gallery of tone pictures, among which the twelfth Étude in B flat minor is never to be forgotten. It is a Night-Piece in the style of Schumann. But all is calculated for human fingers, not for those of Liszt, like Op. 95. And here we feel patiently after the essential nature of the musical Étude. We observe the inner relation between mechanical and spiritual motion. Expression and difficulty grow alongside; the straining of the fingers is involuntarily the straining of the soul; their smooth gliding is the gliding of emotion, and the stress of mind is loosened in the muscles of the fingers as they move over the keys. It is thus that the irreconcilable at last meet.

Parisian and London Pianists at the beginning of the 19th century.

L. Adam. Kalkbrenner. Cramer.

Waltz by Schubert. Berlin Royal Bibliothek.

The Romantics

WHERE definitions fail, the word appears at the right time. The word proves the existence of things, even if they cannot be sharply defined. The word is the artistic form of a transient emotion ; it was made for things which were nameless till its creation ; it was girded with associations which fastened themselves on to this conception. Such a word is Romance. Romance is not a return to the popular, to nature, nor to the mediæval, it is no love for the legendary or the symbolic or the most delicate forms of the most delicate stirrings of the soul. It was indeed the one of these things to one set of persons and another for others ; but in reality it is none of these and all of these. If I say it is an *oppositum* to *synthesis*, or intimateness from the point of view of all possibilities, I have defined it very coldly. But its essential point seems to be its reactionary character. It aims not at raising structures, but at reading souls, and it finds a thousand ways of so doing. These thousand ways cannot be crammed into one definition. We strike only gently the chord of the word, so symbolic, so harmoniously chiming. It is a feeling whose value is not to be analysed.

Near the great architect Beethoven lived the first musical Romantic, the well-beloved Franz Schubert. He felt the burden of existence as only musicians can feel it. But he had inexhaustible fountains of consolation, which sang to him melodies almost more profusely than to Mozart, and he did his utmost to throw the melodies, without too much pedantry or Titan-pride, into songs, symphonies, quartets, and impromptus, as the inspiration took him. He had no long life for working, but he used his time well. It is now many, many years since his death, and still numbers of his works are unpublished. His best teacher was the people, and their songs and dances. The unsophisticated musical feeling, which came to light in this popular song and national dance—the simple natural phrases, the speaking soul, the genuine sense for drama—these were the formative principles of his immortal songs, and these gave the character to his piano music also. Men have been studying his numerous national dances as in a Bible of the dance for fifty years. There are still rare and beautiful flowers to be found among them ; others have been picked out by the virtuosos, and transformed to hothouse plants in many forms, not always so stylish as Liszt's Soirées de Vienne. The case has been the same with his four-hand Marches, whether Caractéristique, Héroique, or Militaire. If we return to their original forms, a surprising air as from country meadows meets us.

He lives entirely in music. From the far land of invention float the melodies, eternally varying, giving colour to the harmonies, and pouring themselves out to their very last note. The ear cannot have enough of them, and, full of the holiest delight, pursues them to the end of their heavenly course. In Paradise there is no time ; and these melodies are a prologue to eternity. Schubert died at thirty-one. His D minor quartet, one of the loveliest compositions ever written, leads us to imagine that he would have been the greatest musician of the century. But he has left us only the works of his youth—a youth of intellectual intimateness and smiling sunshine. In delicacy of musical feeling we put no one above him. He stands before us in the small band of original and delicate minds, whose secret can make the life of higher emotions happy. Let not him who has not delicate fingers touch Schubert. To play him means to have a dainty touch. The keyboard appears unmaterialised : only so much of the mechanism seems to remain as is necessary to render living the conception of this beauty. In peaceful hours we enjoy him most, and confess that there is no tone-poet whom we love so deeply from the heart as Schubert.

In this, those things of their own accord are separated out, in which Schubert did not follow only his natural impulse to the popular song. He was in the first place no master or teacher of musical construction. His scores are simple, and even in his four-handed duets (he has left behind him duets of surpassing beauty) whole passages could often be rendered as they stand by a single player.

Schubert never appears a slave to the arrangement he adopts ; but the movement flows so naturally from his pen that there is no want of harmony between his idea and its realisation. He is just as little a special artist of the form. He has written many sonatas —four-handed and two-handed ; but he cares little for the form. Where he can subject his dainty ideas to this mould, as in the first three movements of the duet in B flat major, he is interesting to us. When he cannot easily do so, he has recourse to variations in the style of the time or to all kinds of academic free fantasias. In this case he speedily becomes antiquated. But we must again remember that he has left us only youthful works. His latest sonatas, particularly those in A major and in B flat major ; his latest chamber-music and symphonies, the wonderful Schumann-like F minor fantasia, and the Beethoven-like duet " Lebensstürme " in rondo form, are more weighty in structure and show him on the way to throw his great conceptions into more recognised forms : in this style he would have grown into a great artist.

The " Wanderer " Fantasia stands on the boundary line. The method of writing a free fantasia on a song-motive—on this occasion one of his own—by which the ordinary four movements are preserved, was then *à la mode*. That the last movement should begin with a fugato, which soon passes over into more general virtuosity, was equally common. In the more purely virtuoso passages, specially in the quite conventional coda, Schubert is the very child of the Viennese school. The free fantasias are rather in Hummel's than in Beethoven's style—preserving a middle path between the two. The form is so free that from the waltz movement of the scherzo to the weighty fugue, from the song of the adagio to the conventional conclusion, almost all the styles of piano music that exist are packed in. But if a song or a waltz rhythm or a special tone expression appears, then we observe with what alacrity Schubert sets about his work. He prepares it beforehand with a certain effort. He caresses the new theme; for example, on the entrance of the melodic E flat major theme in the first movement, in the dramatic deep tremolo in the adagio, and in the pianissimo D flat major waltz in the third movement.

Nothing is more distinctive of Schubert than the development of the Fantasia Sonata Op. 78. The first movement hardly hangs together. A wonderful theme, depending on delicate touch, is mingled with empty technical intermediate passages. The Andante is a Volkslied, arranged as in sonatas; as a whole treated somewhat feebly, but with sudden small intermezzos, at first in F sharp major (bar 47), where suspensions in Schubert's true style sound in softest pianissimo in the middle voices. In the third movement a ravishing minuet meets us, running in cheerful rhythms, with a waltz-like conclusion which anticipates one side of Schumann, and with a dainty trio in B major, in bell-like tones and magical retardations such as Schubert himself hardly surpassed. Thus a G sharp [1] in the chord of the dominant seventh, with which the melodic chain is ornamentally interwoven, was a discovery rich in wonders. And the last movement with its original popular dance, which he overheard directly from the heart of the people where the basses rumble below and the fiddle-bows spring on the strings; with the two laughing trios, in which

---

[1] Cx (C double sharp), bar 11 of Trio.

Johann Strauss is entirely anticipated; national dances with a dainty melody, which conclude so lingeringly in the spiritual chorale-tone (in C major)—pictures like these music had not hitherto known. All kinds of foreign national airs had, of course, been dealt with in artistic style; and Schubert himself, in his brilliant Hungarian Divertissement for four hands, has painted a gipsy picture with all his dexterity in rhythm; but the German national airs had received but scanty attention. Here, at last, we find the German folk-music, which found in the Viennese dance-composers its popular embellishment, and in Schumann its artistic treatment.

With his Impromptus and Moments Musicals, those small impressionist forms, Schubert placed piano-literature upon a new basis. Here is found that form of chamber music which is most peculiar to the piano as a solo instrument with full harmony. It is not a sonata, which is founded by the great laws of universal tonic art; nor a concerto, which drags the piano before a many-headed multitude which delights in distraction; nor an operatic fantasia or variation on an air, which forbids the charm of free improvisation; no technical elaborated étude, nor a scientifically constructed fugato;—but a piece which brings single selected musical thoughts into a short artistic form, no longer in extent than the tone-colour of the instrument permits; yet, with all infelt genuineness, informed with the best effects of the piano, which the player, as he composes in solitude, feels in full intensity. Almost all Schubert's pieces retain something of the spirit of the time. Some are a kind of variations; others études, a third class dances; but they are constantly more than mere echoes of the time; they are founded on an inner genuineness, and much too full in expression to permit of being included under any category of the external. In Beethoven's life we witnessed the way in which a world-embracing genius gradually threw off the traditional form; in Schubert we see how an intimate spirit gradually rises above the style of the time. This development is included between the Sonatas and the Wanderer Fantasia on the one hand,

and the Moments Musicals on the other. At the same period in which the technical musicians accomplished the outward emancipation of the clavier, these short pieces (Kurze Geschichten) made it inwardly free.

As Impromptus the two groups, Op. 90 and Op. 142, were published. Those of the first group have all penetrated deeply into our musical consciousness. All roads lead us back again to the first Impromptu with its simple popular melody in two sections, which is varied in so many extraordinary ways; and with that melodious middle-movement, more joyous and ethereal, than any that had ever been heard before on the pianoforte. Who can forget the second with the light étude-like triplet-swinging in E flat major and the mighty B minor middle section; or the third with its wonderful G flat major melody, its divine modulations and its captivatingly simple conclusion, revealing unexpected melodic wonders in a broken chord of the seventh; or the fourth, a light floating figure with its short Volkslied intermezzi and the long drawn out melody of the trio in C♯ minor—Schumann all over!

The second group of Impromptus (Op. 142) stands below the first in importance. It was with Schubert as with Mozart; good and bad inspirations came to him alike, and he could not discriminate them. Yet they contain the dainty A flat major piece, which demands nothing but a gentle touch; and in the variations of the third Impromptu (which is therefore no impromptu) the likeness to Schumann is once more astonishing. It is a peculiar pleasure to detect Schumann in Schubert, and it is a piece of historic justice which has often been neglected.

More successful, indeed Schubert's greatest achievement, was the "Moments Musicals," which appeared in 1828, the year of his death. The first of these is a naturalistic free musical expatiation; the second a gentle movement in A flat major; the third the well-known F minor dance—in which a dance became a penetrating and sorrow-laden tongue—the fourth the Bach-like C sharp minor moderato, with its placid middle section in D flat major; the fifth a fantastic march with a sharply cut rhythm; and the sixth, perhaps Schubert's most profound piano-piece, that reverie in still chords, which only once are more violently shaken in order to lull us to sleep with its pensive and dainty sorrow, its delicate connections, its singing imitations, its magic enharmonics, and its sweet melodies rising like flowers from the soft ground. The conclusion of the trio, in the style of a popular chorale, with its harmonisation in thirds, is (like many of his harmonic passages in octaves or sixths) exceedingly characteristic of the popular nature of Schubert's music.

We have been turning over the leaves of a book from which Schumann and Chopin might have found matter to fill years of their lives. In form and colour, melody and movement, the model was before them. This modest man, who in his Vienna solitude wrote such things as these for himself, loved a few good friends, but publicity he hated. A composer who never appeared in public—was the like ever seen before? In the aged Beethoven the world understood it; but in this young man it could only reward it with indifference. He remained willingly unknown, like so many of his companions in sorrow who wished to be artists in themselves without relation to others, and without the encumbrance of patronage. The times were altering in music as in painting. The patronage of the State or of the Prince is disappearing; the commissions the artist receives become fewer and more distasteful; he becomes more intimate and is constrained to offer his works to the public, and to supply what it will purchase. Supply and demand rule art as well as anything else: but nowhere is the severance so painful. Pensions are irksome, and official posts are not to be had otherwise than indirectly. The struggle after the ideal which is the life of the artist is purer than it ever was. The type which Feuerbach and Böcklin represent in painting, that new type of artist who can be happy without commissions and without honorarium, is first clearly exhibited by Schubert in the musical world. Publicity, to which Beethoven at first had recourse, and which he would have carried further had fate not opposed, was impossible to Schubert. He had to live on a pension, his applications for posts were rejected, publishers were timid, and very slowly indeed did his songs win their way to favour. Goethe never answered him on receiving his songs; and Beethoven, to whom he shyly dedicated his Variations (Op. 10) as "admirer and worshipper," only learnt to know him in the last days. As he began, so he died. The publishers had still to work through the whole century in order to bring out his works, which they dedicated in very stylish manner to Liszt, Mendelssohn, or Schumann: as Schubert closed his eyes he knew as little as the world that his simple integrity had won a new realm for art.

Some years after Schubert's death, in November 1831, a certain Robert Schumann published as his first work some Variations, whose theme was formed on the name Abegg (A B-E G G). It was easy to see that the Countess Abegg, to whom they were dedicated, was a pseudonym for a good lady, whom the author had once admired as a beauty without otherwise troubling himself much about her. The theme was worked out a little too painfully, and the Variations moved in eclectic style among influences derived from Beethoven, Weber, and the contemporary virtuosos; but their originality was nevertheless unmistakable. It was not the worn-out contemporary style of variations; and many sound traces of that naive dilettantism, which always stands at the cradle of the new, were easily to be detected. Sudden pianissimo effects, single selected technical motives, an original melodic gift for singing with contrapuntal voice-parts and new forms of accompaniment, rapid harmonic changes by the chord of the seventh, legendary romance in the finale alla fantasia, the successive release of the notes of a chord, from the lowest to the highest—all this led men to wait eagerly for Schumann's next work.

This next work bore the title of "Papillons"—a title not unknown in contemporary drawing-room music. But here there was nothing of the drawing-room style. These butterflies seemed to come from the regions where Schubert had found his flowers. Thence they brought a breath of short lyrical songs—a concentrated breath of severe and restrained beauty. A wonderfully penetrating heart-felt tone breathed through them. The world

had now to do with a reflective, deeply musical nature, far removed
from all the merely brilliant virtuosity of the time: it was a
romantic spirit. After the short slow introduction came the waltz,
whose outlines inevitably recalled Schubert; but its emotions were
personally felt. There were melodic passages in octaves for
alternate hands, dying away in the aria with the "nachschlag-
begleitung"[1] down to pianissimo, a splendid fugato-march in
spirited style, episodes of popular songs, sportive whisperings,
sparkling polonaise rhythms, melodious effects working out of
very gentle full chords, canonic melodies in lively motion, repetitions of earlier bars in later sections to represent the external unity
of these little stories, and as a conclusion the "Grossvater" song.
The whole is united contrapuntally with the first waltz. The
carnival is silenced—this appears suddenly in words—the tower-
clock strikes six (and high enough on the upper A); a full chord
of the seventh piles itself up gradually and closes the piece.

No one knew what was the chief impulse which led Schumann
to write these "Papillons." Those who corresponded with him
alone knew that he was thinking of the "Flegeljahre"[2] of Jean
Paul. From Jean Paul he received his spiritual nourishment, and
those to whom his letters came could tell that he hardly sent off
one without including in them a rhapsody for the Bayreuth poet.
In this intermediate world between the highest earnestness and
endless laughter he preferred to live in ironic love and loving
irony. To reflect deeply on immortality, and at the same time
to drink in comfortably the sweet odour of the girdle cake
which the goodwife is cooking in the kitchen—it is in this mixed
light that the poet stands, who has so characterised himself. The
fantastic boundaries of the real and the imaginary world, of the
most insipid flatness of the animal nature and of the most ethereal
heavenly flights, alike attract him. His delicate soul flies to
Nature, and Nature is to him—so he writes to his mother—the

---

[1] See Papillons, No. 2, bar 5. The phrase ("after-stroke accompaniment") is
untranslateable; and the rhythmical formula referred to, though quite common, is not to
be described in words.

[2] "Flail-years" = "wild oats time."

great outspread handkerchief of God, embroidered with His eternal name, on which man can wipe away all his tears of sorrow. But the tears of joy too—and when every tear falls into a rapture of weeping—whence came these tones in the soul of a musician? The world had never yet understood them. It knew them in literary circles, which busied themselves with romantic new creations, where unknown regions seemed suddenly to open themselves between the everyday and the legendary, and which demanded new, painfully twisted words for the wild tumult of their representations. Where pure music had long wandered alone, the poets and the æsthetics had now penetrated; and was now a musician to give them a hand to speak in their tongue? This was a surprising turn. Upon the musical poet came the literary musician. The one could only gain; had the other anything to lose? No; Schumann seemed musician enough to prove that nothing was lost. None of his friends, to whom he recommended the perusal of the conclusion of the "Flegeljahre"—whose masked dance, he said, the Papillons were intended to transform into tones—would have expected this pure and genuine music from him. I imagine they all puzzled their heads to know what the wild Jean Paul had to do with these dainty musical butterflies. And it is to-day even harder for us.

A delicate musician read Jean Paul, and the grotesque figures of this "Walt und Vult" combined in him with a world of tone, which slumbered within him, in those deep regions of associated ideas which stand at the basis of artistic creation. They there formed a special union with their musical counterpart, the simplest, most natural, and least academical creations which the art of tone ever saw—those of Schubert. So early as 1829 Schumann, who was then a student, wrote to Frederick Wieck from Heidelberg: "When I play Schubert, it is as if I were reading a Romance of Jean Paul set to music." Jean Paul and Schubert are the gods in Schumann's first letters and other writings. He cannot shake off the ethereal melancholy, the "suppressed" lyrical tone, in Schubert's four-handed A major Rondo: he sees Schubert, as it were, in bodily shape, *experiencing* his own piece. No music, he said, is so psychologically remarkable in the progress of its ideas and in its apparently logical leaps. There is a rare fire in him when he speaks of Schubert. How eager is he for new publications from Schubert's remains! Yet, while he is devouring a volume of his national dances, he is weeping for Jean Paul. In the Papillons, we hear, there was Jean Paul; and what we find in them, is Schubert. What was to come of this conjunction?

This question was very satisfactorily answered in the next work (Op. 3). This was a collection of Études with a textual introduction on motives after Paganini, but adapted to the piano. Considered as a whole it was technical to a degree, yet without disguising the real Schumann. And what was the meaning of the Introduction? Every great pianist had already written his "School" or wanted to write it. Did these barren finger-directions speak for the virtuoso Schumann?

The Intermezzi (Op. 4) answered in the negative. These were genuine pure music without any external pretensions. It was possible already to recognise the true style of Schumann: the characteristic features were repeated. Dotted motives, built up in fugato style; delicate melodies with the "nachschlag" accompaniment and with other melodies superimposed; reflective repose in chords; syncopated rhythm; parallelisms of the air in octaves; all these were as before. In the slurred thirds and the sequences, and especially the diatonic runs, which seem to gather their strength as they go, the model was not Schubert but Sebastian Bach. There was something in this not merely of his absolute, self-contained music, but even of his means of expression. At this time of course this could do no harm. In the fifth and sixth intermezzos Schumann's personality would seem to have entirely ripened. This marked propensity to "anticipations," those pianissimo unisons, those sharp detonations of C and C sharp, D and D sharp; the singing legato middle voices developing in the canonic manner, the absolute transference of whole passages by means of a single note foreign to the scale, generally effected by an anticipation; all this had grown into a definite musical picture, extraordinarily sympathetic, in which soul and technique were united. With stern sadness the hands grip one within another, to bring out the "suppressed lyric" of the piano; and a delicate noble spirit guides them, which delights to express strange things in strange forms. With stern sadness, as in the style of Jean Paul, and right in the midst of the music, where an answering voice intrudes itself, Schumann writes over the notes the words, "Meine Ruh ist hin"—my peace has departed. This is not as text, but merely as a comment by the way.

Then came Op. 5, free variations in romantic style, on a theme by Clara Wieck; and Op. 6, called "Davidsbündlertänze." They were dedicated to Walther von Goethe, and bore as motto the old proverb:—

"In all' und jeder Zeit verknüpft sich Lust und Leid ;
Bleibt fromm in Lust, und seyd dem Leid mit Mut bereit."

[In all and every time, our joy and sorrow meet :
Gird up thy loins and go, bravely thy fate to greet.]

In the later revised edition Schumann cut out this good old saying, as he omitted so much of the first and heartfelt edition. "Two readings may often be of equal value," says Eusebius once in the aphorisms. "The original one is usually the best," adds Raro. Why did not Schumann follow his own Raro? Raro was the most delicate of the "Davidsbündler." He was in his irony, which had drunk deep of worldly wisdom, raised far above the storm and stress of Florestan and the gentle, simple complaisance of Eusebius. In Florestan there was much of Beethoven, in Eusebius an echo of Schubert. Raro was to surpass and combine them in a higher unity. But Raro is just—rare.

The "Davidsbündler" declare war on the Philistines, and of an evening bring their dances together, which are then published in a single volume. Florestan contributes the stormy ones, Eusebius the gentle ones; while Raro puts in his word as seldom as in actual life. Such bands of Romanticists we have heard of before ; we think of Hoffmann's Serapion Brothers, and their zeal against the Philistines. Herz and Hünten, and all the musical lions of the drawing-room were to be put aside. There was still music after Beethoven. David's companions meant, like their prototype, to put the Philistines under a harrow. Even the explanatory notes of his " Bündler " were cut out by Schumann in his later revised edition. He smiled perhaps at the beautiful fancies of his youth, when he seemed to carry three temperaments warring in his soul. And yet this fictitious society was the truest expression of his romantic soul, in which living music and literary reflection met together. They were his fellow-workers in his life's work, whom he could never renounce.

The moment had come when the world busied itself with Schumann in somewhat wider circles. It asked after his private circumstances, and gained the answer—surprising, and yet no longer utterly surprising—that here an academically educated man had become a musician—a phenomenon long unknown, and only possible in this new era of art, in which one could give oneself up to composition without having to wait for a commission for each single work.

Schumann had attended the Zwickau Gymnasium in due course ; and at eighteen, in 1828, he entered the legal profession at Leipzig. His piano-lessons under Frederick Wieck of course attracted him far more than jurisprudence ; and when, after an interval spent at Heidelberg, he returned to Leipzig, the die was cast. The letter to his mother in which he announces his decision is to-day interesting for the light it throws on his intentions. Naturally, he thought of the career of a virtuoso ; and, in order to make his fingers supple, he hung one of them in a sling while practising, with the result that first the finger and then the whole hand was maimed, and Schumann was saved for pure composition. Composition is soon intimately knit with love for Clara Wieck, the daughter of his teacher, whose great talent was to compensate him for his own lost power. We cannot forget his youthful letters to Clara, which form the conclusion of the edition of " Schumann's Letters," which she issued. Never were more lyrical letters written.

Engraving by M. Lämmel.

Chopin.

Anonymous Lithograph, after portrait by Ary Scheffer (1795-1858).

He dedicates to Clara his whole power of creation ; it is she that lives in all his pieces, and to create was to think of her. Before this he tells her legends and supernatural tales. " Look now at your old Robert ; is he not still the frivolous ghost-tale teller and terrifier ? But now I can be very serious too, often the whole day long—but don't trouble about that—they are generally processes in my soul, thoughts on music and compositions. Everything touches me that goes on in the world—politics, literature, people. I think after my own fashion of everything that can express itself through music, or can escape by means of it. This is why many of my compositions are so hard to understand, because they are bound up with very remote associations, and often very much so because everything of importance in the time takes hold of me and I must express it in musical form. And this, too, is why so few compositions satisfy my mind, because, apart from all defect in craftsmanship, the ideas themselves are often on a low plane, and their expression is often commonplace. The highest that is here attained scarcely reaches to the beginning of what is aimed at in my music. The former may be a flower, the latter is the poem, so much the more spiritual ; the one is an impulse of raw nature ; the other the work of poetical consciousness."

In these words Schumann penetrated into his own heart ; and there is nothing to be added to this characterisation of his literary music. The new type existed in its purity ; namely, the musician, standing on the height of the representative art of the time, of which type Wagner was the best expression. There is a strange likeness in these two opposed natures. What in Wagner passed over into the external, in Schumann passed into the intimate. Where the one carries us along with him in an intoxicating rush, the latter is a personal enjoyment for retiring souls. The one lives in the orchestra, and plays the piano badly ; the other dreamed first for the piano, then for the chorus, and never was able to express himself tolerably through the orchestra. Wagner never burst into tears, like Schumann, when he before his wanderings played for the last time on the beloved instrument which had heard all the sorrows and joys of his youth.   And Wagner never wrote to Madame Cosima as Schumann wrote to Clara : " You speak in your last of a cosy place where you would like to have me—do not aim too high—I ask no better surroundings than a piano and you close by.   You will never be a kapellmeisterin in your life ; but inwardly we are a match for any pair of kapell-meisters, are we not ?   You understand me."

This man of delicate feeling, who wished to reduce piano-culture to a system, was editor of a paper, which he founded at Leipzig in the year 1834, along with certain friends and men of like tastes, of whom he seems to have valued most Schunke, who died very soon.   This " New Magazine of Music " was Schumann's special medium, and in it he published his splendid and very spirited criticisms and aphorisms ; later, when Brendel purchased it from him, it was of equal use to Wagner, his exact opposite. Till 1844 Schumann edited it for the most part personally ; and his position aided the spread of his works, which laid themselves out so little for popular success.   Still more effective was the career of his betrothed, who because of certain awkward obstacles only became his wife in 1840.   This was his most productive year. It saw the appearance of a hundred and thirty-eight songs, and of the cycle of Heine's lyrics (Op. 24).   If the betrothed Clara and the piano were spiritually united, the married Clara and the song were equally so.   Thus the songs stand precisely midway between his youthful piano-writings and the orchestral and choral efforts of his later years.   And indeed the piano succeeds better in them than in any song hitherto written.   The accompaniments of " Du, meine Seele " or of the F sharp major " Ueberm Garten durch die Lüfte," are minute and scrupulous pieces of artistic work.

The eighteen " Davidsbündler," Schumann's first complete piano-work, were composed in 1837.   Clara contributed the first bars—a cheerful musical motto.   Schumann was fond of accepting his first bars as gifts from friends.   The Romancist was fond of these incursions into actuality, this poetry in the real.   As the letters A B E G G had once taken his fancy, so later did A S C H.

And once he wrote in Gade's family album a piece on "Gade, Ade" (Gade, farewell).

Schumann's music is characterised in few strokes; it is never hard to recognise its features. The interwoven melodies, the love of "anticipations," the rollicking humour, which might almost be borrowed from old drinking songs, the contrapuntal collisions of

Clara Schumann, née Wieck.

the bass on which the light waltz flutters down, the cheerfully pensive codas, the restlessness of his syncopated rhythms, the sweet lulling romantic tone mingled with wild and vigorous march-motives, the full effect of broken chord passages of mounting fifths, the conclusions of the sections abruptly broken off by a staccato chord—all these were to be seen in spring-like freshness in the "Davidsbündler." We have there the "einfaches stück" of Eusebius, the free recitative in No. 7 beginning with arpeggiando chords for the left hand. Next, "Florestan's lips quiver." Then follow the extraordinarily beautiful E flat major (No. 14) with its airy melancholy; the staccato, passing humorously over into the "Wie aus der Ferne," and finally "Happiness speaks out of his eyes." Nothing so wonderfully simple, so old-new, so true, so German, had been painted on the piano since Schubert. And here was a yet more modern spirit—a mind whose depths were not merely over-flowed by the streams of music, but were pictured in delicate musical emotion. The construction is clean and simple; the language refined and lofty; the whole the consolidated improvisation of a mind standing at the highest point of representative art. More perfect improvisations it did not lie in the nature of the piano to produce. It was the high-water mark of piano literature.

I pass rapidly over Op. 7, one of his earliest composed pieces, the toccata, brilliant in colouring, delicately chased, bold in construction, wonderful in technique; and Op. 8, a concert allegro, in which he, certainly in an unusual way compared with the literature of the time, sacrifices a little to popularity, and thereby crushes out certain beauties. I pass on to Op. 9, the "Scenes Mignonnes" of the carnival, in which neither technical nor concert problems were to be mastered. The motive of the carnival is A S C H, which is the name of the home of one of his musical lady friends and which contains all the letters of Schumann's name which are adapted to the stave.[1] A bustling ball-play develops itself, Pierrot and Harlequin appear, a Valse Noble unites the parties, the mask of Eusebius is seen through, and the gentleness of Florestan is resumed, the Coquette frisks by, Papillons flutter round, and the letters A S C H dance a rapid waltz. Chiarina and Estrella, not unknown characters, are represented; and Chopin appears in person between them. A short recognition scene in the time of the Polonaise, in which we hear the dainty causeries among the marching rhythms—the miniature ballet of Pantaloon and Columbine—a comfortable allemande, into which Paganini suddenly darts with his most extravagant leaps; in the distance a gentle confession of love;—all comes again together in

[1] S = E flat or A flat.

the polite and festal promenade of the couples. There is a pause ; and then reminiscences run through the memory ; one melody restlessly pursues another ; room is made ; the final effect comes ; the "Davidsbündler" begin an abusive march against the Philistines ; they roar out the Grandfather· song—"Grandfather wedded my Grandmother dear, so Grandfather then was a bridegroom, I fear"—and the people enjoy it, till they all, with a "Down with the Philistines," join in, and a galloping stretto finishes the boisterous amusement.

The inscriptions Schumann inserted later. He took a literary delight in putting in an "Estrella," as it is seen in old copper engravings. It was the pleasure of the delicate man of taste in labelling. But he laid no stress on this nomenclature ; the relations indicated were as wide as before, when there were none of these labels. We are reminded of Couperin, whose miniature porcelain pictures were ticketed just like this moving panorama of tunes, and in surprisingly similar style. In both the titles were nothing but a halt in the midst of full musical representation ; they involved no limitation, no point of departure. Under like tickets, works came into the world which were separated in time and in tone by whole centuries. Schumann himself almost thought the titles a trifle too theatrical. The Davidsbündler, he said, are related to the carnival like faces to masks.

Among the works that followed, technical and purely musical gifts alternated. As Op. 10 we have further Paganini Études, with wide stretches, contrapuntal, transformed in the spirit of Schumann. Here, as before, the order of publication did not correspond to that of composition. The F sharp minor sonata (Op. 11) was begun contemporaneously with the Impromptus. It was dedicated to Clara. It is a romantic deepening of the sonata form, cast throughout in these small lyrical sections which are peculiar to the time, but here are held together by an internal unity. We must feel this unity in order not to cut up the work into mere fragments. An oceanic vastness spreads over it, whose tone is struck in the broad introduction. It has a first theme, contrapuntal in style, and a second of full-voiced melody; the working-out attaching new ideas half in imitative, half in étude fashion. On the third, the A, which drags itself over, the aria begins its deep-felt lament, in three melodies with the genuine Schumann-like coda, sighing itself away under the final slurs. The fresh staccato canon work of the scherzo carries us with it. Two wonderful trios introduce themselves, the second with the remarkable recitative. The conclusion is formed by a modest movement which is put together like a mosaic out of a stormy quaver theme, two cantabiles, a syncopated motive, a section in full chords and a stretto. We shall only feel the unity if we give our playing a touch of improvisation. In a word the case is this; in a sonata of Schumann what most charms us is the movements regarded separately; and in the movements, the separate passages. This Sonata, like the others of his works, must be considered as a volume of lyrical poems.

The "Phantasie-stücke" were the next work. These again are a completed picture, for the most part broader in conception than the Davidsbündler, with which they were contemporaneous in composition. They were the ideal of delicate piano composition, and have remained so down to the present day. The sweet "Abendruhe," the stormy "Aufschwung," the dainty "Warum," the capricious "Grillen," the gloomy "Nachtscene," in which Schumann was thinking of Hero and Leander, the "Fabel," alternating in Ritornell and Staccato; the "Traumeswirren," and the beautiful "Ende vom Lied," whose humour sounds again wonderfully in the intellectual augmentation at the conclusion— all this formed an extraordinary picture-gallery. The height of art was attained in the "Nacht," where the dark rolling accompaniment, the solitary sighs in the gloomy air, the deep returns to darkness, the gently sounding and wild shrieking cries and emotional songs, over the gurgling accompanying figure which runs through the whole, made one of the immortal piano-pieces.

A more purely technical work was the Études Symphoniques, written in 1834 simultaneously with the Carnival, on a theme of

Fricken's.   These variations are as significant for Schumann as the Goldberg variations for Bach or the Diabelli variations for Beethoven.   They are a breviary of all specialities in expression. All Schumann's characteristics were here: the strongly accented fugue, the tied notes with repeated chord accompaniment, the cantabile with broken chords, the staccato chords in canon, the dotted rhythms of Var. IV., the complicated syncopations of Var. V., the bold phrasing of Var. VI., the Bach-like style of Var. VII., the hurrying rush of semiquavers in Étude IX., the duet of voices with tremolo accompaniment in Var. IX., the march with contrapuntal treatment on pedal. points which concludes the work—all was here ; and all was made into a delicate étude in which that union of technique and poetry was constantly completing itself in fresh form.

In the Sonata (or concerto) " without orchestra " (Op. 14) which he recast later without introducing much warmth of feeling, we observe chiefly the strong influence of Bach, which informs the last movement.   If we look closely, indeed, we shall be often reminded of Bach in the last works, particularly in the Symphonic Études.   Certain slurred ornamental figures, certain tricks of accompaniment, the play of dotted and triplet rhythms, the canonic carrying-out of the theme, left no doubt that Schumann had been trained on Bach, and that he had strengthened his musical consciousness by the study of a music in which there is not a superfluous line.   The Letters make this certain.   In 1832 he sat over the Wohltemperiertes Klavier, his Grammar, and occupied himself in analysing the fugues down to their minutest ramifications.   " The use of such a process is great, and has a morally strengthening influence upon the whole man ; for Bach was a man, through and through ; in him there is nothing half-finished, nothing halting ; all is written for eternity." All this has a special and peculiar influence on Schumann.   The abstract music of a Bach is mingled with the concrete representative secondary aims of romance, which find an entrance all the more easily as this absolute art, free from all words and all that is ephemeral, is by far the most expressive to the profoundly musical spirit. Bach's art expresses every phase of feeling, and the emotions are so wide-embracing that they never find a boundary in the domain of reality. This art is the original realm of all transcendental desires. "The profound power of combination, poetry and humour in the new music," wrote Schumann in 1846, "has its origin for the most part in Bach. Mendelssohn, Bennett, Chopin, Hiller, the so-called Romantics, as a whole, stand far nearer to Bach than to Mozart; for as a whole they know Bach through and through. I myself daily confess to this high power, to purify myself, and to strengthen myself through him."

Along with Bach was mingled in his mind the author Hoffmann. There was a remarkable elective affinity in the sympathies of his nature. The "profoundly-combining" Bach took the place of Jean Paul, and the story-teller Hoffmann took the place of Schubert. The twists and turns of a writer, whose style might be called "contrapuntal," found their continuation in the musician who brought all counterpoint into a wonderful "incommensurable" harmony; and the popular simplicity of a musician found its complement in the dreamy lyricism of a genius who had formed perhaps a more beautiful anticipation of the whole music of our century than its actual state has realised. This poet, himself a musician, valued the most romantic of all arts, "one might almost say, the only genuine romantic art; for its subject-matter is the eternal: music opens to man an unknown realm which has nothing in common with the external world of sense, and in which he leaves behind all defined feelings in order to give himself up to an inexpressible longing." And the poet leads us into a realm of magic. In the "Kreisleriana," the garden into which the author leads us is full of tone and song. The stranger comes up to the young squire and tells him of many distant and unknown lands, and strange men and animals; and his speech dies away into a wonderful tone, in which he expresses unknown and mysterious things, intelligibly, yet without words. But the castle maiden follows his enticements, and they meet every midnight at the old tree, none venturing to approach too near the strange melodies that sound therefrom. Then the castle maiden lies pierced through under the tree, and the lute is broken ; but from her blood grow mosses of wonderful colour over the stone, and the young Chrysostom hears the nightingale, which since then makes its nest and sings its song in the tree. At home his father is accompanying his old songs on the clavicymbal, and songs, mosses, and castle-maiden, are all fused in his mind into one. In the garden of tone and song all sorts of internal melodies rise in his heart, and the murmur of the words gives them their breath. He tries to set them to the clavier, but they refuse to come forth from their hiding-places. He closes the instrument, and listens to see whether the songs will not now sound forth more clearly and brightly ; for—" I knew well that the tones must dwell there as if enchanted."

Out of a world like this floated all sorts of compositions into Schumann's mind, as once from the " Flegeljahre " of Jean Paul. Thence came the " Scenes of Childhood," where we listen to tales of foreign lands and men, and dream by the hearth, and play Blind-Man's Buff, and then bend forward to hear, for the Poet is speaking. They are his miniature painting ; of a gentle ineffable grace. Only a " Romantic " can love children thus. Schumann himself had a particular fondness for these little pieces, whose smallness was their very essence.

From Hoffmann also came the inspiration of the " Kreisleriana," so called after Hoffmann's tale of the eccentric Kapellmeister Kreisler. In 1834 Ludwig Böhner, the original of Kreisler, met Schumann. Once "as famous as Beethoven," he jeered at men till they now jeer at him. In his Improvisations, here and there, we catch a glimpse of the old brilliancy; but elsewhere it is all dark and waste. " Had I time," says Schumann, " I should like to write *ana* of Böhner to the papers. He himself has given me plenty of material. In his life there has been too much both of joy and of sorrow." Here was a happy conjuncture for Schumann's genius. A suggestive bit of life, and its poetic

Louis Böhner, the original of Hoffmann's Kreisler. Engraved by Freytag.

setting by Hoffmann, which had first appeared to him as literature, was transformed into music, and a work was born whose title, as so often, he borrowed from a fiction with whose contents it had but little connection, except as suggesting the groundwork. The "Kreisleriana" was his greatest work. The artist who brings life itself, gently transfigured by literary art, into musical emotion, never before or since became so clear a personality. The piano has advanced into the midst of a life-culture. A thousand threads run from all sides into this intimate web in which the whole lyrical devotion of a musical soul is interwoven. The piano is the orchestra of the heart. The joys and sorrows which are expressed in these pieces were never put into form with more sovereign power. For the external form Bach gave the impulse; for the content, Hoffmann. The garlanded roses of the middle section of No. 1, the shimmering blossoms of the "inverted" passage in the "Langsamer" of No. 2, the immeasurable depth of the emotions in the slow pieces (4 and 6), the bass unfettered by accent, in the final bars of No. 8, leading down to the final whisperings, are all among the happiest of inspirations.

The Kreisleriana are dedicated to Chopin; the Fantasia Op. 17 to Liszt. We are on the height on which the first artists of the piano are greeting each other; on which breathes the purest atmosphere of this intimate music; we are on the heights of a culture which has become the dominating power of the world. The Fantasia is, so to speak, a confession of this devotion. In its first movement there is an undefinable romantic feeling as of the words woven round a legendary theme (he called it first the "Ruin"), with mysterious passages, answering voice-parts, mystic ghostly calls. In the second there is the grand triumph, a pane-

The last piece in Schumann's "Kreisleriana," main movement. After the autograph in the possession of Baroness Wilhelm von Rothschild, Frankfort a.M. Differs from the printed edition, being simpler and more massive.

gyric on technique and toil—he called it the "Gate of Victory." In the third is the poetic transfiguration (at first called "Star-picture"), with its ethereal dances and the dying sound of harps, and the sweeping mist, broken chords with pedal, resolved in rubato, over which descend the mournful melodies.[1] The first

---

[1] This sentence refers to the marvellous and perfectly inexpressible passage in the Fantasia Op. 17, beginning forty-one bars before the "Mässig, durchaus energisch."

movement is not free from the variation-technique of the time; the second is a tribute to virtuosity ; the third, a half Schubert. Contrasted with the Kreisleriana of 1838 we recognise an earlier style of 1836, and we wonder at the strong power of progressive development in Schumann—a power which, strange to say, some would deny to him. But the Fantasia was so happily *felt* that it despised time and still to-day stands in the forefront. As there are Études which seem to hold out a hand to Romance, so here Romance held out a hand to technique ; and the Fantasia, in its three forms, remained a classic monument of all the contemporary tendencies. When Schumann published it he cut out the old inscriptions, its profits being devoted to assisting in erecting the Beethoven monument at Bonn, and wrote above the first movement this motto from Schlegel: "Through every tone there passes, to him who deigns to list, in varied earthly dreaming, a tone of gentleness."

In the productive year 1838, before the Scenes of Childhood, Schumann had written three books of " Novellettes," which were now published for the first time and dedicated to Henselt. Springing from his happiest period the music flows as if of its own accord, and its framework is admirable. They are the most subtle pieces conceivable for the piano, and the most popular of his compositions, neat and regular music. Their construction is transparent ; the sections arranged for contrasted effects. In the first piece we have the March, the Cantabile, and the Canon ; in the second the glitter of semiquavers and the delicate rocking Intermezzo ; in the third the humorous Staccato and the wild B minor section; in the fourth the dance and the song mingle with the staccatos of the sequences; in the fifth a Polonaise, in a style approached by few, and Intermezzi in legato, cantabile, and staccato; in the sixth and seventh the effective contrasts of scherzo, canon, and cantabile ; in the eighth an air in duet alternates with several trios ; all kinds of sections are attached, a voice from afar, and free repetitions, as if everything left over had been thrown into it. They are unsurpassed, wonderfully dainty pieces ; but the Kreisleriana were an experience.

The charming smoothness of the Novellettes was no longer alien to Schumann's feelings. The older he grew the more he strove to attain a "dry light," which might easily prove dangerous to his romantic temperament. He began to despise the exuberance of his youthful works. We cannot, in reading the last piano works of Schumann, restrain a certain feeling of pain. Where once the stream bubbled and sparkled, it now flowed too evenly ; where before the music was *felt*, it is now constructed. A new ideal comes slowly into the circle of Schumann's sympathies, and that was Mendelssohn. He not only admired Mendelssohn's greatness, placing him perhaps even above Chopin, but, as his works show, he envied his constraining plastic art, which possibly he mistook for monumental calm.

In piano-literature Mendelssohn is the composer for young girls, the elegant romancist of the drawing-room. From the sphere of polite literature, where passion must be trimmed and neat, and where there is no sentence passed without amiability, and a smiling *laissez-faire* rules the day, there penetrates into glowing romance the limitation of this neatness, and a formality well adapted to the drawing-room. The old Volkslieder, the simple Ritornells, the tones of aspiration in forgotten old airs, the dances of elves, the moonlight love-scenes, are all brought on to a parquet for the delectation of comfortable people. It is a gilt-edged lyricism, without any unbefitting exhibition of unseemly feeling ; a mere art of perfumery compared with Bach and Schubert. The development of the pieces shall exhibit nothing to shock ; it shall run on in the most intelligible manner. A dainty accompaniment-figure is formed, which plays some bars alone ; then follows the melodious and soothing theme, which moves in certain sequences and delights to rock itself to and fro on related degrees of the scale. The strophic divisions are clearly defined ; small cadenzas mark the main sections ; and at the conclusion there appears a miniature canon or a vigorous episode, which leaves behind a good impression on the mind of the satisfied listener.

At the head of this enormous branch of piano-literature stands

Mendelssohn. His "Songs without words," of which six books appeared in his life and two more after his death, gave the decisive form to this class of Short Story in music. All the technical devices of the time, the wide stretches, the broken accompaniments, the multiplicity of rhythms, are here adapted to the drawing-room. The Volkslieder are put, as it were, into evening dress. That in A minor is surrounded towards the conclusion with octaves, which are merely technical, and without emotional significance. The Funeral March, compared with that of a Beethoven, is as if it were written for a set of marionettes. The Spring Song is, so to speak, set on wires. And all is so beautiful, so objectionably beautiful! It tells us all through that it is beautiful, and the composer moves his head to and fro with the music, and says, "How beautiful it is!" Until at last, when we have grown to man's estate, we can endure it all no longer ; or at most we take up once again from time to time this or that song, preferably one in quick time—perhaps the Spinning-Song, the best of all.[1]

From these drawing-room romances of Mendelssohn one piece is to be taken apart, as equally pleasing both to young and to old. This is the Elf-music. Such music, with its gay dancing of gnomes, intermingled with a slightly sentimental air, was wonderfully suited to Mendelssohn's genius. He never surpassed his overture to the Midsummer-Night's Dream, written at seventeen. There are four of these "Elf" or "Kobold" pieces for the piano. The first, in the Character-Pieces, Op. 7, begins in E major, shoots

---

[1] These remarks, though severe, are just, if they are not allowed to apply themselves to *all* of Mendelssohn's work without proper discrimination. Many of his pianoforte works and songs are abundantly feeble ; but we, in England at least, must always owe Mendelssohn a debt for having provided an easy path by which amateurs have been led, now for many years, towards the high and true romance of men like Schubert, Bach, and the others. But it is necessary, and indeed the special duty of an Englishman, to advise young persons who read this book, that Mendelssohn *at his best* is what they should get to know, and that unless they have "Elijah" and "St Paul" by heart, the adverse criticism of the composer of those works is denied them. Even in these two great oratorios it requires no practised Diabolus to find their weaknesses—but what shall an honest man say of " Yet doth the Lord see it not," or "The nations are now the Lord's," in spite of the wretched weakness of counterpoint in the fugal parts of the latter movement ? The man who could write such things is a great man and a true "romantic."

rapidly past, and ends very daintily in the minor. The second, Op. 16, 2, begins on the contrary in E minor, and concludes in a very spirited fashion in the major—a very poetical little Battle of the Mice, with tiny fanfares and dances, all kinds of squeaks, and runnings to and fro of a captivating grace. The third is the Rondo

Head of Mendelssohn, after Hildebrand.

Capriccioso (Op. 14), for which all piano-players have a deadly hatred, but which is much prettier than we are inclined to think to-day, when it is worn out. Finally we have the F sharp minor Scherzo, which was written for the "Album des Pianistes," with dotted, staccato, and singing themes, and stands out among his pieces.

Mendelssohn was one of the few great musicians, whose whole

life, from cradle to the grave, was lived in sunshine and happiness. From his joyous youth to his European renown as head of the Leipzig Conservatorium his life was a round of serenity, and at its zenith he might well die.   Sunshine and happiness are in his works; storm never breaks in, no sigh moves to tears.   His storms and sighings never forget their artistic calm.   His pieces cast friendly glances on all sides, and are quite conscious of the friendly glances they receive in return.   As beautifully as their author played — he played rarely but willingly in concerts — they present their technique, so popular, so charming; sounding more difficult to play than they are.   The technical content is chiefly rapid staccato, whether of single notes or chords; the ornamentation of melodies in arpeggio; brilliant repetitions obtained by rapid alternation of the two hands; free obligato use of the pedal; and a showy use of a facile right hand.

These find their most popular expression in the conclusion of the Serenade, in the first movement of the D minor Concerto, and in the E minor Prelude.   Popular even ad nauseam are the Concert-pieces, the B minor capriccio (the favourite fantasia with march-conclusion), and the two piano concertos, all of which are practically in one movement, with partial repeats.   In technique these appear to owe an obligation to Weber, for whom Mendelssohn had a heartfelt admiration.

The third group of Mendelssohn's piano works, along with the " Short Stories " and the concertos, are the " Bachiana," or, more properly, " Handeliana."   An æsthetic historic sense is a rooted characteristic of the romantic spirit.   Mendelssohn's studies in Bach and Handel had a great influence on his development, and are plainly shown in some of the " Seven Character-Pieces," with their soft, gentle, old-world conduct of the melodies, and the clever fugal movement which seems to set an ancient counterpoint on to Mendelssohnian harmonies.   Here belongs the Fantasia, Op. 28, with its three contrapuntal movements ; also the famous E minor fugue and its companions in Op. 35, with the appended chorale and the pompously smooth partwriting, fall into this place.   It is constructed entirely differently from the fugue of Bach, which grows up from within ; it is a grafting of a fugato on the trunk of a drawing-room piece. Finally, we recall the "Variations sérieuses," composed in 1841, the purest, most solid, most massive work that Mendelssohn ever wrote for the piano, without a suspicion of triviality, filled full with intellectual outlines and harmonies, a splendid erection, but—throughout dependent on Schumann.

We have thus returned to Schumann, whom Mendelssohn so nobly repaid for his admiration. This elegant composer, who, whether as poet, as concertist, or as a follower of Bach, was always equally clear and plastic, might well appear to Schumann the fulfilment of his own aims. He had not wavered as to whether he was called to be a musician, though he had perhaps regarded business as the easier course. At his pieces he had toiled as Heine toiled at one of those smooth-flowing poems of his. The doubt may well have often recurred to him whether the flow was checked. But from this Mendelssohn the music flowed so easily from the fingers, and stood so clear and transparent before him. At one time he believes that the stream is clear, and he rejoices over the speed with which he finishes twelve sheets in a week. This work was the " Humoreske," which entirely puts aside the earlier fragmentary romance, and throws all, joy and sorrow, into the same crucible. Thus we gain a piece bearing all the marks of decadent imitation of Bach's traditions, and even of those of Schumann himself, in spite of isolated, delicate, lyrical traits, which occur specially in the G minor section (Einfach und Zart). We are now in March 1839. Schumann writes to Clara, asking her why she chooses the Carnival to introduce him to people who do not know him. Why not rather choose the Fantasie Stücke, in which one does not nullify the other, and in which there is a comfortable breadth ? " You like best storm and lightning at once, and always something new that has never been." Then also he put his " Arabesque " and his " Blumen-stück " together, which has nothing but the title in common with Jean Paul. As a matter of fact, nothing was new, and everything had been. It had become a question whether the limits of the possibilities of the piano had not already been over-passed. As Op. 22 he brought out the Sonata in G minor, which he had composed earlier; a piece, compared with the F sharp minor, rounded and of satisfying content. The final pithy move-ment he replaced by one of neater and smoother character. It is sad to hear him, in his letters, speaking with great *empressement* of the Nacht-stücke (Op. 23) and then to find that there is nothing special in them. As Op. 26 appeared the "Carnival Jest" (Faschings-schwank) which brought back his old style of the "short story," but forced into a sort of sonata-arrangement. The vigorous "Reveillé" in F sharp major, the fine painting of the restless bustle, the beautiful Romance, the delicate simplicity of the Scherzino, with its canonic conclusion, the singing Intermezzo, which in breadth and value on the whole surpassed Mendelssohn—all these have ill prepared us for the great falling off in the Finale. This piece was Schumann's last great utterance on the "subjective" piano. In the meanwhile the Song had taken him captive, and dominated his whole nature. In Schumann development pro-ceeded almost according to classes. After the Song came chamber-music, then chorus, then the symphony.

Among his later piano-pieces we find all sorts in various styles—partly interesting as showing an advance upon himself, partly, alas, mere decadent imitations of himself. The fulness of ideas and of titles is quite astonishing in his "Jugendalbum," in his "Albumblätter" containing the dainty Slumber Song, and in the "Bunte Blätter" containing the Geschwind-marsch. The most delicate aftermath of Romance proper was the "Waldscenen" in which the "Eintritt" and the "Verrufene Stelle" are worthy of a musical Hoffmann. The Hunting Song is in the style of Mendelssohn. As late fruits of the intimate piano lyric appear the sweet variations for two pianos, which we cannot choose but love, the four-handed Eastern Pictures (Bilder aus dem Osten), in which Chopin plays a part, and the Songs of Early Morning, and to Bettina, which show a beautiful touch of a later style, often reaching the borders of motives from Parsifal. But most important were certain concertos. Of these the limpid A minor, dedicated to Hiller—the first movement of which was composed earlier—in its freedom and colouring recalling Beethoven, and finally showing traces of Chopin's influence, is a perfect work. Finally, we must not omit the Concert Allegro (Op. 134) dedicated to Brahms, a brilliant creation, often recalling Bach, with a theme very much in the style of Brahms, and many interesting repetitions of earlier figures of Schumann's own. Why has it been almost forgotten?

Like Schubert throughout his music, so has Schumann in his chamber-music left us his youth. He broke off the regular practice of it at about the same time of life as that at which Schubert died. During the next fourteen years a slow decline in the artistic freshness of his works made itself noticeable; and finally, alas, his genius deserted him.

At this time some one wrote: "Thalberg is a king, Liszt a prophet, Chopin a poet, Herz a lawyer, Kalkbrenner a troubadour, Madame Pleyel a sibyl, Döhler a pianist." The reader will observe that Schumann is not even mentioned in this list. In Paris, as yet, he did not count. There was an utter absence of the frivolous in his music, and it had none of the qualities which were likely to conquer the great world. Chopin scarcely ever required his pupils to play the works of Schumann, and would seem to have had very little taste for them. On the other hand, it was Schumann who gave an impulse to the popularity of Chopin's works in his magazine, as early as the appearance of the Variations on the theme "Reich' mir die Hand" (Op. 2). Indeed, the rapid and enduring fame in Germany of Schumann's only true rival was due to Schumann himself.

"Chopin a poet." It has become a very bad habit to place this poet in the hands of our youth. The concertos and polonaises being put aside, no one lends himself worse to youthful instruction than Chopin. Because his delicate touches inevitably seem perverse to the youthful mind, he has gained the name of a morbid genius. The grown man who understands how to play Chopin, whose music begins where that of another leaves off, whose tones show the supremest mastery in the tongue of music,—such a man will discover nothing morbid in him. Chopin, a Pole, strikes sorrowful chords, which do not occur frequently to healthy normal persons. But why is a Pole to receive less justice than a German? We know that the extreme of culture is closely allied to decay; for perfect ripeness is but the foreboding of corruption. Children, of course, do not know this. And Chopin himself would have been much too noble ever to lay bare his mental sickness to the world. And his greatness lies precisely in this, that he preserves the mean between immaturity and decay.

His greatness is his aristocracy. He stands among musicians in his faultless vesture, a noble from head to foot. The sublimest emotions, towards whose refinement whole generations had tended, the last things in our soul, whose foreboding is interwoven with the mystery of the Judgment Day, have in his music found their form. At this Judgment Day appears to be expressed what man kept dark within himself, and shuddering sought to hide from the light. Now it has become free without becoming plebeian; it has been uttered without becoming trivial. This miracle is sung by geniuses, who are not cold as marble, nor of such unreal beauty that we, to our horror, are constrained to believe that there is an anti-human classicism. No; the angels bear those delicate features as they weave nobility and joy into one. These are Polish piquancies, tender and shining eyes of inner fire, with happy heavy lids, and gently curved outlines, in which pride and spirit blend together; speaking lips, which have something sweet to say, and gentle, melting contours.

Chopin gave recitals but rarely. In his youth—who was ever, as a youth, without visions of a virtuoso-life?—he sometimes did so; but even then with little enthusiasm. If he was heard in Paris, it was at very select matinées at the Pleyel salon, to which only with difficulty was admission to be obtained. The exiled aristocracy of Poland, the world of Parisian art and letters, and ladies, sat around and listened. *Réunions intimes, concerts de fashion,* as Liszt called them, were the purest piano-recitals ever given. The artist knew his audience ; and in that small circle there was free play for the isolated poesy which sounded from the instrument. A delicate genius had won back for the piano its reserved nobility. There was here no *fracas pianistique,* no noisy circus-scene before a many-headed, unknown, indeterminate public ; but courtly culture without the court. When in 1834 Chopin gave a great recital in the Italian Opera, he was undeceived by the want of response which he found, and necessarily found, in those great halls, which only dissipated his dainty playing. He said to Liszt, " I am not fitted for public playing. The public frightens me, its breath chokes me, I am paralysed by its inquisitive gaze, and affrighted at these strange faces ; but you, you are meant for it. If you can't win the love of the public, you can astonish it and deafen it."

Chopin once said of himself that he was in this world like the E string of a violin on a contrabass. His finely-strung nature sought retirement, and fate had given him precisely that longing for rest and harmony which of necessity made the contrabass of this world excessively painful to him. He ran restlessly from one abode to another, till he found in the Place de Vendôme the best for dying in ; he became more and more retiring, called for peaceful pearl-gray carpets, and gave full play to all his decorative emotions, which are the external proof of a harmonic soul. The art of his life was driven into isolation, into inclusion in the sacred recesses of his musical poems ; and he knew well how so to level his life to the external observer, that the biographers—apart from his one great passion—had never so uneventful a life to record. The wellknown description of an evening with the master, which Liszt gives in his fanciful but yet so true biography of Chopin, is so rich in character that reality itself could hardly have done it better. A melting twilight in the room, the dark corners seeming to produce themselves into infinity, the furniture covered with white hangings, no candle except by the piano and by the fireside.

We distinguish Heine, Meyerbeer, the tenor Nourrit, Hiller, Delacroix, the unemotional Minkiewicz, the gray-haired Niemce-wicz, and George Sand with propped arm leaning back in a chair. The people stand round Chopin in the twilight, and hardly know whence these magic tones come. [The English reader will recall the exquisite description of Chopin's playing in Crawford's romance "With the Immortals."]

We can easily see why Chopin could never compose duets· Not only did he devote himself exclusively to the piano—he wrote nothing in which the piano does not bear a part—but he broke with the custom of writing duets for one or two pianos. A single Rondo for two pianos, of the year 1828, was found among his re-mains. How he smiled once at Czerny, who " had composed another overture for eight pianos and sixteen persons, and was very happy over it." Chopin opened to the two hands a wider world than Czerny could give to thirty-two. And further, he selects and rejects with great care before publishing. He prints nothing which does not absolutely satisfy his mind both as a whole and in its details.

Between his youth in Poland—which was soon closed to him on political grounds—and his last journey through England and Scotland, his stay in France stretches like a peaceful background of exclusively artistic activity. A thousand anecdotes cluster round him, but only a few of them have stood the test of criticism and comparison. In his "Life of Chopin"—and there are few musical biographies equally good—Niecks has collected every-thing that is told, and all the arguments against the authenticity of the various tales. Even upon that famous scene, in which the Countess Potocka sings the dying Chopin to his eternal slumber, the traditions are contradictory. There are few letters to help us. Chopin was too reserved to write them. It was said that he would rather go right through Paris to decline an invitation by word of mouth than write his excuse. And of the few letters he actually did write, the best appear to have been burnt in the sack of Warsaw. Nevertheless there is a certain charm in being thus obliged, as it were, to see him in shadow.

A sweet tie bound him to his native country. The fundamental characteristic of the Poles, who united the merits of the Gaul and of the Slav, that character of modesty and resignation, of sadness and of reminiscence, flowed all the purer into the works of the artist. It was easy to see that almost every one of Chopin's compositions, even if it was *not* a Mazurka, sprang from the rhythm and sentiment of the

George Sand, in man's dress. Lithograph by Cecilia Brandt.

Mazur (Magyar) music; but it had been all steeped in the spirit of the Parisian life. A *milieu* of his own was here, of a charming and cultivated kind, of which there are but few; the *milieu* of fair Polish ladies, who in Paris lived for their aspirations and their temperaments. As Liszt said, the French alone saw in the daughters of Poland a yet unknown ideal: the other nations had not the slightest suspicion that there was anything worthy of admiration in these elusive sylphs of the dance, who smiled so happily of an evening, and in the morning lay sobbing at the foot of the altar; in these apparently distracted travellers, who, if they journeyed through Switzerland, drew the curtains of their carriages lest the sight of the mountain-landscape should erase the memory of the limitless horizon of their own native plains. Is not this a paraphrase of Chopin's music?

That enigmatical daemon, whom fate had allowed to grow up within the walls of Paris—George Sand—was Chopin's one grand passion. This was his one overmastering emotion—but its influence never faded. The beginning and the end of their association were varied a hundredfold. His love for her seems to have begun in hate and to have ended in it; hers began in dreaming, and ended with emotion; and, as she carried through the episode in actual life with *bel esprit*, so she clothed it poetically with the same. Who can reproach a Don Juan nature with wickedness? George Sand must have been wicked to play her vampire-part to the end. But there was nothing petty about the style in which she played it.

The Powers were cruel who brought these two persons together. Now in Paris, now at George Sand's country place at Nohant, now in travel, Fate compelled them to play this fearful comedy, in which, at bottom, neither truly knew or comprehended the other. The woman remained a *bel esprit*, and the artist remained a dreamer. And in the midst of the comedy stands the ridiculous idyll of Majorca, in which these two persons live near each other, in a prison of their souls. The man delicate and pining, with agile limbs, slight hands, slight feet, silky-brown hair, transparent complexion, finely-curved nose, quiet smile, voice muffled "like a creeper whose calyx rocks on the delicate stem, dressed in wonderful colours, but of such airy texture that it tears at the slightest motion." The woman, with an ideal Greek countenance on a somewhat thick-set body; a face that might seem to have come down from earlier ages, as Heine describes it, but softened by a surprising gentleness—Musset's "femme à l' œil sombre." They sit in the midst of the cypresses, oranges, and myrtles in the deserted monastery of Valdemosa with its chapels, churches, carved statues, and moss-grown stonework. In the evening the populace come out and dance ghostlike boleros with castanets, or at other times the wind howls as if possessed and the rain falls without intermission. Eating is impossible; ships cannot come through the storm. A Pleyel piano, brought there with difficulty, stands in the deserted halls, and Chopin sits at it and shivers. He longs for home; and she is soon compelled to recognise that nothing increased his chest-complaint so much as this winter in Majorca, which she had aided him in planning.

This winter in Majorca was that of 1838 and 1839. It has long been believed that it gave rise to Chopin's Preludes. Some have even fancied they recognised in the dropping motives of some of them, especially the E minor, the B minor, and the D flat major, the effect of the constant rain of Majorca. The truth is that a large part of the Preludes were written, or half written, before this, and that only the last touches were given to them in Majorca. Nay, it is even possible that the mighty and fiery A major Polonaise was conceived and finished under the gloomy sky of Majorca. Dates are difficult to obtain, and also of very little importance. Chopin writes his works so entirely from the heart that they have very little dependence on the moment of their composition. The single case of an impulse of this kind would seem to be the news of the sack of Warsaw, upon which he is said to have written the stormy C minor Étude. Poetic influences, also, Polish or French, move him only as it were on the circumference. He is a delicately emotional nature, but far from a literary one.

Chopin's habit of conceiving his pieces as great wholes is precisely what renders an analysis of his works impossible. Chopin, with all the charms we know so well, with all his wide embracing harmonies, his spirited voice-outlines, is but one, and one whole: and this single Chopin takes now one, now another, isolated form, in which, from the original motives, ever fresh creations are fused together. In every piece he is entirely present. There are, it is true, a few weaker pieces of his youth; and Fontana has published a large stock from his remains (these are numbered from Op. 66 on)—a thing to which he would have objected; he hated this stirring of dead bones. But these pieces have now vanished even from the practising repertoire of the following generations. Certain lines can always be drawn over his general work. We see him, at first, plainly dominated by his only true forerunner, Hummel, for whom he felt a passionate admiration, and whose method of execution he has only further enlarged; so that in Chopin's daintiest colourations a keen observer can detect the relics of the old "manieren" and ornamental flourishes. The E flat major Rondo, the Concert-Polonaise, and, above all, the two Concertos in E minor and F minor, show clearly the influence of Hummel, notably in their jerky insertion of étude-like murmuring motives, their simply broken accompaniment to the cantilena, their brilliant effects in the high registers, their easy drawing-room phrases, and their surprisingly Mozart-like charm in melodic line. But the concertos, the most fairy-like in the whole range of that class of literature, already point to regions so far out of the reach of Hummel that they cannot be exhaustively summed up under that category. Scarcely to be separated chronologically from them are the pure commencements of the genuine art of Chopin, which is clearly visible in the first Mazurkas, and stretches far into the forties. Even those remarkable spirited variations in B flat minor, dated 1833, on an operatic theme of Herold, in which Chopin seemed to make a concession to fashion, are not removed a hair's breadth from the distinction of his best style. In 1840, a year so fruitful for Schumann also, appeared Op. 35 to 50. Chopin was thirty-one, the age at which Schubert died. At last a certain later style has been marked off; restrained, contrapuntal, and yet unfettered. His most brightly-coloured examples he gave in the wildly poetical Barcarolle, the spiritual B major Nocturne, and the full-bodied Fantasia-Polonaise.

Chopin's work shows but few departures from his regular lines. Of these we may mention the beautiful pasticcio of the F minor Fantasia, which should be played with a sort of ex-tempore laxity; the Barcarolle; the Tarantelle; the Bolero; and the refined Berceuse, in which, over the uniform accompaniment, a splendid succession of motives ascends or descends; which form an epitome of Chopin's "manieren," as the Goldberg Variations were of Bach's, the Diabelli of Beethoven's, or the C sharp minor of Schumann's. Apart from these his pieces fall into symmetrical groups, each of which has its own pronounced character.

His sonatas remain most strange to us; they are sonatas in the strict sense as little as the other sonatas by the Romantics. Chopin cares so little for form that he avoids the recurrence to the first theme. The whole falls into fragments: the B flat minor has its wild first theme and its dainty second; the capricious Scherzo, the Funeral March, which, alas! has become so popular (it was introduced into the Sonata only by an afterthought), and the spirited unisono storm of the last Presto, right on to the fortissimo concluding bar. But from the B minor Sonata, the sultry Largo, and the last movement, a kind of giant boating-piece, strike us as most remarkable.

Chopin finds his true form in the Ballades and Scherzi. This is the extempore form, which even in the Impromptus has for long not been so unfettered. The dividing lines of the sections are drawn from free invention, and the thought is constrained by no scheme. An artistic order introduces the rhythm of the arrangement with which the moment would have been obliged to dispense. It is naturalism lifted into the sphere of discrete art.

The improvised form is shown in the Preludes still more purely, but with less pretension. They are a succession of musical aphorisms, from the sketch to the finished piece, running through the gamut of all forms.

In these Ballades, Scherzi and Preludes, we reach again one of those solitary peaks of piano literature in which improvisatorial invention and artistic construction meet again in a higher unity.

The Études crown the efforts of this period, to bring technique and tune into the friendly relation peculiar to them. While we admire their mechanical value in point of polyrhythmical effects, wide stretches, double trills, independence of the left hand, airy piano-effects, freedom of the wrist, and quickness of finger-change, we praise their poetry, the grace of the C major or the magic of the A flat major, the solemnity of the C sharp minor, or the intoxication of the G flat major, the Titanic force of the C minor, or the melancholy of the E flat minor.

The Nocturnes—with the silken web of the D flat major in their midst—are the high songs of melody which Chopin nowhere else has framed with such entrancing aspiration or such broad exclamatory sighs. But the dances are the high songs of rhythm, to which never yet was so intellectual a homage paid. The Polonaises have the *galant* and knightly features of the old Polish nobility ; and Chopin's head rears itself in them more proudly than one would have expected from his feminine nature. But the Mazurkas are bourgeois little joys, half bathed in sorrow, half crushing their pain in the jubilation of the rhythm—an unparalleled series of intellectual inspirations. In the Waltzes we have only a higher kind of Mazurkas, with less of the national spirit, like Poles in the Parisian drawing-room. The slow Waltz in A minor, not without reason, was dearest to Chopin's own heart.

Chopin's playing was the rapture of his contemporaries. All agree that his individuality could only be made intelligible by himself. How long did Moscheles torment himself with the remarkable harmonic transitions which he found in Chopin's compositions ! But when he heard the master himself, all doubt vanished ; what had seemed violent now became self-intelligible. Chopin's playing was dainty and airy ; his fingers seemed to glide sideways, as if all technique were a glissando ; even the Forte was in him not an absolute but a relative forte—relative, that is, to the gentle voice of the rest ; and it rises, the older he grew, so much the less by force than by a subtle play of touch. All execution has made way for a certain free extempore poesy ; the *rubato* softens the harshness of bar-accent. Liszt's definition of the rubato is well known—" You see that tree ; its leaves move to and fro in the wind and follow the gentlest motion of the air ; but its trunk stands there, immovable in its form." Chopin seems never to have carried the rubato so far that this trunk itself would have stirred. Once already had a player arisen who cultivated this graceful and airy kind of execution. Field, a Scot by birth, Clementi's pupil, a pale and dreamy man, had anticipated the delicate breadth of Chopin's touch ; and the world had been enraptured with his melancholy renderings by means of apparently motionless hands. Alongside of not very important sonatas, concertos, and rondos, he had published a series of song-like pieces, which he called " Nocturnes," and in which he put to special use his longing melodies, his dreamy *portamenti*, his rose-chains of airy colourations. Compared with Chopin's Nocturnes, these must necessarily appear pale and even monotonous; but in his whole essence, in the form of his pieces, and the delicacy of his touch, Field was a prelude to Chopin—as Dussek or Louis Ferdinand were in their kind. When Chopin once played before Alexander Klengel, Clementi's pupil, the latter was strongly reminded of Field. And when Chopin, after his arrival in Paris, conceived the idea of taking further lessons under Kalkbrenner, whose delicate playing he admired above everything, the latter likewise thought that the style reminded him of Cramer, but the playing of Field. "Were you Field's pupil?" he asked. Chopin's true teacher, the forgotten Elsner of Warsaw, had had no share in it. Chopin had formed his own playing, as he formed his own style. In early years he had a mania for width of stretch, and even invented a device for stretching the fingers. The experiment was fortunately more successful than Schumann's attempt to increase the independence of the fingers by means of a sling. The difference is noteworthy : Chopin aimed at a richer impression of voluptuous fullness in the chords ; Schumann at increased independence of part playing.

Chopin, as a sensitive artist, laid special stress on the kind of instrument he used. In his youth he would only willingly play on Graf's pianos ; in Paris only on those of Pleyel, whose silvern muffled tone was specially attractive to him. In those of Erard he thought the tone too insistent. "If I am in a bad humour I play an Erard, and easily find there the tone ready-made. But if I am in the humour, and strong enough to make my own tone, I use a Pleyel." The fingering, also, he regulates for himself. For the sake of a better execution he never objects to put his thumb on a black key in suitable places, or to glide with one finger over two keys, or to let longer fingers pass over the shorter without using the thumb. In his Études he has expressly written marks for many such naturalistic fingerings.

The special character of Chopin's method, which in this literature created an epoch, consisted in an effective use of three voices.

Of course it is not meant that he constantly writes strictly in three parts; quite on the other hand, he has made a quite unique use of the unison in the B flat minor Sonata, in the fourteenth and eighteenth Preludes, and in the second movement of the F minor Concerto; and there are plenty of examples in him of the simple accompaniment of a simple melody. But the peculiar charm of his technique begins only in the parallel application of three voices (I am not using this term in the contrapuntal sense), in the laying alongside of three motived systems, three musical thoughts, three principal paths. In the Berceuse, for example, upon the heels of the one voice over the accompaniment treads instantly a second, and the threefold combination of accompaniment and two overparts is carried through in all possible variations. The two overparts are no less present in several passages, which appear on paper merely as zigzag runs, which bind together continuously the two melodic lines. In favourable cases, as in the boldly accented chords toward the conclusion of the B flat minor Scherzo, this peculiar line-counterpoint is carried to an extreme. The fusion of unfusable things in melody, rhythm, and harmony is the new synthesis by means of which this art advances. The charm of certain melodies of Chopin is increased by their taking up intervals foreign to the key, which affect us half with Eastern, half with ecclesiastical associations, but on closer inspection these are seen to be merely due to the collision of two melodic lines.[1] There are, for example, resolutions of suspensions, which are postponed for the moment; the main melody of the First Ballade, the whispering second Intermezzo of the famous B flat major Mazurka, the D in the C sharp minor Nocturne, the A in the B minor Prelude, are instances. It is a *rubato* of melody : a musical, not a rhythmical rubato. If a section of a Mazurka in Op. 30, 3 is repeated pianissimo, it does not shock us, if certain notes already played reappear a semitone lower, precisely as if the dynamic weakening had a musical weakening as its result. It is an effect of intellectual

---

[1] Cases of this kind are common in Purcell and Bach. Examples are easily quoted. One of the commonest with Purcell is the collision of ♮7 and ♭7 in perfect cadences.

naturalistic charm. Everywhere the straight line is by preference avoided. Suspensions (retardations) are boldly prolonged at the conclusion of a bar, as in the B flat major Mazurka or in the stretto of the G minor Ballade. The melodies wind themselves round invisible axles, and the *fioriture* play in turn round the supports of the melodies. The time is ignored, incommensurable passages can only be worked in by the *feel*, triplets and duplets are mingled with each other, or a wonderful pseudo-rhythm, as in the F major theme of the A flat major Ballade, makes us waver pleasantly between two time-emotions. There is constantly a combination, by the two independent hands, or by the independent movement of an upper or under group of fingers in one hand: this is the extreme attainment of artistic finger-mechanism on a harmonic instrument.

The sensuous charm of sound in Chopin's music rests essentially on this *use* of the individualisation of the fingers. Formerly the fingers had only been tools, which rendered on the piano the general many-voiced piece. Now, however, a music had arisen from the essence of the fingers which was quite peculiar to the piano. The pedal held the dissected music again together. The left hand continues its own melodic lines under the right, as we find in the E minor Prelude, in the C sharp minor Étude, in the middle movement of the C sharp minor Polonaise, and the Scherzo of the B flat minor Sonata, in the F sharp major Impromptu, in the G minor Ballade, in the A flat major Waltz (Op. 34, 1), or in so many Études with characteristic full figuration in the left hand. Or in passages which run swiftly enough to allow this little acoustic deception to grow into a charm, the two melodic passages or one melody unite with their retardation notes into those zig-zag contours which became Chopin's distinguishing mark. There is a long spirited series from the first Hummel-like pieces in the E minor Concerto, through the ethereal sounds in the middle movement of the third Scherzo, to the B minor Scherzo which forms its wild main movement entirely by means of this mannerism. The concluding trills of the concertos, the arpeggios of wide chords;

the ornamentations in the middle of the chords, take a share in the using-up of the polyphony for sound effects ; until at last we meet the threefold or fourfold web in the concluding sections of the Barcarolle.

We have, in these last phrases of Chopin been reminded of the influences of Bach, and in fact, the extreme individualisation of the fingers leads us of necessity back to Bach, in whose works the fingers are called upon to perform the last possibilities of many-voiced music. Throughout it all Chopin knew that Bach is nature in music. When he was practising for his recitals, he played, not Chopin but Bach.

[The English pianist and composer, William Sterndale Bennett, contemporary and friend of Mendelssohn, equally popular as a musician both in Germany and his own country, demands notice in this place. If England has not succeeded in forming a definite musical style for itself in the nineteenth century, at least it can take credit for having possessed one composer who may be called "unique" in the true sense of the word. As far as his powers extended, Sterndale Bennett achieved the highest distinction. There is no one *like* him—his pianoforte music (on which alone he can afford to take his stand) ranks quite by itself in expression, character, and technical difficulty. Those who class him with Mendelssohn look merely on the surface, and show themselves incapable of making a worthy distinction.

Sterndale Bennett's music is never *weak*, although for the most part cast in a delicate mould. On the other hand, he seems to have felt that the "grand" style was out of his reach, and that it was no part of his business to act the strong man. Accordingly, he seldom shows any inclination to venture too high a flight. This alone suffices to distinguish him from Mendelssohn.

Probably most pianists, when speaking of Sterndale Bennett, would naturally think first of the Three Sketches (Op. 10, Nos. 1,

2, 3), "The Lake," "The Millstream," and "The Fountain." And it would be difficult to better this as a specimen list—the first as a perfect expression of natural tranquillity, the second as an example of Sterndale Bennett's peculiar technical difficulties, and the last as a complete imitative picture.

The "Six Studies" (Op. 11) are quite characteristic. Their musical value is very evident to the hearer; it is only the player who can appreciate the perfection of execution they demand. No. 3, in B flat, is the gem of the set. No. 6, the octave study in G minor, approaches real power in the first section. The *cantabile* second subject is an exemplification of the quite inimitable style of the composer. Amongst other miscellaneous pieces the following must be named—the Fantasia in A, Op. 16, dedicated to Schumann, especially the first movement, with its lovely melody on arpeggiando accompaniment—the Caprice in E (with orchestra), Op. 22, an excellent proof of Sterndale Bennett's mastery of the "concerto" manner—the Rondo piacevole in E, Op. 25, where one notes the wonderful grace of the first subject, the expressive power of the second.

Sterndale Bennett comparatively seldom rises to emotional heights; however, see his Op, 28, No. 1, the Introduction and Pastorale in A, particularly the early bars of the Introduction, where, if he does not attain the seventh heaven of a man or an archangel, he at least reaches the clear empyrean of the happy skylark. He touches the same high level towards the close of the Pastorale itself. For other examples of his capacity for the expression of deep feeling compare also the third and fourth movements of the "Maid of Orleans" Sonata, Op. 46, an idyllic work, almost unknown, and scarcely ever played. Description of this Sonata would be useless: it should be studied. It shows Sterndale Bennett at his best and worst—it shows all his strength, and some of his peculiar weaknesses.

Space prevents more than the mere mention of other works in which the pianoforte takes a prominent part:—The Concerto in F minor, Op. 19 (played by Sterndale Bennett himself "at the concerts of Leipsic ") ; the violoncello and piano duet, Op. 32 ; the Sextett for two violins, viola, violoncello and contrabasso, with pianoforte, Op. 8 ; the pianoforte Trio in A, Op. 26 ; and, not least important, from the point of view of this book, the twelve songs, the accompaniments of which are of ideal beauty.]

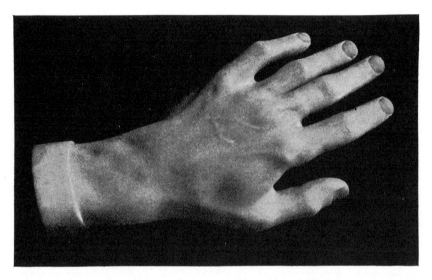

Chopin's Hand.   From a marble in the National Museum at Budapest.

An Afternoon with Liszt. Lithograph by Kriehuber.
Kriehuber.   Berlioz. Czerny.   Liszt.   The violinist Ernst.

Liszt and the Present Time

Photograph of Liszt, taken in Budapest.

AT the beginning of the era of present-day piano-art, perhaps also at the culmination of all independent and advancing piano-art, stands Franz Liszt. The artistic phenomenon of Liszt is yet so near to us, that it is still misunderstood. Even to-day he has fanatical friends and bitter foes : blind assailants and diplomatic defenders. And through it all, the whole world of piano-playing stands under his influence.

This was possible because Liszt was a developed artistic nature, who did not fall in with the established scheme, was by everybody differently understood, differently loved, differently hated. We can distinguish three types of artists. The one is the rapid composer, whose new thoughts readily find their new suitable form. The second class is that of the artists of the will—great innovators, like Manet and Degas among the painters, who worked not so much by their visible productiveness, as by their personal influence, exerted from day to day; an influence which after their death seems almost inconceivable. The third consists of the compilers, classics in the historical sense, who form a synthesis of all the constituent parts, a unity of opposites, into which history continually diverges, a conjunction of all begun and severed paths, the complete culture of a time made living. Liszt belongs to none of these types; he belongs to the last two *together*. The union of the innovator and the classic forms his essence; and in understanding this lies the complete comprehension of him. He possessed a double power, which influenced the world as it did, because the world never saw the one half of his nature before the other.

Liszt the revolutionary cast his seed wide into the world. His system of patronage, founded on artistic feeling, not merely smoothed the way for Wagner and Berlioz, but assured to every suppliant the preservation of a modicum of self-respect and a modicum of hope. He pointed out to the modern musical development, in a kind of theoretical praxis peculiar to himself, the paths which led from the revolutionary principles of Berlioz to the popular musical realism of to-day. He scattered over both hemispheres the seeds of intimate personal instructions, of great and small disclosures; so that even now eternal gratitude to this most kind-hearted of all artists is felt over the world.

Liszt the compiler is a new Liszt. Here the revolutionary remained apart, and the new Liszt came forth, who rushed in undreamed-of splendour through real and imagined worlds. He gathers cultures, a princely collector, with the crown of rare desert

ETUDES
pour le
Piano
en douze Exercices
composés
par
F. LISZT.

——— Oeuvre I ———

Travail de la Jeunesse.

Liv I. 16 Gr.   Liv.II. 20 Gr.

Leipzig, chez Fr. Hofmeister.

2340 - 41

Title-page of Hofmeister's Edition of Liszt's Op. I.

upon his head. The world did not know that this same man could pass through times of quiet creation and thought. He is a man of the world of the highest *savoir faire*, a writer of bewitching elegance, a conqueror who makes nought of the boundaries of peoples, a king despising kings, a demigod as conductor of tumultuous musical festivals, and in his works, which seem to appear daily in countless, uncontrollable numbers, a classical combiner of that which is and that which has been. It was he who united composition and interpretation, music and poetry, romance and virtuosity, Olympian and Titan, Beethoven and Paganini. Everything that the piano had experienced, the mystic longings of the old counterpoint, the love of variation of Bird and Bull, the ornamentation of Couperin and Rameau, the sensuous delight in sound of Scarlatti, the absolute art of Bach, the charm and formal beauty of Mozart, the pain of Beethoven crying for release, the intellectual confessions of the unique triumvirate, Schubert, Schumann, and Chopin—the rays of all met in him. A true combiner, he did not jumble these cultures in a learned and academic fashion together in himself, but he developed their common medium, in which they could test their mutual effects, with ever new charms.

The life of Liszt necessarily prepared him for this mighty combination. It is a co-ordination of cultures, each of which, singly experienced, might have sufficed for an ordinary mortal. He passed through six such lives in the various parts of his existence. As "petit Litz" he lived the life of a precocious much-loved child ; then in Paris he penetrated to the depths of a romantic idealism, which drew closely together the men of that fruitful epoch ; next, with the Comtesse d'Agoult he lived for five years the free and productive life of a wandering artist : then he experienced the glories of European renown as a virtuoso ; next, he exerted himself in Weimar as the pioneer of the modern style ; and finally, in Rome, Buda-Pest, and Weimar, he lived the peaceful life of a ruler, having attained the heights of worldly honour and equally those of that conquest of the world which found its symbol

Liszt in his youth. Lithograph by Kriehuber.

in his priestly robe.   Lina Ramann had the courage to make three
volumes of biography out of this unparalleled life, in which the
unique material is spoilt by doubtful German and uncritical
enthusiasm.   Liszt is in her books not the subject but the hero of
the tale ; and the wickedness of women is the theme.   The

After Dantan's Caricature of
Thalberg.

Comtesse d'Agoult receives the same
measure as George Sand in Niecks'
"Life of Chopin."   It is remarkable,
how in the archives which are arranged
after the death of great men, so little
is said of humanity and so much of abstract right.   Is the moral order of the
world so inexorable that even its fairest
opponents must be docketed and ticketed
in accordance with it ? [1]

In the romantic Thirties, and in Paris,
men thought otherwise.   In the freedom
of that society Liszt's personality received its stamp.   In Paris he remained
after the tour of the world which he
made in childhood, on which Beethoven
had kissed him ; and in Paris he learned

the elegance of a man of the world, and
a depth of pantheistic thought.   These were his two opposite poles.
And very soon this mental culture raised him far above all his
contemporaries in his profession ; Chopin alone was worthy to
be placed at his side.   It was a good preparation for those

---

[1] Some of us would be inclined to follow this train of thought in another direction.
The question would not be—May great artists break the law and be blameless ? (the Pope
practically held that they might ; if Benvenuto Cellini does not lie about his own case)
but—What right has the public to obtain a full account of any man's private life ?

Vulgar curiosity, and an unacknowledged desire on the part of the reader to find that
the great man is " even such a one as himself," have more to do with the popularity of
certain biographies than their writers would care to acknowledge.

The " Life " of a great man should be a faithful report of his Greatness.   His
weakness and folly, often exceeding that of commonplace people simply because of the
vastly greater range of his temptations, is no business of ours, and should never be
printed, except in so far as it is necessary to make clear the plain story of his career.

Lithograph of 1835 by Staub.

Liszt at Weimar, 1884.

triumphs of virtuosity that were soon to come, which were to transform him from a delicate Parisian into a European citizen. The splendour of virtuosity lay like the eternal sun over Paris. From time to time something would happen to cast even that splendour into the shade. In the twenties came Moscheles ; then the wonders of the little Liszt; and now the appearance of Thalberg. Thalberg, the natural son of a prince, a ravishing and brilliant person, a cavalier through and through, came to Paris in 1835 and took her by storm. He had a luxuriant,

After Dantan's Caricature of Liszt.
From the Nicolas-Manskopt collection, Frankfort-on-Main.

fascinating execution, in which the silken glitter was that of the *fontaine lumineuse* ; and he had besides the peculiarity of holding the middle melody supported by the pedal, both hands taking part, while they enfolded it in arabesques of chords. In the rivalry with him Liszt was the complete and foursquare man : no longer the " petit Litz," standing on the height of the time, but the mature Liszt, with his " profil d'ivoire," who left the time far behind. Liszt and Thalberg were both *gentlemen.* They never showed such animosity as their respective partisans, who split Paris as once it had been split by the Gluckists and

Facsimile of Liszt's

Hungarian Storm-March.

The "jeune école" of Parisian Pianists.   Lithographed by Maurin.
Standing—J. Rosenhain, Döhler, Chopin, A. Dreyschock, Thalberg.
Sitting—Edward Wolff, Henselt, Liszt.

the Piccinists.   But their rivalry had nevertheless something
dramatic in it, and in it lay a regard for piano-culture never
yet seen.   The crisis of the struggle was reached on the 31st
of March 1837, when the Princess Belgioso ventured to invite
both Liszt and Thalberg to a benefit-concert, at which the price
of the tickets, forty francs, was proportioned to the character of
the company.   Hitherto each had performed on his own account;
and each had been applauded for himself.   Both came ; and both
played.   The following conversation gives the decision of the
audience—" Thalberg est le premier pianiste du monde ! "   " Et
Liszt ? "   " Liszt, Liszt est—le seul ! "   It seemed a drawn
match.   But meanwhile the depth of Liszt's artistic character
was conquering though unobserved.   Liszt had in an article
severely censured the empty compositions of Thalberg.   Fétis,
the musical historian, took the other side, and maintained
strongly that not Liszt but Thalberg was the man of the new

school. A few years only had to pass, when people grew sick of playing Thalberg. The broader humanity of Liszt's art had won the victory over external glitter in popular dress—a victory which Liszt's personality could not gain over that of Thalberg. Thenceforward Liszt's supremacy was uncontested.

In the same year, 1837, Liszt made a confession, in an essay written for the *Gazette Musicale*, which was the greatest flattery

Liszt in his youth. Engraved on steel by Carl Mayer.

that ever the piano received from one of its masters. Liszt refuses to go nearer to the orchestra or to the opera. "My piano is to me what his boat is to the seaman, what his horse is to the Arab : nay, more, it has been till now my eye, my speech, my life. Its strings have vibrated under my passions, and its yielding keys have obeyed my every caprice. Perhaps the secret tie which holds me so closely to it is a delusion ; but I hold the piano very high. In my view it takes the first place in the hierarchy of instruments ;

it is the oftenest used and the widest spread. . . . In the circumference of its seven octaves it embraces the whole circumference of an orchestra; and a man's ten fingers are enough to render the harmonies which in an orchestra are only brought out by the combination of hundreds of musicians. . . . We can give broken chords like the harp, long sustained notes like the wind, staccati and a thousand passages which before it seemed only possible to produce on this or that instrument. . . . The piano has on the one side the capacity of assimilation; the capacity of taking into itself the life of all (instruments); on the other it has its own life, its own growth, its individual development. . . . It is a microcosm, a micro-theus. . . . My highest ambition is to leave to piano players after me some useful instructions, the footprints of attained advance, in fact a work which may some day provide a worthy witness of the labour and study of my youth. I remember the greedy dog in La Fontaine, which let the juicy bone fall from its mouth in order to grasp a shadow. Let me gnaw in peace at my bone. The hour will come, perhaps all too soon, in which I shall lose myself and hunt after a monstrous intangible shadow."

It is due in very great measure to the example of Paganini's violin-playing that Liszt at this time, with slow, deliberate toil, created modern piano-playing. The world was struck dumb by the enchantment of the Genoese violinist; men did not trust their ears; something uncanny, inexplicable, ran with this demon of music through the halls. The wonder reached Liszt; he ventured on *his* instrument to give sound to the unheard of: leaps which none before him had ventured to make, "disjunctions" which no one had hitherto thought could be acoustically united: deep tremolos of fifths, like a dozen kettle-drums, which rushed forth into wild chords; a polyphony which almost employed as a rhythmical element the overtones which destroy harmony; the utmost possible use of the seven octaves in chords set sharply one over another; resolutions of tied notes in unceasing octave graces with harmonies thrown in the midst; an employment hitherto unknown of the interval of the tenth to increase the fulness of tone-colour; a regardless interweaving of highest and lowest notes for purposes of light and shade; the most manifold application of the tone-colours of different octaves for the coloration of the tone-effect; the entirely naturalistic use of the tremolo and the glissando; and above all a perfect systematization of the method of interlacing the hands, partly for the management of

Cartoon representing Liszt and his Works. 1842.

runs so as to bring out the colour, partly to gain a doubled power by the division, and partly to attain, by the use of contractions and extensions in the figures, a fulness of orchestral chord-power never hitherto practised. This is the last step possible for the piano in the process of individualisation begun by Hummel and continued by Chopin. The three systems of notes, instead of two, appear more frequently; in fact the two hands appear

Der General Bass wird durch List in seinen festen Linien überrumpelt u. überwunden.

"General" Bass surprised and overcome in his fortress by Liszt. (*List* means craft, or stratagem. Observe Liszt's wings, *flügel*, which word also means grand piano. General or "thorough" Bass is a personification of the "classical" school.)

for the most part to play a group of notes which seem to be conceived for three. And precisely by this means the two hands run inside and through one another, as if they were only a single

Liszt and Stavenhagen.

tool of ten fingers. The music appears again to become a corporate unity of tone, as it had already once been in its first beginnings. But, it has now become, out of a universal music, a music for the piano. An historic mission is fulfilled.

Liszt invents a fingering for his purposes which has no other principle than that of the most absolute opportunism. Scales, struck by one finger, trills played with changing fingers, strenuous parallel octave passages, heavy fingering in order to drag out parts which otherwise glide too lightly—everywhere, in place of the academic rule, there is an attempt to grasp the effect of the moment, a moulding after the impulses of the expression. And thence arises a soul-giving power even down to the most trifling passing-note, until the man and the playing are one. Liszt did the miracles of a prophet in his recitals, tumultuous assemblies, in which it actually happened that the people did not stir from the place till one o'clock in the morning.

So early as 1839 he was able to venture on the first pure piano-recital ever given, after Moscheles had paved the way with his mixed piano-recital without orchestra. Not only could he fill up a whole evening with performances on this instrument alone ; he was able to fill with his performances twenty-one evenings in the short space between December 27, 1841, and March 2, 1842. This was the brilliant period of his virtuoso-years ; twenty-one recitals in Berlin within this short space ! In the history of piano-playing they are festival weeks, holy days, in which by the greatest of all pianists a world-literature was made living on the keys, so that all Europe resounded. At that time we hear of a critic wondering how this marvellous man could actually improvise along with an orchestra ! So little were people accustomed to playing by heart, which since Liszt's time has become the universal rule.

Liszt's innumerable compositions for the piano, which were first completely named in Ramann's book, remind us again of the three types of artists of which we spoke above. We find in them Liszt the compiler, who makes use of the experiences of centuries ; and we find Liszt the innovator, who points out new ways in motives which we might think were only seen in Wagner, in naturalisms which developed music, and in technical means of expression ; but we do not find in him a composer of genius, who can hardly hold himself back from his inspirations, and who with unforced ease, creates new forms for the new ideas. We shall, as time advances, suffer less and less from illusions on this point. And Liszt himself was content to be an innovator without being a creator. He was a clever artist who knew his own limitations accurately. He invents a theme which is spirited, new, and characteristic; and when he has invented the theme he sits down and arranges it according to all the powers of technical expression; and varies it in forms whose technique is their content, so that technique and content become identical. This is the last

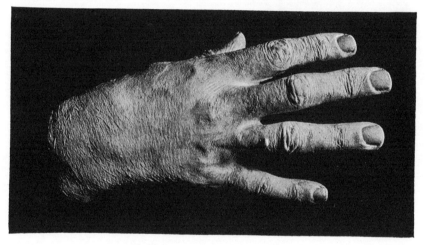

Plaster Cast of Liszt's Hand. Weimar.

effect of the Étude-principle, in which an idea finds, not its form, but its technical expression.

This special method of Liszt is preserved at its best in the twenty Rhapsodies. The Magyar *Dallok* had appeared already as studies. But these Rhapsodies far surpass them in polish. Hungarian national airs, with their rushing rhythmical and unrhythmical *verve*, were here for the first time taken up into the circle of art, and supplied the motives from which he poured forth a pyrotechnic display of brilliant variations, whose technique has not a single useless note, and whose working-out is indescrib-

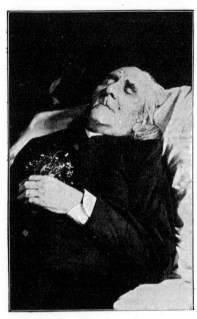

Liszt lying in state.   Bayreuth, 1886.

ably delicate and harmonically interesting. Nos. 2., 6. 9. (Pester Karneval), 12 (to Joachim), and 14 (to Bülow), are not unjustly preferred to the rest. No 14, with its astounding development from the funeral march to the joyous stretto, has remained one of the most marvellous piano-pieces on record. In it an un-paralleled technique is revealed, while the piece is not thereby rendered hollow or superfluous.

The charming Spanish Rhapsody, the Chopin - like "Consolations," the wonderfully impromptu-like "Apparitions" and "Harmonies Poétiques et Religieuses," that grand con-geries of various differently arranged and differently put together Études and drawing-room pieces, the "Années de Pélerinage" (three volumes) with the Tarantelle, the Paganini Études with the Campanella, further collections of Études till we reach the Twelve Études d'exécution transcendente, the "Dream Nocturnes," the "Mephisto Waltzes and Polkas," the "Caprice Valses," the "Chromatic Galop"—I will only refer to a few pieces which possess a special historic or artistic interest. In 1834, as his first romantic production, appeared the "Pensée des Morts," in mixed time, *senza tempo*, with mottos from Lamartine, for whom, with Chateaubriand, he felt the highest literary admiration. In the same year came out "Lyon," a realistic piece on the uprising of the Lyons working-classes, and one of the few piano-compositions relating to contemporary events. "Sposalizio" and "Il Penseroso" (1838, 1839) are notable as pieces inspired by the impressions of the representative arts, as the somewhat feeble "Fantasia quasi

Sonata" (1837) arose from the perusal of Dante. The whole of these are romantic confessions in which the arts greet each other in friendly wise. In importance, however, they are far surpassed by the later piano works; above all by the five best original pieces, the Legends, the Concertos, and the B minor Sonata.

The Legends of 1866 are in honour of his patron saint, St Francis. The first shews him in an ecclesiastical theme, sweeping over the waves, which are represented by the usual variation. In the other he is preaching to the birds. It is a wonderful free

Music-room in the "Altenburg" at Weimar, with Liszt's giant piano by Alexandre, Paris. In the background a clavier of Mozart's.

impromptu, in which a church air is set over against the twitter of the birds, which is marked by masterly technique. The birds seem to be listening to the saint; their twittering seems likely to give way to his pious harmonies; but at the conclusion we see them again in a cheerfulness which leads on to a ravishing cry of birds. It is the most poetical piece that Liszt ever wrote for the piano.

The Sonata in B minor (1854) dedicated to Schumann, has one movement but many themes. Six motives of varied colouring are knitted into one web, which unfolds itself into a splendid picture. A royal brilliancy lies over the whole. More free and lively are the two single-movement Concertos. The one in A major has its characteristic line C sharp B C B, which is to be followed out into the cadenzas ; a main theme with all kinds of subordinate themes, in a natural threefold quickening from slower reflective sections. The E flat major is constructed on the opposite model—its characteristic line is E flat, D, E flat; D E flat, D, D flat. This work is probably the most frequently heard of Liszt's concerted pieces. It is more *giusto* in essence, with slower by-themes— especially the beautiful Adagio with the Tristan-like motive and the Pastorale middle section—swinging up in Bacchic style. On the return to the main theme all the motives alter into a more cheerful strain ; the adagio gives way to a martial movement, and the Pastorale is taken up by the piano with increased ornamentation. In the place of the old formal scheme a psychological process had entered ; an inward conversation of the piano with the orchestra and its instruments.

From the point of view of number, still greater than the original pieces are the arrangements, which embrace a whole world, from variations to complete transformations of themes, from the " Dance of the Dead " on the Cantus of the Dies Irae to the Rhapsodies, from his arrangements of Bach to his Paraphrases of Wagner, from the innumerable songs and waltzes of Schubert to the settings of Beethoven's symphonies, and the symphonic poems of Liszt's own. Here was a huge mass of material, which was transmitted spiritually and artistically to the public by means of the piano. And in the hither and thither of the arrangements we trace the most labyrinthine paths. Schubert's Marches, for example, were first transcribed for four hands, then arranged for orchestra, and finally re-transcribed from the orchestral setting for the pianoforte. Liszt's arrangements are no mere transcriptions ; they are poetical re-settings, seen through the medium of the piano. He assimilates the composition before him into himself, and reproduces it on the piano as if he had conceived it, with all its special peculiarities, for the piano alone. Such things seemed often to be the very best expression of his genius. This great series begins with the transcriptions of Paganini's Capriccios, and that of the "Symphonie fantastique" of Berlioz; and it reaches its height in the two-handed settings of Beethoven's symphonies. The pieces have become genuine piano-compositions, in which a full score is reproduced by specific fulness of chord, and a sweeping chord by broken harmonies

Döhler. Lithograph by Mittag, after the picture of Count Pfeil.

sustained by the pedal. The piano is no longer merely one pillar of the musical structure; it has become the architect of an art of its own. This art of its own becomes yet more visible when it deals, not with the transcription of ready-made works, but with paraphrases of given sections, which were to be released from their surroundings. Liszt made many operatic fantasias of this kind, and did not always utterly oppose the taste of the time, which did not object to dissolve a characteristic melody into flourishes, or to

Sophie Menter in her youth.

make a sad and trembling motive tower into unexpected heights. Of this his Tannhäuser March and his Don Giovanni Fantasia are proofs. But the rule, nevertheless, is that he never undertakes anything contrary to the character of the passage to be paraphrased, and that — as he does most successfully in the Rienzi Fantasia—he does not overlay the melody with cadenzas and ornamentations from without, but extracts them, as it were, from the substance of the piece itself.

Only those parts of the opera does he bind together in his paraphrase, which stand in an inward relation to each other. It is now entirely drawn from a leading idea, and is related to the earlier externally-connected operatic fantasia as the symphonic poem to the symphony.

The immense difficulties of Liszt's compositions retarded their popularity for many years. Clara Schumann and Sophie Menter were amongst the first brave performers to introduce them into their repertoires. To-day they almost overburden the recitals, and include much of little value, which would hardly survive except as the *disjecta membra gigantis*. His influence was of a kind never seen before. He created a type of recital in which his imitators often copy the Master down to his very hair. His missionaries travelled over the whole

Clotilde Kleeberg, 1888.

Madame de Belleville, 1808-1880. Pupil of Czerny. Well-known pianist. After the picture by Agricola.

world from the circle which he gathered round himself at Weimar in the summer months. Their ideal is his creation ; the perfect, memoriter, technically and stylistically adjusted mastery of the great and many-sided piano literature, without regard for century or nation.

Liszt's contemporaries in piano - virtuosity are almost forgotten. Their name vanishes like a dream. Others succeed in their place ; generations press eagerly on each other's heels. There was the wild and headstrong Mortier de Fontaine, who was the first to venture on playing Beethoven's Op. 106 in public. Döhler, Dreyschock, Rosenhain, Jaell and his wife, Wilhelmina Clauss - Savardy, Sophie Menter, like her in objectivity, the more vigorous Annette Essipoff, afterwards the wife of Leschetizki, who now holds the very centre of piano-teaching in Vienna. In our time are Madame Carreño, so masculine in her convincing interpretations, and Clotilde Kleeberg, her opposite, so sympathetic and delicate, the truly womanly executant of Schu-

Carl Filtsch, infant prodigy. Pupil of Chopin. Died very young.

"Anton Rubinstein, pupil of Mr A. Villoing, Moscow. To Dr. Aloys Fuchs, as a souvenir from the young Anton Rubinstein, Moscow. Vienna, April 5, 1842."

mann and Chopin. Madame Essipoff was a pupil of Anton
Rubinstein, from whom a by-stream ran out alongside of the
world-embracing school of Liszt. Rubinstein's and Bülow's playing represented the difference which was bound to arise between
the classical and the spiritual interpretation of piano-works. Rubinstein was the great subjective artist, who gave way entirely to the
mood of the moment, and could rush on in an instant in such a

Hans von Bülow. Taken in the year 1879.

way as to leave no room for the cool criticism of a later hour. But
Bülow was the great objective artist, the teacher and unfolder
of all mysteries, the unraveller of the knottiest points in Beethoven's latest works, which he understood to their innermost
details. In his playing the intellect had the gratification of
clear-cut sharpness, while the heart retained the emotion long
after the artist left the platform. Both artists were in their
kind finished and complete, and both were of incalculable

Last Portrait of Rubinstein.

influence on whole generations. The impressionist Rubinstein and the draughtsman Bülow had each the technique which suited him. The one rushed and raved, and a slight want of polish was the natural result of his impressionist temperament; the other drew carefully the threads from the keys, occasionally showing them with a smile to his audience, while

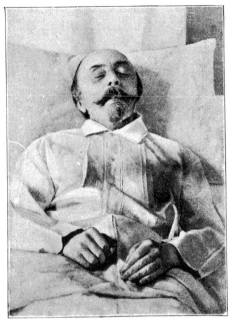

Bülow on his deathbed. Cairo, 1894.

every tone and every tempo stood in ironbound firmness, and every line was there before it was drawn.

Rubinstein and Bülow were both interpretative natures. Rubinstein composed much, Bülow little ; and Rubinstein's compositions are hollow while Bülow's are fragmentary. In their compositions the two men are at their worst ; the pathos of Rubinstein became maudlin, and the severity of Bülow became simple harshness. The best that Bülow ever wrote for the piano was the piano-arrangement of Tristan, which is unparalleled in its expression of pain ; but his best work of all was his annotations to Beethoven's Sonatas and Variations. Rubinstein's innumerable Dances and National Airs are played indeed, but they are practically forgotten ; his Tarantelles, Serenades, Sonatas, Concertos, get nearer to sinking every year. Rubinstein's experiences, his activity in St Petersburg, his final stay in a pension at Dresden, were rather external than internal changes. Later in his life

Reinecke in his youth.   Most famous of
modern Mozart players, afterwards Director of the Leipsic Conservatorium.   After
the picture by Seel.

he was able to spend more money
on his gigantic plans.   In a cycle of
seven piano-recitals he undertook to
give a complete picture of the historical development of his art.   It is
well known with what self-sacrifice
he gave these recitals, and how
nobly he followed the unique principle which great virtuosos should
set before themselves, namely that
those who have should pay for the
art, in order that those who have
not should receive it gratuitously.
Bülow's experiences, on the other
hand, were internal.   His change
from Wagner to Brahms will be regarded by every student of great
souls, not as a desertion of his colours, but as a mental phenomenon.   In Bülow's nature there was at bottom nothing in
common with Wagner ; and it may well be that he never saw
Wagner except through the glasses of the concert, of execution, of display, not of the stage, or of sensuous perception.
Bülow was not stage-bitten, nor was he even a man with a
head full of the philosophy of the stage ; he was a downright
worker, a teacher, to whom indeed teaching came so natural that
he for a considerable time gave lessons with Raff in Frankfort and Klindworth in Berlin.   When he gave public recitals he
did not, like Rubinstein, crowd a history of the piano into a few
evenings.   He took by preference a single author, like Beethoven,
and played only the five last Sonatas, or he unfolded the whole
of Beethoven historically in four evenings.   He would have
preferred to play every piece twice.   Great draughtsman as he
was, he hated all half-lights and colourations ; he pointed his
pencil very finely, and his paper was very white.   If he laid
his pencil down, it was only for a short time ; and if he played

Portrait by H. Katsch.

Johannes Brahms.

Photograph from life by Marie Fellinger, Vienna.

any work, the composer was a made man. Over the variations of Tschaïkowski could be read, "Joué par M. Bülow dans ses concerts."

Teacher and virtuoso — these mark great pianists into two groups, or at least into two temperaments ; and it was this marked difference which was signalised by the appearance of Bülow and of Rubinstein. In all, the severance is perfected according to the natural aptitude and inner development. Of course over every virtuoso at a certain time there comes the wish to busy himself with teaching, but only in a small circle ; but on the other hand we observe that the decision to follow the teaching profession is instantly taken by those artists who have no turn for publicity, or do not like to face the competition which to-day is more keen than ever. The extreme of the virtuoso type is seen in certain international geniuses, who continued rather the tradition of Thalberg than that of Liszt. Thalberg, in the fifties, like Henri Herz in the forties, toured in America and Brazil. Rubinstein also, in the sixties, visited America. The most travelled of all was the Irish pianist and composer Wallace, who, for the sake of his health, toured and gave concerts through Australia, New Zealand, India, South America, the United States and Mexico — long before Thalberg's Brazilian journey. To-day a tour in America is almost a matter of course in the life of every virtuoso. Countries like France and Italy are shut off from a great inter-national intercourse of this kind, since their concert-life, and especially their cultivation of the piano, has never duly unfolded itself. The opera is there all powerful. But England, as a hundred years ago, invites to her shores the great men of the Con-tinent, and sends them back loaded

Paula Szalit.

with treasures. As London pianists Hartvigson, the pupil of Bülow, Borwick, and Dawson, stand in the front rank. Russia, formerly a colony of foreign emigrants, has now, by Anton Rubinstein's foundations in St Petersburg, and by the like activity of his highly - esteemed brother Nicholas in Moscow, awaked to a noble concert-life, in which the rivalry of the two capitals is remarkably balanced. It was inevitable that in nearer and further states ever more numerous pupils of German or Parisian masters should settle and labour as teachers. In America, so early as the sixties and seventies, a great number of naturalised teachers was known, among whom Wolfsohn is perhaps most distinguished. His eighteen evenings of historically arranged piano-music, which he gave so early as 1877 in Chicago, are deservedly famous.

Tausig, the pupil of Liszt, who by his brilliant technique and his extraordinary sense for style was the wonder of his contemporaries, left behind him various good arrangements and compositions perhaps too obvious in their virtuosity. He was born in Warsaw and died at thirty. He would have meant to our time a teaching power of the first magnitude. The crown of piano-playing in our time has been won by Eugene d'Albert, born in 1864, a small man with giant power, a loveable person of astonishing artistic seriousness. He was a pupil of Liszt, and on him the mantle of Liszt has fallen in our generation. His greatest virtue is his classic temperament. In his memory rest safely stored the greatest works from Bach to Tausig. If he takes one out, he takes with it the sphere in which it stayed unspoilt—the style of its execution. The piece stands fast in its construction; not a phrase appears inorganic, not a rhythm accidental. The seriousness of Brahms's Concertos, the murmuring of Chopin's Berceuse, the Titanic power of his A minor Étude, the grace of Liszt's Soirées de Vienne, the solemnity of Bach, move under his hand in the concert, without one taking the least from another. It is objectivity, but we do not cry out for subjectivity; it is personality, but we do not miss the *rapport* with eternity.

Liszt's pupils Reisenauer and Stavenhagen endeavoured on a similar ground to play a part as more general interpreters. But chance and change played them many tricks. Others, again, had and have their special excellencies. Paderewski, idolised in England and America, is the delicate, emotional, drawing-room player; Sauer, the bravura pianist; Siloti, the interpreter of Russian piano-music; Friedheim, the Liszt-player; Karl Heymann, the graceful. Barth, the pupil of Bülow, is severe; Rosenthal, an amazing technician; Ansorge, one of the most intellectual; Gabrilowitsch, who drives the horses of Rubinstein; Vladimir von Pachmann, with all his extravagancy, at least plays Chopin's Mazurkas with absolute faithfulness to their national character; Busoni shows great passion; Lütschg has an extraordinarily strong wrist; the miraculous child Paula Szalit transposes fugues on the spot; Josef Hofmann, once an "infant prodigy," is now an astonishingly individualistic artist; and Eduard Risler has an inimitable soft touch. Since the triumphs of Planté, indeed, Risler is the first French pianist to achieve a universal re-

nown. He is a pupil of the eminent Parisian master Diémer. He has discovered those last delicate *nuances* which lie precisely between tone and silence. His tones seem not to begin and not to cease; they are woven out of ethereal gossamer. While d'Albert plays with the whole upper body, seeks the keys and rivets them fast, breaks the sforzatos, and soothes the pianissimos ; Risler is a statue at the piano, externally a Stoic; but his gliding and crossing fingers, so soon as they have struck the first chord, become the most sensitive agents of an emotional soul. Under Risler's treatment the commonplace becomes a novelty. Out of Liszt's sermon of St Francis to the birds he draws the last poetical breath ; Beethoven he bathes in a warm brilliancy of his own ; and, not to be charged with too much sweetness, he flings himself loose with the overture to the Meistersinger, so that we fancy the whole orchestra to be playing, and we have an assurance that it is not weakness, but an active artistic restraint which gives to his touch its never-to-be-forgotten delicate profundity.

Piano-playing, in such an unparalleled advance, became of necessity a profession, which at one time enticed to deceive, at another rewarded abundantly. It is a profession which on one side leads to royal wealth, on the other to that extreme of misery which is the half of all art. The collision, which in our age is inevitable between industry and art, revealed the terrible abysses which yawn between the claims of a profession and those of art. While in a Frankfort paper we can read advertisements in which a young lady teacher offers two piano lessons a week in return for the daily four o'clock coffee with the family, young Hofmann, at nine years of age, gave, in New York alone, within three months, thirty-five recitals, from which his impresario, out of a gross receipt of over twenty-five thousand pounds, took at least ten thousand for himself.

The piano has become an essential part of life. Those who cannot play it stand outside a great company which cultivates it as an engine of social and home intercourse. In households where there is no piano we seem to breathe a foreign atmosphere. To-day we need no longer explain the piano from the church or the theatre, from the ballet or the volkslied, from the artistic song or the violin; it has on the contrary become an active centre, which has given its form to our whole musical culture; nay, more, which has even given the stamp to our whole conception of music, not only in the minds of all amateurs, but in the minds of many professionals. Whether the young girl spends her time with Chopin's E flat major Nocturne, or whether a false sentiment attaches itself to the "Maiden's Prayer" or the "Cloister Bell"; whether the waltzes of Lanner delight a quiet mind or Strauss calls to the dance; whether the eager pupil plies her healthy sport in Cramer's, Schmitt's, or Czerny's Studies, or the rising virtuoso exercises himself mechanically in scales after d'Albert's fashion, while he simultaneously reads new notes, or as Henselt plays Bach while he reads his Bible; whether amateurs enjoy themselves with the piano-abstracts of operatic fragments; or whether artists like the Kapellmeisters Fischer and Sucher, offer those Fantasias from Wagner over which they have spent their lives; whether the professor allows himself the enjoyment of private piano-literature, or performs standard works before thousands in the concert hall;—all these are accidents of culture, they are phenomena which offer a picture of that intimate interdependence of

Madame Carreño.

music and actual life which has developed so fruitfully since the art ceased to be the private possession of a clique, and which has established it on an absolutely new foundation. Of course, the more general piano culture has become, the more has it been in turn used up as a profession, and the more easily were its wings fettered. Our chief men also have ceased to improvise during a recital. Only our "comic artists" do so at the present day. And of a power of magical improvisation, exercised in private such as Beethoven and Liszt so often displayed, we now hear less and less. The recitals, in great part, deal with the interpretation of known works, which often—like Beethoven's E flat major concerto—are repeated *ad nauseam*. We have learning, we have playing, but we never see the enthusiasm which can be evoked by the stress of immediate creation. Piano-playing is a universal business even to the extremest limits of an amateurism which cannot strike a single chord instantaneously, nor dot a single note correctly. It is a long line from the little yawning schoolgirl, through the teacher running up and down stairs, to the virtuosos who play in the winter and give instruction in the summer. With excess of zeal comes sin. Nowhere in an art is a sin so often committed as in the choice of masters popular to-day. From false economy, musical culture, which is so profound and so difficult, is intrusted to the most incompetent, and fortunes are squandered in ruining the music in a child. In a paper once was to be read a somewhat humorous satire, entitled, "Directions for use," in which the teachers were thus handled : "For beginners the choice of a master is recommended—there are masters at all prices—very good lessons can be had for sixpence ; but masters with long hair charge three shillings and upwards—for male adults the choice of a mistress is recommended, because pleasure and love are thus excited together."

In order to put a check on amateur teaching a movement has of late years been set on foot to forbid untried teachers to occupy any position. As yet, however, the movement wants legal enforcement. Kullack and Klauwell in Cologne, Breslaur in Berlin,

publisher of the *Piano-teacher* (a
paper now twenty-one years old),
have founded seminaries for intend-
ing teachers. In 1896, in Cologne,
out of four hundred students only
thirty received a diploma of teaching
capacity—but no means at present
exists of forbidding the others to
teach. Consider the enormous crowds
that pass out of our music-schools.
An infinitesimal proportion may perhaps decide for a virtuoso career.
Of the rest half remain amateur,
the other half go in to the teaching
profession. The overcrowding may

easily be imagined. The largest music-school in the world, the
English "Guildhall School" of Music, had till lately 140 professors, 42 teaching-rooms, 2700 students; and will shortly be
enlarged till it has 69 rooms and 5000 students. I have made
special inquiries at the Berlin Conservatorium of Klindworth and
Scharwenka. My numbers are I think exact to a few figures. In
1895-6, out of 387 students, 41 men and 208 women took piano
only; 8 men and 15 women took piano with some other subject.
In 1896-7, out of 383 pupils, 40 men and 239 women learnt piano
alone, and 4 men and 8 women learnt piano with something else.
Of these 247 women, besides, about 43 are English or Americans.
Since on the average we reckon two years for a course, there go
from this school alone, every year, more than fifty women-teachers
into the world. Some of them perhaps may win a doubtful testi-
monial in a dearly-bought Berlin concert; others, who aimed at
virtuosity, may, after a pitiful experience, themselves sink into
teachers. Of the frequency of piano-performances in concerts
the following figures may give some notion. I have counted the
more important Berlin concerts in nine weeks taken at random—
159 in all. Among them are 58 piano-concerts, partly combined

with performances on other instruments, partly interesting through
the personality of the pianist; mere accompanying of songs being
of course not reckoned.

The number of music-schools has increased specially in the
capital cities. In France the Parisian High School has a great
repute; in Russia the Moscow and St Petersburg Conservatoriums;
in Belgium the Brussels Conservatoire, under the guidance of
Dupont, who is also distinguished as the editor of old piano-
works; in London the Royal Academy of Music [and the Royal
College of Music]. In Germany we have in Frankfort the Hoch
Conservatorium under Bernhard Scholz, and the Raff under Max
Schwarz; Stuttgart has somewhat declined through the deaths
of Lebert and Starck, the editors of the great Theoretical and
Practical School; but Cologne has greatly gained in importance
under Wüllner. In Leipzig under Mendelssohn, Moscheles and
Plaidy, piano-playing took the first place; new technical devices
like the pedal-clavier—that is, with organ pedals for the low notes
—were freely admitted, as in our days the Janko-keyboard. But
with the inevitable reaction, this school has decayed, and its
importance in piano-art is not what it was. In Berlin the Royal
" Hochschule " with Barth, Raif, Rudorff, and others, at its head,
experienced a like fate. Private institutions have come to the
front. Tausig's School for higher piano-playing (1866-1870), was
very distinguished. From it went Joseffy to New York and
Robert Freund to Zürich. The New Academy, founded by
Theodor Kullak, was also famous. It was afterwards replaced
by another Institute founded by his son. The Stern Conservatorium, now directed by Gustav Holländer along with Jedliczka;
the Klindworth, at which for a time Bülow and Moszkowski
laboured; and that of Scharwenka, which, after Xaver Scharwenka's departure for America, was for a time united with the
Klindworth;—are known to all.

Like the practical "schools," the theoretical have also become
innumerable. I take as a few of the most important works the
following: Adolph Kullak's "Aesthetic of Piano-playing," re-

edited by Bischoff, a unique and profound work on the theory of the art, as a hundred years' experience and the careful observations of the author have enlarged it ; Hugo Riemann's "Comparative Theoretical and Practical Piano School, presenting system, method, and materials, in a historic and organic connection " ; and, among the innumerable " schools " and volumes of exercises, the various thoughtful works of Germer. Two main principles have come to occupy the first place in the newest school-practice. First, the systematic carrying out—not merely of a musical mechanic of the hand, but its thorough gymnastic. This was the natural advance,

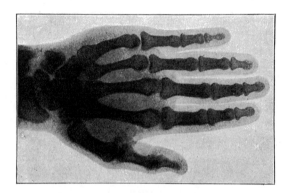

Hand of Eugene d'Albert. Röntgen ray photograph by Spies.

which carried yet further the teaching of Czerny. The hand is adapted for piano-playing—as in the systems of Thilo, Virgil, and others—by gymnastics of the fingers, and stretching of the muscles. Thus a great part of the gymnastic cultivation is got over before actual musical practice begins. In this work the dumb keyboards, which to-day are constructed with great delicacy, have borne a great part. They now admit of legato playing and of different degrees of strength in touch.

The second great principle is to take into account in instruction the peculiarities of the pupil's hand. It stands to reason that the same exercises will not do for all hands. One hand demands this, the other that. This method is carried out with the utmost precision by the greatest of teachers, Leschetizky. A similar principle prevails in modern teaching of singing. We no longer endeavour to base voice-cultivation on the universal vowel A, but on that vowel which comes most natural to the organ of the pupil.

The arrangement of the keys is the sacred tradition of centuries. It presents the tone-system, as it were, lengthways, and is the natural expression of a melodic musical concept. The separation of the black and the white keys has been introduced in accordance with a certain theoretical principle, which allows the difference of position in our scales over the black and white keys to appear somewhat complicated. Our keyboards are constructed entirely on the C major scale ; the tones outside this scale are thrown into the black keys, and thus appear in a subordinate position : thus all other scales have a strange form and often a somewhat difficult fingering. But since the seventeenth century our conception of music has gradually, from melodic, become harmonic ; we hear vertically as well as horizontally ; we hear the beauty of all chords as sounded together, and, unconsciously, we fill in the harmonies to every melody we hear. It would have been natural if the keyed instruments had adapted themselves to this altered musical conception, and had resigned the original conception of the scale to make way for harmonic conveniences. Nothing, however, is slower to be reached than the determination to revolutionise from the foundation a technique adopted in the schools, since no one is willing to make the sudden break with the old and the sudden start with the new.

Attempts had already been made to break the monopoly of the C major scale, and to form a regular chromatic scale of twelve similar keys. In our own day Paul von Janko has improved this system by repeating every regular chromatic series three times in terrace-style one above another, so that not only wider stretches, but also, without much movement of the hand, a surprising control of full chords and of rapid passages is attained. The tones are thus brought more narrowly together as the monopoly of the C major key is destroyed ; and the result betokens a decisive advance in the conception of modern music. This conception still embodies a compromise between the old scale-keyboard and an arrangement of the keys, which, founded on harmonic ideas, has promise for the future. Janko's keyboard is slowly gaining converts. Great houses, like those of Ibach, Duysen, Kaps, and Blüthner, are taking it up. Hausmann in Berlin, and Wendling in Leipzig, are the chief supporters of the scheme. In America we hear stories of remarkable results. Only by the development of such a new keyboard, which will have to answer the demands of the modern conception of music, will it be possible to draw new tone-effects from the piano. Its utmost capacities, in its present form, have been exhausted, it would seem, by Liszt.

Meanwhile the construction of the instruments has advanced to an unexampled perfection. It is only a hundred years since Stein began his laborious attempts on the new pianoforte. To-day a network of factories is spread over the whole world, in which innumerable faultless instruments are made, which put to use all the results of experience in the treatment of wood and wires. The modern pianos have already attained so completely the ideal of the hammer-mechanism that we are beginning to hark back to the forgotten tones of the cembalo. In Paris these aims have their strongest support in Diémer, who plays his Couperin on clavecins, and at the same time wins new renown for the oboe d'amour and the viol da gamba in the chamber-concert. Already quill-claviers are being more frequently constructed, and the reaction against the predominance of the pianoforte finds its satisfaction in their sweet and thrilling sounds.

It is impossible to review all the piano-factories of both hemispheres, or to register all their innovations. I must content myself with mentioning the system of " overstringing," invented simultaneously by several persons ; the felting of the hammers, introduced by Pape ; the third pedal of Steinway which holds on single tones without affecting the others ; the use of a cast-iron frame and of cast-steel strings; and the vertical stringing of the upright "cottage" piano, which is developed out of older forms. Bechstein's factory in Berlin stands at the head of German manufacture ; but there are also Duysen, Blüthner, Schiedmayer, Irmler, Westermayer, Kaps, Ibach, and innumerable others ; Bösendorfer in Vienna, Knabe in Baltimore, and Steinway in New York, who have succeeded to the renown of Chickering ; besides the many other older-established firms. Bechstein, so fundamentally sound ; and Steinway, with his patent fulness of tone, are the two rivals for the laurel at the end of the century.

Henry Engelhard Steinway, born in Brunswick, began, in the fifties, his New York business in very small circumstances. A three-storied house was the factory, and one piano a week was the output. In 1859, however, the firm was in a position to build a great establishment, which now, after several enlargements, covers more than four acres. The output advanced with giant strides : numerous patents were taken out for the improvement of the resonance and the fulness of tone : in 1872 the Emperor Alexander bought the twenty-five thousandth piano, and in 1883 Baron Nathaniel de Rothschild of Vienna bought the fifty thousandth. Besides the factory, the firm possesses in Astoria great estates, the timber of which covers not less than a hundred and fifty acres. There they have their yards, saw-mills, turning-mills, foundries, metal-workshops, and mechanical wood-bending and carving apparatus. The parts are sent from Astoria to New York to be fitted together. When completed, the pianos are exhibited in Steinway Hall (14th Street) with a view to sale. More than ninety thousand have been completed up to date, of which a large proportion has been transmitted to Europe through the London and Hamburg branches.

Bechstein has adopted a similar division of his work. He has two factories, the one in the suburbs, for the preparation of the parts and the drying of the wood, the other in the town for the fitting together of the pieces. This latter is in close connection with the shop. Karl Bechstein, like Steinway, began in the fifties on a very small scale, and in 1860 founded his great house in Johannisstrasse. In 1880 he acquired the first portion of the suburban estate, on which to-day four factories stand. The victorious brilliancy of modern ingenuity is to be seen in the whole establishment. The probation through which the wood has to pass in the yards, then in the dry-rooms, in the store-cellars, and finally when sized in the store-houses of the factories, before

it can be used, is a grand guarantee of its suitability. Two important rooms are devoted to steam-power. The one is the planing-room, where sides and lid are planed together by machines of such extraordinary power that the shavings hum about under centrifugal force, and are carried off by an exhaust apparatus. The other is the foundry, where all the metal work is carried on, from the boring of the cast frame to the preparation of the screws. Next, in the upper storeys, in the more distant factories, begins the process of fitting the piano together from the rough parts. The action is provided by a separate factory, the Nürnberg wires are spun, the walls of the grand pianos are glued together in from twelve to twenty thicknesses, the frame is bronzed, the wood inlaid, the ornaments put on, every tiny screw, every spindle

Upright Hammerclavier (pianoforte), Italian, beginning of 19th century. Two pedals, one to raise the dampers, the other a "jalousie schwellung" (*i.e.* Venetian shutters, like an organ swell or the harmonium "forte" action). Richly inlaid. Engraved crowns on the fronts of the keys. De Wit collection.

is touched up with rare attention, till the instrument gains its speech, and is tested, for the last refinements, in separate rooms. Since the completion of the last building, they reckon on a yearly output of not less than three thousand five hundred pianos, on which eight hundred workers are employed. The proportion of grands to cottages is as three to four, a proof of the enormous popularity of the cottage, for which as a piece of furniture it is so easy to find room, but which, even in its best specimens, can never give to the musician the fulness of tone and the resonance of a grand. The demand for Bechsteins is greater than their factories can meet. It is remarkable that half of them go to

Bechstein Cottage Piano, "English style."

England and the English colonies through the London branches ; while Germany, Austria, Russia, Italy, Spain, and South America, share the other half. In a business of such magnitude it is no mere ostentation to record these figures, which simply supply the necessary statistics of the general trade.

So long as the piano was merely an instrument for more or less gifted musicians, it was unnecessary to consider the question which to-day, when it has become a general means of social pleasure, stands in the foreground—namely its treatment as a piece of furniture. The "square" instrument has only certain parts, particularly the lower extremities, in which the style of the time could be expressed. The legs and the feet were, in the time of the Ruckers, *baroque ;* as in the time of the Streichers they adopted the style of the Empire, and in our day that of the Renaissance. The rest of the body was fixed in its main lines by the given natural forms ; and has altered very little in architectural relations in the course of centuries. The piano was in the fortunate position, even in the times when as yet little attention was paid to constructive logic, of being a construction, which, from its very aim, gained the most beautiful form. With its gracefully-bending walls, and its natural and yet characteristic shape, the grand piano, in many furnishing schemes of the insipid fifties or the glaring eighties, in many a jerry-built and cheaply appointed house, stood as the single solid and carefully wrought article in the place. The cottage, on the other hand, which too often is meant to be nothing but a piece of furniture, and which with its encasing wood-walls offers only too much opportunity to fashionable taste, has sunk deep into the domestic style, and even to-day has hardly freed itself from these false influences. It would seem that the cottage piano was invented in 1739 by the priest Don Domenico of Mela in Gagliano. Only at the commencement of this century did it begin to spread on this side of the Alps. It offered a grand field for dubious artistic experiments. Now it was treated merely as a sideboard, now as an Egyptian pyramid, now as an altar with figurative paintings, now as the *corpus vile* for all kinds of marqueterie-experiments. I know only one cottage piano that expresses its essence in characteristic style, and develops its form without grimaces : this is the "English" type, plain and unadorned, introduced into the trade by Bechstein, a principal feature of which is that the legs are continued above the keyboard in a very graceful style, as candle-brackets.

When the grand piano is used as an object for decoration,

the result is usually unsatisfactory. The contradiction between its plain form and gaudy ornamentation becomes very marked. Earlier ages saw clearly that the walls of the piano and its lid are best left plain, and adorned with paintings. But to-day the cases are more frequent in which specially magnificent pianos are so carefully fitted up with plastic ornamentation in all styles with pillars, reliefs, and other descriptions of carving, that one can only smile at the waste of labour. In the over-rich rococo adornment, which was presented by a piano built by Bechstein some time ago for the Empress Frederick for a particular apart-

Bechstein Grand Piano *de luxe*, "Rheingold." 1896.

ment, a trained eye can to-day find no pleasure. More tolerable are the splendid grands, richly adorned with paintings, in which, in Germany, Max Koch is chiefly concerned. The Wagner piano for the Prince of Anhalt-Dessau, or the Rheingold piano, both by Bechstein, are also worth noticing. The latter has the daughters of the Rhine for legs, a waving ornamentation on the walls, and carved bulrushes on the lid; it is one of the most interesting monster-pianos built in our time. In England Alma Tadema is the piano-painter most in request. For Henry Marquand of New York he prepared an instrument, adorned with precious stones and with painting, which was priced at £15,000. His own piano is also extraordinary. The ornamentation chosen is in the style of mediæval mosaics, with expensive surface ornamentations. Under the lid are framed and adorned parchment strips, on which Liszt, Tschaïkowski, Gounod, and others, inscribed their names. This was appraised at £2500. A piano built in London for Carmen Sylva had ivory legs. Perhaps a varied ebony and ivory ornamentation, which springs from the appearance of the keys, taking advantage of the splendid surface provided by these materials, would be more promising than any kind of rococo or Gothic design. Ivory is still in strong demand for pianos. Ninety thousand instruments are yearly issued from the hundred and seventy London houses; and these take ten thousand tusks.

Ever since composers began to write easier pieces the demand for pianos has been greater. The market has of course been well supplied. In 1896 appeared over 2500 "books."[1] of piano solos, 2000 songs with piano accompaniment, more than 250 books of duets, and 300 pieces for piano and violin. Among these figure many new editions of old works, which to-day form a literature by themselves. The arrangement of historical material, as it gives its character to the calling of the modern pianist, is also reflected in it. We have excellent editions, like the Berlin "Original Texts" (Urtexte), "Bischoff's Bach," published by Steingräber, "Klindworth's Chopin," published by Bote and Bock, "Bischoff and Neitzel's Schumann," "Bülow's Beethoven's Sonatas." Breitkopf and Härtel have extended their Popular Library over the widest area. They have arranged their piano-publications into a uniform piano-library, which soon will embrace 10,000 numbers. Nay, the "Moonlight Sonata" is already to be purchased for a penny. And yet we must confess that really beautiful editions of bibliographical value are not to be found. An edition in artistic binding, on thick paper, in elegant engraving, following the best original copy, with none of those instructive but unornamental marks of fingering or

---

[1] Meaning separate publications—ranging from single pieces to large collections in one volume.

phrasing, and at the same time well
adapted for opening out without in-
jury, and calculated for perfect typo-
graphical pictures on every page —
why is there no such edition of
Beethoven, when people can be found
who will pay ten or twelve thousand
pounds for a piano?

Where the historic tendency is so
well marked, creativeness has degene-
rated. Since the middle of the century plenty of good sound stuff has
been written for the piano ; but it
must be confessed that piano-music

has shown no tendency to strike out a new path. No com-
manding or révolutionary personality, like Schumann, Chopin,
or Liszt, has arisen. Almost all modern production is but the
popularisation of Liszt, or a respectable mean between Chopin
and Schumann.

Ferdinand Hiller began the endless succession of these eclectic
musicians. But the last of the solid old style was Alkan, a solitary,
eccentric, misanthropic, but withal interesting old man. He was
born in Paris in 1813, and remained there. He was one of the
many pupils of Zimmermann, that modest but most influential
teacher. Alkan's pieces were highly esteemed by Bülow, who
gave him a place in his list of Étude-masters. In his works,
which are chiefly Études and Preludes, there speaks a Berlioz,
with an elemental and realistic power. He stands in his kind
half-way between Chopin and Liszt. Some pieces, like the
highly original Op. 39, 1, do not easily fade out of the memory.
The seventh of the twelve Études, dedicated to Fétis, is a
remarkably significant Chopin-like Ballade in Berlioz' style,
with kettle-drum rolls, and other most peculiar harmonic and
orchestral effects. In the "Allegro Barbaro" of the fifth Étude
he gives full play to his propensity to exotic phrases of foreign

colouring. He works with uncanny, lengthy unisons, or with cutting climbing ninths. An out-and-out romantic, he delights not merely to rush into the middle of his pieces with explanatory words—"Mors" is one of these—but he has hit upon the most original titles that ever an association of ideas led a composer to adopt : "Pseudo-naïveté," "Fais Dodo," "Heraclitus and Democritus," "Railroad," "Odi profanum vulgus," "Morituri te salutant." To play his pieces is as difficult as to construe the Talmud.

A constant succession of romantic writers of Études or small

Stephen Heller.   Ferdinand Hiller.   Adolf Henselt.

pieces stretches from that era to our own. First stands the intellectual Volkmann ; next, the somewhat too dainty Kirchner, a regular album-writer, who went so far in his admiration for Schumann as to publish "New Davidsbündler" and "The New Florestan and Eusebius." Adolf Henselt, who lived at St Petersburg, practised an extraordinary longdrawn legato technique. He is still esteemed for his tolerable F minor Concerto, and for his second and fifth Études, especially the well-known "Si oiseau j'étais." Stephen Heller, who lived in Paris, wrote a hundred and forty-nine works, almost exclusively for the piano.

He is a combination of Schumann, Chopin, Mendelssohn, and water; but we light occasionally on passages of some inspiration. His well-known Saltarellos and Tarantelles, his effective " Forellen " (Trout) Fantasia, and his excellent " Danses Bois," are in the taste of the time. More important was his pretty idea, in the Freischütz Studies, of uniting operatic motives and étude-practice in an organic and poetic combination.

Tschaïkowski.

The lesser Romantics and Romanticists were meanwhile working diligently in Paris. A group of successful piano-composers of this class reaches down to our own day. The chief names are Fauré, Widor, Vincent d'Indy, Chabrier, César Franck, Dubois, Cécile Chaminade, Paul Lacombe. The drawing-room romance, which in Chaminade unfortunately tends too often to shallowness, exhibits often a Mendelssohnian classicism, of which dainty specimens are given in Lacombe's Toccatina, and in the Toccata of Chaminade herself. The literature for two pianos is well illustrated in Chabrier's Romantic Waltzes, which are unusually spirited. César Franck's symphonic variations, serious and academic, and St Saens' Concertos, more interesting in their effective technique than in content, stand out from the mass of orchestral piano-work.

An equally important group is that of the Russians, headed by the emotional and highly-strung Tschaïkowski, whom Bülow, not without justice, honoured with his special admiration. Tschaïkowski's variations are one of the soundest and most genuine of modern piano works; and the B flat minor concerto has a swing and rush that carries us away.   His Sonata, not only by its application of national themes, but specially by the national colouring of the episodic parts, down to the light and shade of the figurations, is unique among piano pieces.   He was simpler and more popular in his numerous drawing-room pieces, which

From painting by Fritz Erler.

constantly reward study by a spirited phrase or unusual harmony. The school of older and younger Russians has worked on the same popular lines.   To this school belong Borodin, Cui, Liadoff, Rimsky-Korsakoff, Mussorgsky, Glazounow, Naprawnik.   A third group is that of the Scandinavians, who gained importance in Europe about the middle of the century, not merely in fiction and painting, but in music also. But they were rather inspired than inspirers. Their leader is Grieg, whose well-known concerto Op. 16, in spite of certain eccentricities, has a very flowing course suggesting the united influence of many predecessors. His themes

are good specimens of a music which is not the product of experience, but of invention. Scores of variations and dainty isolated pieces keep the same happy and attractive medium between the shallow and the interesting. They are in any case more important than Gade's Mendelssohniana. For a long time less known, but far deeper and more genuine than Grieg, is Halfdan Kjerulf, whose works have been republished by Arno Kleffel (Simon). Humorous little pieces in the post-romantic style, but of concentrative ability, deserve the highest praise a Romantic can receive; they are like Schubert in spirit. Among the later Scandinavians, Schytte and Sinding have tried no new paths; Stenhammer, also of importance as a virtuoso, has given us works of pith and character, which may rank among the first.

In England and America, in later times, Graham Moore and Macdowell may claim notice as lesser Romantics. The former is not free from triviality; the latter invents with more delicate genius, and has written a very respectable piano-concerto. But Germany may still boast that she retains the supremacy.

From the group of German post-Romantics, which found in Franz Brendel a very fertile composer of programme tone-pictures, two great personalities drew apart. Adolf Jensen was the inheritor of Schumann's emotion, Johannes Brahms of Schumann's musical character. Jensen, whose character is the mean between Chopin and Schumann, has left behind him music which will not die, in his clear-cut and splendidly worked-out Suites, in his emotional "Wanderbilder" and Idylls, in the unique Eroticon, which characterises the different forms of love in separate movements, and in the four-handed wedding music, which is lovely and full of power. But Brahms inherited from his patron Schumann, not youth, not this simple thinking and inventing, but manhood, in which music became an absolute self-supported world. He worked in the world of tone, with no trace of virtuosity, with not a suspicion of a concession to the understanding of the mere amateur. His Sonatas and Concertos, the sparkling Scherzo Op. 4, the Variations, the Études, even the four-handed waltzes and the unique "Liebes-lieder" waltzes—for four hands with voices—there has, in our time, been no music written so free from the slightest condescension. Stubborn, at times repellent, even in her smiles not very gracious, this music seeks to make no proselytes; but whomsoever she wins as a friend, she holds fast and allows that rarest of pleasures—the pursuit of lofty aims, and the quiet rapture of a student.

Over against these two originals stands Joachim Raff, the eclectic. We have grown accustomed to count his eclecticism no reproach, for never did man more bitterly experience the sorrow of art. His great legacy of piano-pieces will at least give a good picture of the time. In them the most commonplace demands of art are mingled with the most

heart-felt lamentations—as they never mingled except in our age. They are a long catalogue of virtues and vices, from the hapless Polka de la Reine to the Sonatas, in which, whether for piano alone, or more especially for piano and violin, he attained astonishing heights; from the ravishingly graceful suite-movements to the romanticism of his lyrical songs. And over all broods the unrest of the time.

Among living Germans the same two main groups are in general to be distinguished : the artists of the serious, self-sufficient music, and the poets of the lighter, post-romantic *genre*. Rheinberger's sound and solid Sonatas and smaller pieces are the purest representatives of the more absolute conception of music, and they deserve the highest praise. Richard Strauss, also, in his earlier years, came out with some remarkably original piano-pieces, which betrayed a strong sense for absolute music. I would mention particularly the pithy Burlesque for Orchestra and Piano. In such serious and solid endeavour Wilhelm Berger stands out among the younger masters. But—as in the middle section of his great variations for two pianos—he must beware of a too great fluency, which is the stumbling-block of all absolute musical emotion.

Eugene d'Albert, in spirit, resembles Brahms. This appears most clearly in the eight massive Piano-pieces of his Op. 5, which live by their infelt music, and are in that respect to be numbered amongst the noblest fruits of modern piano-literature. This inclination to absolute music appeared even in his first work, a very interesting Suite, and has received further active expression in certain arrangements of Bach, which take a front rank along with those of Busoni. Among his piano-concertos, the second, which is included in a single movement, is without serious rival, at least among works that have appeared since Liszt, in wealth of invention and variety of colour. His secular turn will probably continue itself in his later works, which, in consequence of his devotion to opera, will necessarily cease to be influenced by Bach and Brahms.

Paderewski stands perhaps on the dividing line between the severer absolute musicians, in whose style he composed his Variations and Humoresques à l'antique, and the daintier drawing-room romantics, with whom he associates himself specially in numerous fiery Polish dances. His Concerto in A minor is absolutely bathed in this national spirit.

Xaver Scharwenka strikes a similar note. Something of Chopin at his best still lives in him ; and his Concertos, above all, have given him a name as a composer. His brother Philip renounces the virtuoso, and appears rather as a teacher and former of taste. He has created a rich piano-literature, which prefers to deal in graceful and *galant* forms, and holds itself utterly aloof from storm and revolution. Scharwenka has the rare merit of having successfully cultivated four-handed piano music; and his " Herbstbilder " and " Abendmusik " belong to the most tasteful productions of this class. Among his multiform " Jugend-stücke " the " Kinderspiele," in several volumes, are the most successful. A similar activity has been shown by Wilhelm Kienzl, who has been able to work the light romantic *genre* in all its aspects. Kienzl is one of our most fertile piano-composers. His pieces are all occasional, thought out for delicate orchestral effects, and thus are extremely unassuming. His "Boat-Scene" gained the special approval of Liszt, while his Dance Airs and Dance Pictures belong to the most popular class of piano-works. His

illustrated cycle "Child-love and Life," which appeared with text in four languages, seeks to apply to the piano the method of intuitive instruction. The cycle "From my Diary" is the best example of the specially subtle and suggestive touch, by which Kienzl attains his detailed orchestral effects; while the two volumes, "A Poet's Journey," are to be regarded as his ripest work.

Moritz Moszkowski, who has not yet laid aside his career as a virtuoso, and only the other day appeared with a new piano-concerto, is among the most remarkable in the band of modern piano-poets. A delicate and polished virtuosity, as it appears in the Etincelles and the Tarantelle, is allied with a characteristic force in form, which has made his four-handed Spanish dances, and his " From Foreign Parts," so popular.

History shows that the piano only flourishes in a pronounced opposition to the opera, which is the other extreme, the triumph of all arts united. The opera seeks to realise the impossible; it calls into requisition a whole world of forces in order to grasp in a sensuous manner the heights of life. It forms a Titanic resolve to build mountains out of sand ; an intoxication, an extraordinary consciousness of victory, gives wings to this most daring of experiments. A great man once appeared, who made Dionysus his lord, and sought to win from the stage a mirror of the world and worldly honour. We stand on the fair ruins of his splendid failure. We have been instructed, we have been elevated ; but the tragedy of the theatre is too deep. Then come the hours in which we flee to the household-ingle of chamber-music, and strive to disentangle its enlacing lines, in which we see the whole of life included, since it depicts itself without the need of foreign aid. The piano will further be the central point of this introspection. Let us have no concertos, in which this delicate instrument is dragged before the crowd and has to fight a duel with the orchestra. All beautiful compositions notwithstanding, the piano is no concerto-instrument. In concertos the delicate ear is outraged. The piano will not adapt itself for new ideas in the hall, in the midst of virtuosity, or against the orchestra. It must become chaste ; it must turn in faith to Bach's Wohltemperiertes Klavier, the Old Testament, as Bülow called it, of the musician's creed, and to Beethoven's Sonatas, the New.

It is noteworthy that in Schytte's " Silhouettes," or Variations on the same theme in the different styles of various Masters, he nowhere fails so badly as with Bach, who is marked by retardations in the middle voices, or with Beethoven, who is characterised by gloomy rhythm. The true path seems to have been lost. The line through Bach, Beethoven, Schumann, and Brahms, is the only safe line for the piano; and it is the line in music furthest removed from the opera. In those great natures, whether they knew it or not, was a strong repugnance to the opera; and Brahms, whose eulogists said he was the last of his race, will perhaps one day be viewed as the connecting link between the old and a new musical culture.

It is in chamber-music alone that we have the right to look for great triumphs in the immediate future; triumphs of which Klinger's "Radierungen," Brahms's "Clarinet Quintet" or Smetana's "Aus Meinem Leben," are at once the anticipation and the guarantee.

It is for our children to see to it that the great traditions of the past are not forgotten; and that the building which it will fall to them to erect is not unworthy of its foundation.

Postscript

Prosniz's " Handbuch der Klavier-litteratur," which goes down to 1830, and the new edition of Weitzmann's " History of Piano-playing and Piano-literature," now in preparation, supply a complete apparatus of all the sources of information necessary to the student. Thus I have been able in this work, to the exclusion of all dryasdust references to authorities, to present the development of piano-literature from the point of view of culture and of human interest. For procuring the material which lies in the works themselves and contemporary writings, I am indebted to the labours of Dr Kopfermann, Director of The Royal Library of Music at Berlin. I am enabled to give the illustrations by the extreme kindness of Mr Otto Lessmann, the Baroness Wilhelm von Rothschild, Mr Nicolas Manskopf, Mr Edwin Bechstein, Mr de Wit, Madame Bülow, Madame Marie Fellinger, and others.

Errata

P. 43. The note on Agricola is a mistake. M. Agricola is of the early 16th century. Bach's pupil was J. F. Agricola, for whom see p. 122, *note*.

P. 48. *For* "Tielman Sufato" *read* "Sufato Tielman."

P. 63, line 2. *For* "brown" *read* "yellow."

P. 63, line 2. *For* "dark grey" *read* "gris de Maure."

P. 70, line 27. According to the latest investigations Scarlatti died in *Naples* in 1757 ; thus he must have returned from Spain to Italy. (*Cf.* "Gazette Musicale," Napoli, 15th Sept. 1898.)

P. 114, line 19. *For* "Hezekiah's" *read* "Gideon's."

Addendum

P. 16. *Note*. That one of the earliest indications of the 18th century suite is to be seen in the Elizabethan "Parthenia," viz., in the association of Prelude, Pavan, Galliard.

Index of Names and Matters

List of Full-page Engravings

List of other Illustrations and Facsimiles